THIEF OF THIEVES

CREATED BY ROBERT KIRKMAN

ROBERT KIRKMAN
STORY

JAMES ASMUS
WRITER

SHAWN MARTINBROUGH
ARTIST

FELIX SERRANO
COLORIST

RUS WOOTON
LETTERER

SEAN MACKIEWICZ
EDITOR

SHAWN MARTINBROUGH
FELIX SERRANO
COVER

THIEF OF THIEVES, VOL. 2: "HELP ME."
ISBN: 978-1-60706-676-7
PRINTED IN U.S.A.
First Printing

Published by Image Comics, Inc. Office of publication: 2001 Center Street, 6th Floor, Berkeley, California 94704. Image and its logos are ® and © 2012 Image Comics Inc. All rights reserved. Originally published in single magazine form as THIEF OF THIEVES #8-13. THIEF OF THIEVES and all character likenesses are ™ and © 2013, Robert Kirkman, LLC. All rights reserved. All names, characters, events and locales in this publication are entirely fictional. Any resemblance to actual persons (living or dead), events or places, without satiric intent, is coincidental. No part of this publication may be reproduced or transmitted, in any form or by any means (except for short excerpts for review purposes) without the express written permission of the copyright holder.

For information regarding the CPSIA on this printed material call: 203-595-3636 and provide reference # RICH - 486444.

IMAGE COMICS, INC.
Robert Kirkman - chief operating officer
Erik Larsen - chief financial officer
Todd McFarlane - president
Marc Silvestri - chief executive officer
Jim Valentino - vice-president

Eric Stephenson - publisher
Ron Richards - director of business development
Jennifer de Guzman - pr & marketing director
Branwyn Bigglestone - accounts manager
Emily Miller - accounting assistant
Jamie Parreno - marketing assistant
Jenna Savage - administrative assistant
Kevin Yuen - digital rights coordinator
Jonathan Chan - production manager
Drew Gill - art director
Tyler Shainline - print manager
Monica Garcia - production artist
Vincent Kukua - production artist
Jana Cook - production artist

www.imagecomics.com

For SKYBOUND ENTERTAINMENT

Robert Kirkman - CEO
J.J. Didde - President
Sean Mackiewicz - Editorial Director
Shawn Kirkham - Director of Business Development
Brian Huntington - Online Editorial Director
Helen Leigh - Office Manager
Feldman Public Relations LA - Public Relations

For international rights inquiries,
please contact: foreign@skybound.com

WWW.SKYBOUND.COM

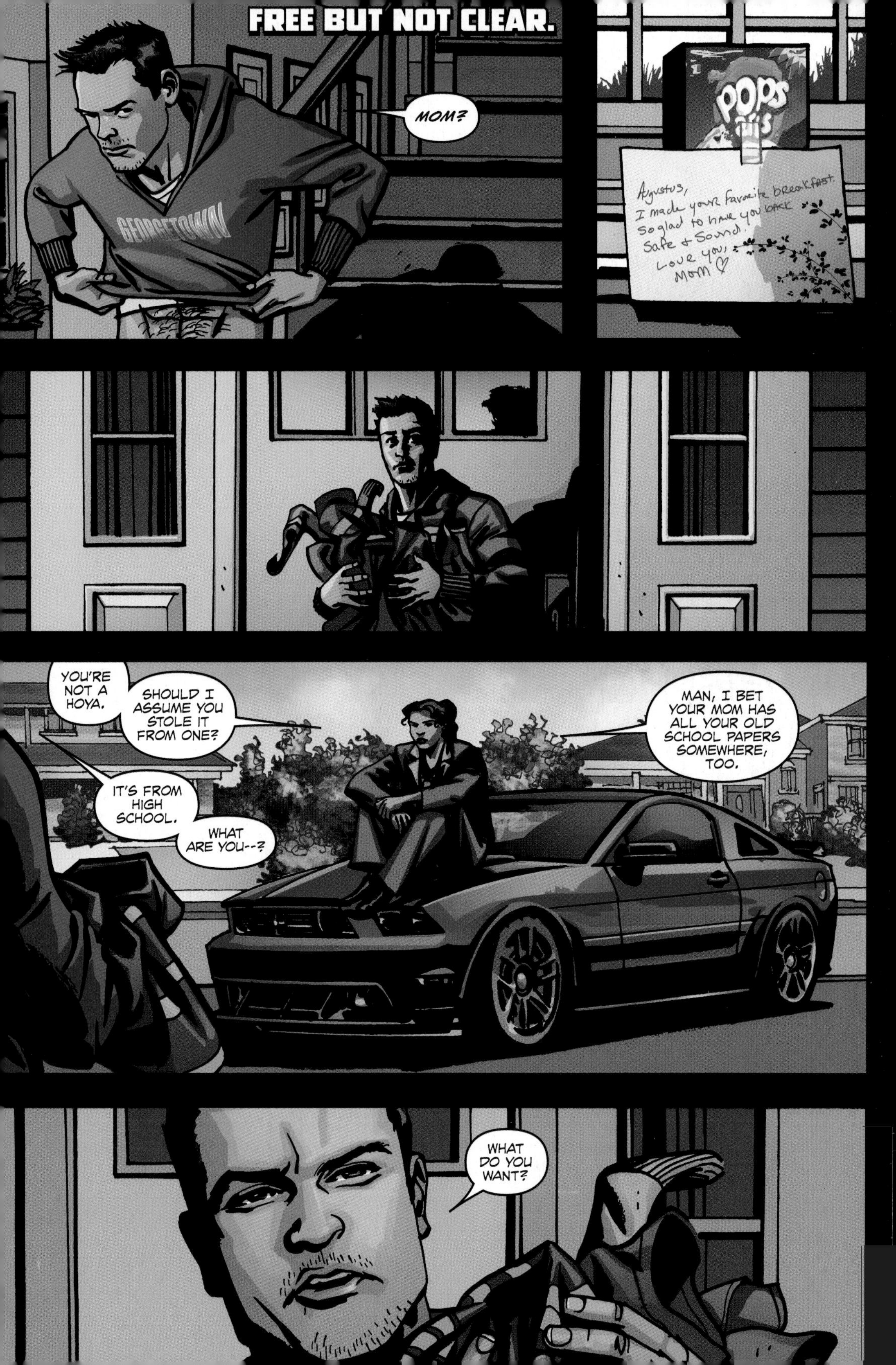
FREE BUT NOT CLEAR.
MOM?
GEORGETOWN
POPS
Augustus,
I made your favorite breakfast.
So glad to have you back
Safe & Sound.
Love you,
Mom
YOU'RE NOT A HOYA.
SHOULD I ASSUME YOU STOLE IT FROM ONE?
IT'S FROM HIGH SCHOOL.
WHAT ARE YOU--?
MAN, I BET YOUR MOM HAS ALL YOUR OLD SCHOOL PAPERS SOMEWHERE, TOO.
WHAT DO YOU WANT?

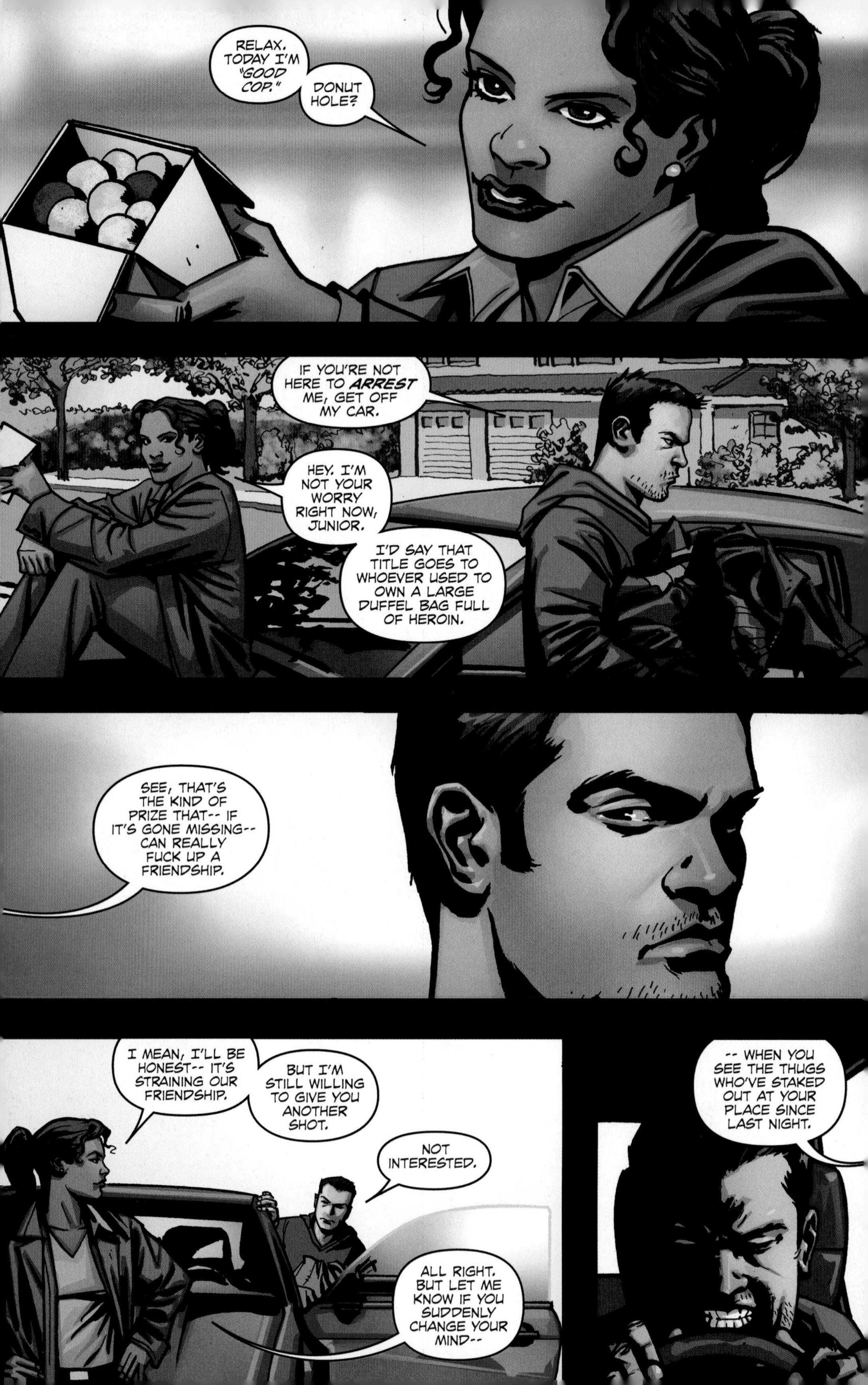
RELAX. TODAY I'M "GOOD COP."
DONUT HOLE?
IF YOU'RE NOT HERE TO ARREST ME, GET OFF MY CAR.
HEY. I'M NOT YOUR WORRY RIGHT NOW, JUNIOR.
I'D SAY THAT TITLE GOES TO WHOEVER USED TO OWN A LARGE DUFFEL BAG FULL OF HEROIN.
SEE, THAT'S THE KIND OF PRIZE THAT-- IF IT'S GONE MISSING-- CAN REALLY FUCK UP A FRIENDSHIP.
I MEAN, I'LL BE HONEST-- IT'S STRAINING OUR FRIENDSHIP.
BUT I'M STILL WILLING TO GIVE YOU ANOTHER SHOT.
NOT INTERESTED.
ALL RIGHT. BUT LET ME KNOW IF YOU SUDDENLY CHANGE YOUR MIND--
-- WHEN YOU SEE THE THUGS WHO'VE STAKED OUT AT YOUR PLACE SINCE LAST NIGHT.

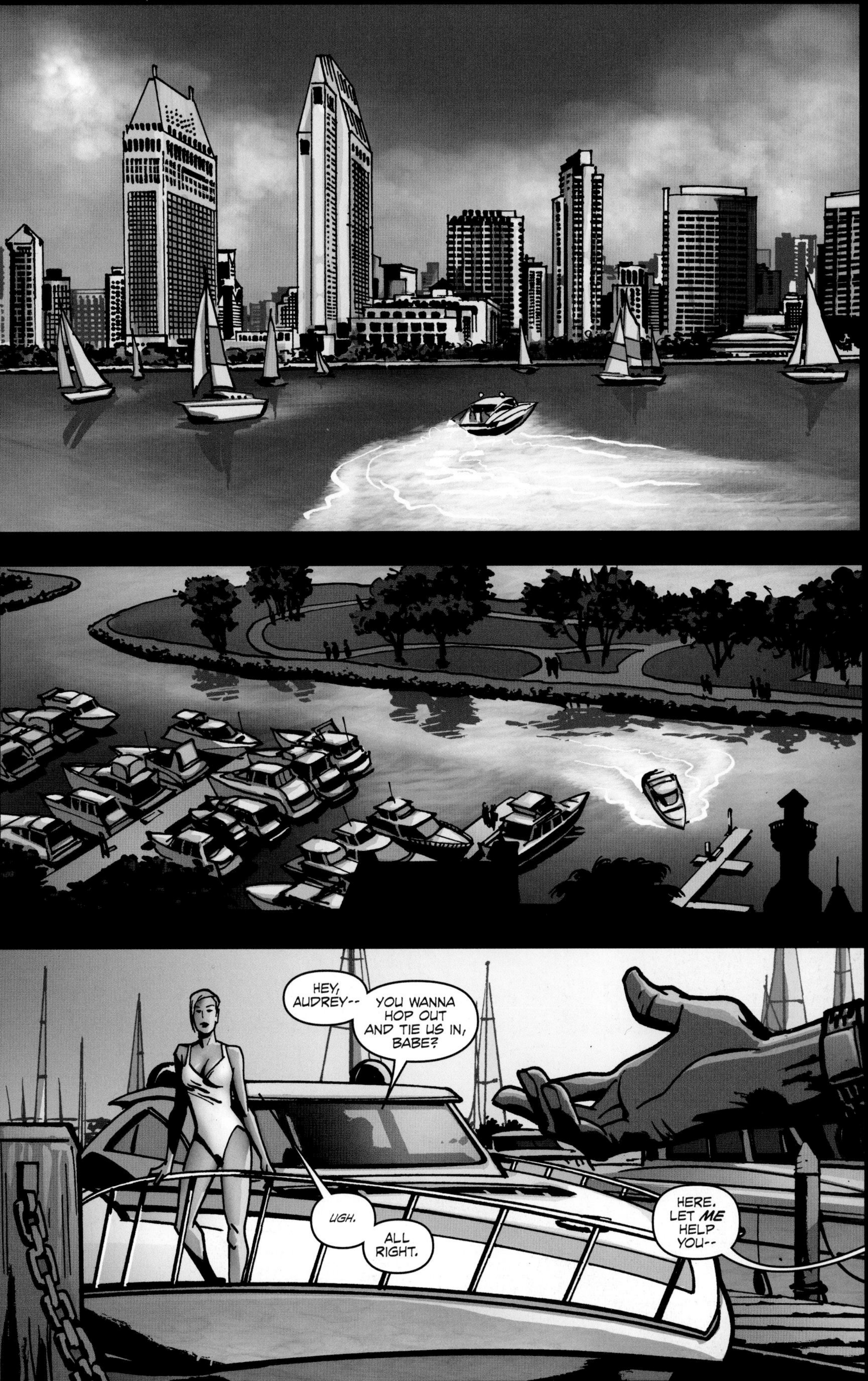
HEY, AUDREY--
YOU WANNA HOP OUT AND TIE US IN, BABE?
UGH.
ALL RIGHT.
HERE. LET ME HELP YOU--

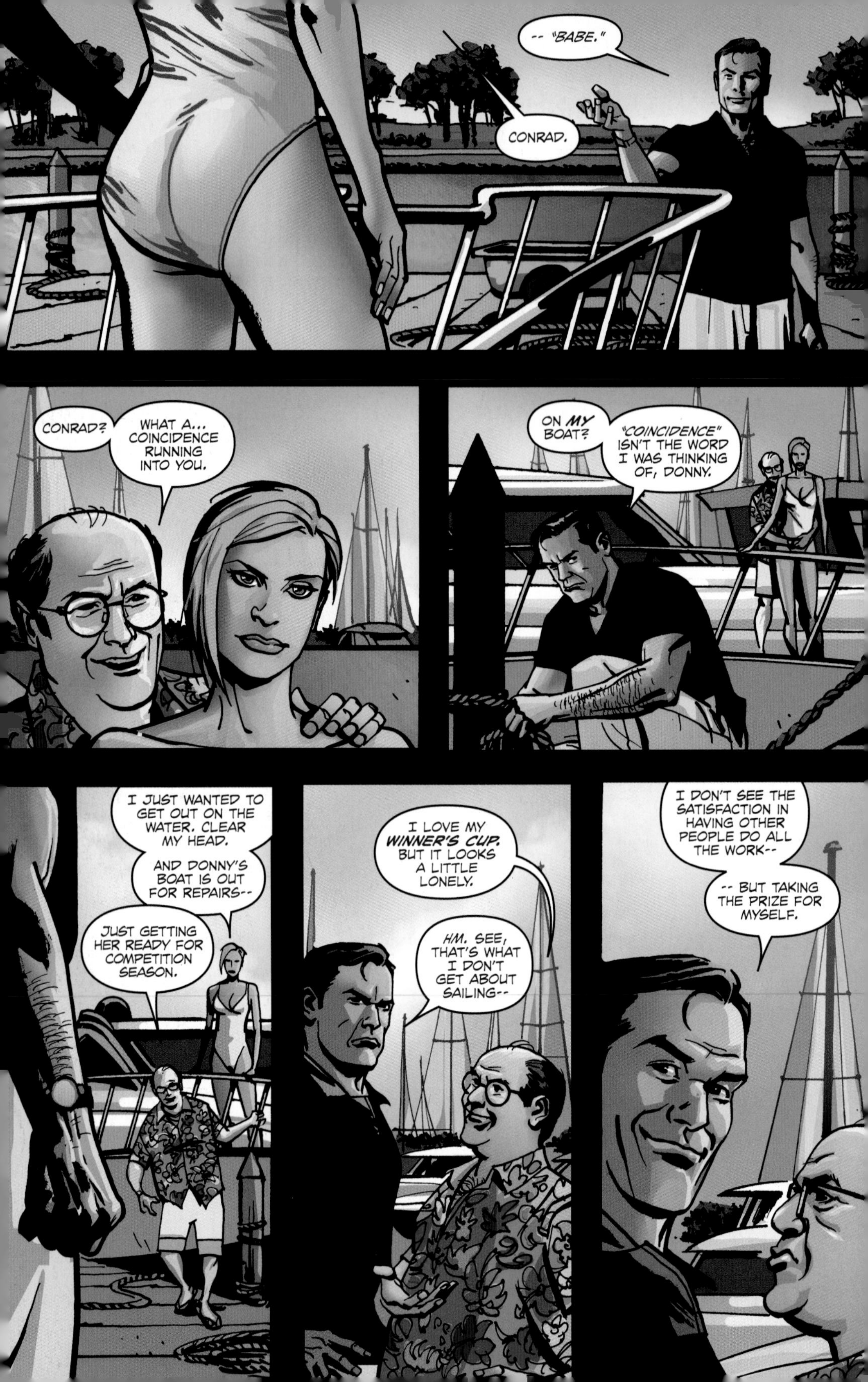

-- "BABE."
CONRAD.
CONRAD?
WHAT A... COINCIDENCE RUNNING INTO YOU.
ON MY BOAT?
"COINCIDENCE" ISN'T THE WORD I WAS THINKING OF, DONNY.
I JUST WANTED TO GET OUT ON THE WATER. CLEAR MY HEAD.
AND DONNY'S BOAT IS OUT FOR REPAIRS--
JUST GETTING HER READY FOR COMPETITION SEASON.
I LOVE MY WINNER'S CUP. BUT IT LOOKS A LITTLE LONELY.
HM. SEE, THAT'S WHAT I DON'T GET ABOUT SAILING--
I DON'T SEE THE SATISFACTION IN HAVING OTHER PEOPLE DO ALL THE WORK--
-- BUT TAKING THE PRIZE FOR MYSELF.

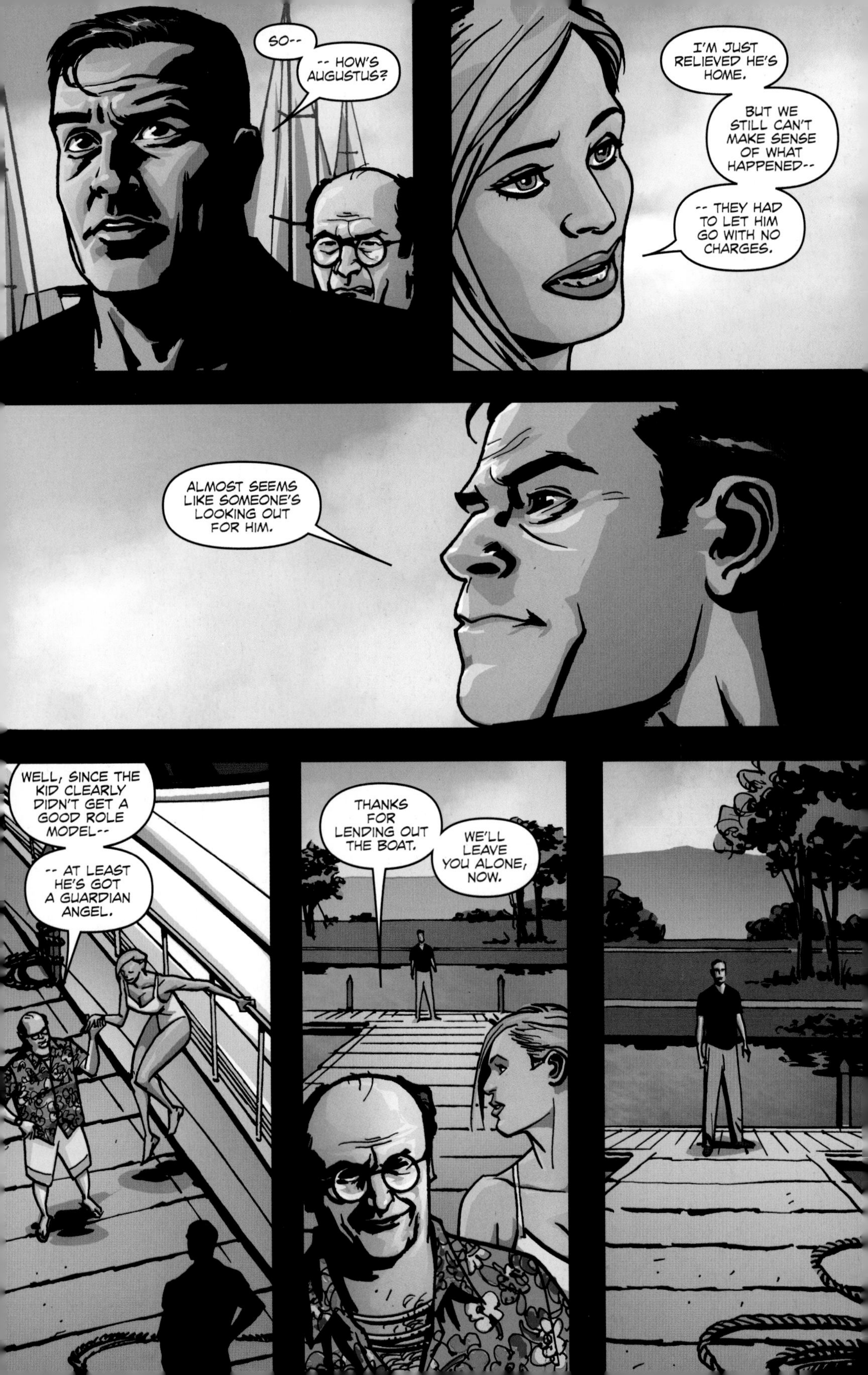
SO--
-- HOW'S AUGUSTUS?
I'M JUST RELIEVED HE'S HOME.
BUT WE STILL CAN'T MAKE SENSE OF WHAT HAPPENED--
-- THEY HAD TO LET HIM GO WITH NO CHARGES.
ALMOST SEEMS LIKE SOMEONE'S LOOKING OUT FOR HIM.
WELL, SINCE THE KID CLEARLY DIDN'T GET A GOOD ROLE MODEL--
-- AT LEAST HE'S GOT A GUARDIAN ANGEL.
THANKS FOR LENDING OUT THE BOAT.
WE'LL LEAVE YOU ALONE, NOW.

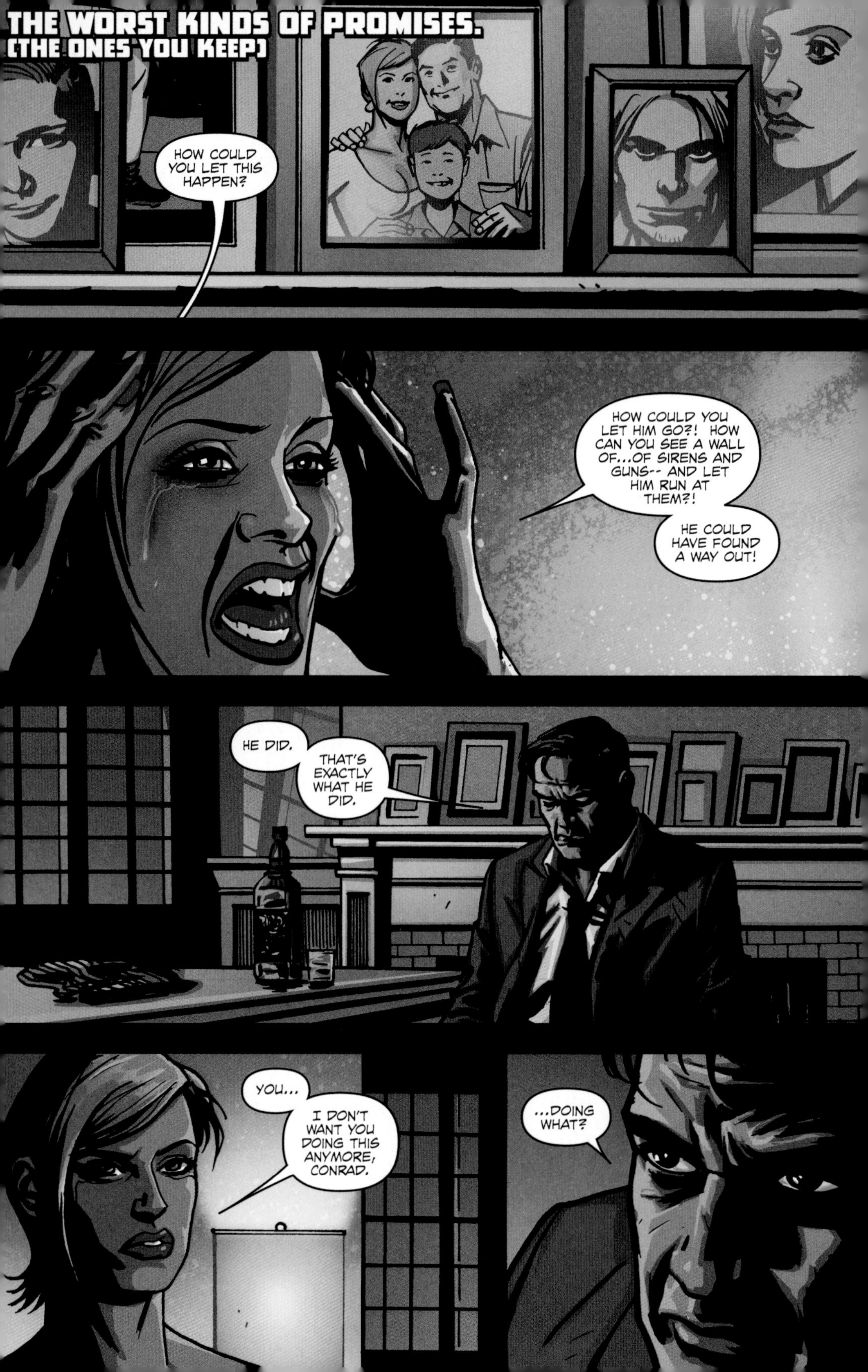
THE WORST KINDS OF PROMISES.
(THE ONES YOU KEEP)
HOW COULD YOU LET THIS HAPPEN?
HOW COULD YOU LET HIM GO?! HOW CAN YOU SEE A WALL OF...OF SIRENS AND GUNS-- AND LET HIM RUN AT THEM?!
HE COULD HAVE FOUND A WAY OUT!
HE DID.
THAT'S EXACTLY WHAT HE DID.
YOU...
I DON'T WANT YOU DOING THIS ANYMORE, CONRAD.
...DOING WHAT?

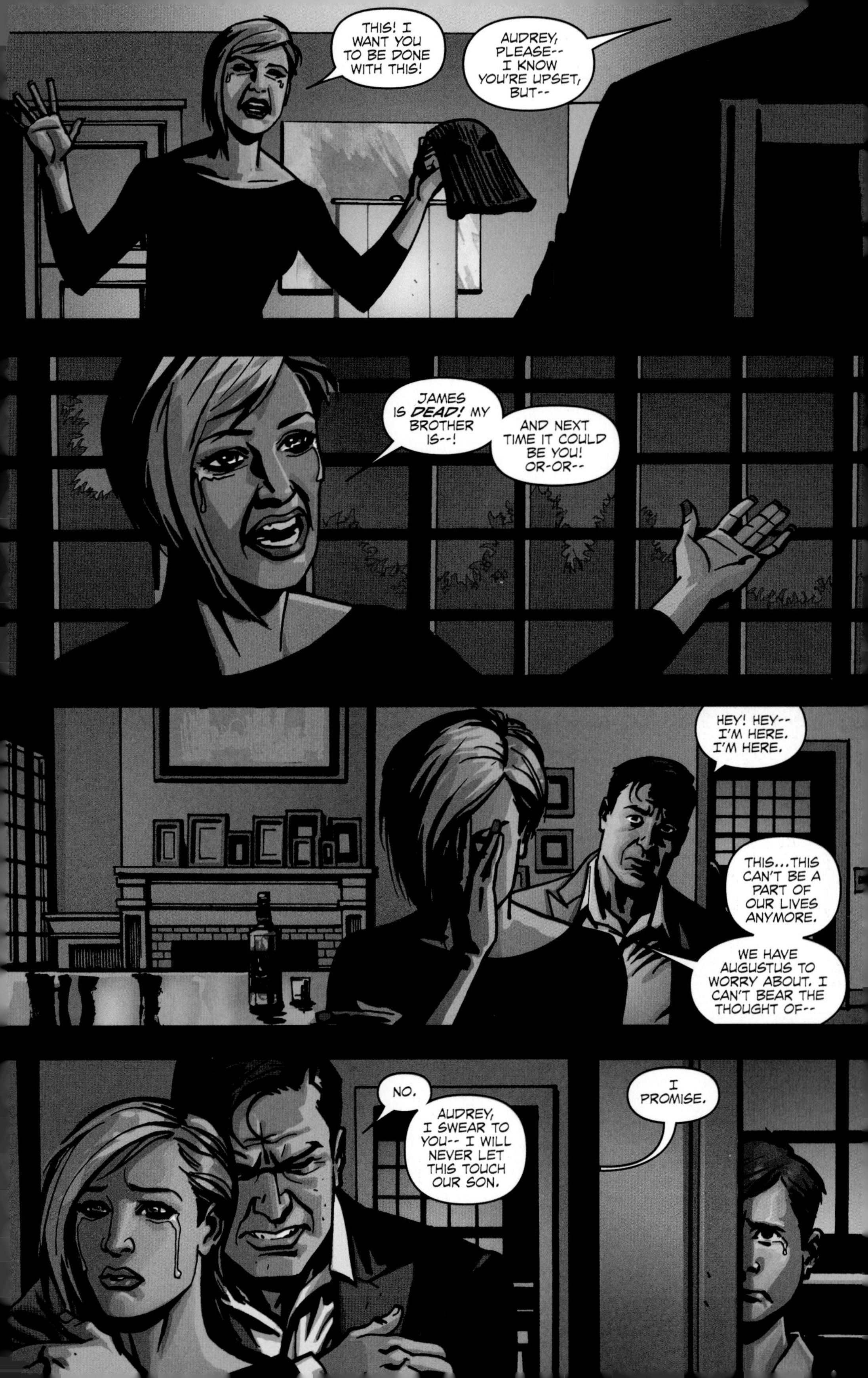
THIS! I WANT YOU TO BE DONE WITH THIS!
AUDREY, PLEASE-- I KNOW YOU'RE UPSET, BUT--
JAMES IS DEAD! MY BROTHER IS--!
AND NEXT TIME IT COULD BE YOU! OR-OR--
HEY! HEY-- I'M HERE. I'M HERE.
THIS...THIS CAN'T BE A PART OF OUR LIVES ANYMORE.
WE HAVE AUGUSTUS TO WORRY ABOUT. I CAN'T BEAR THE THOUGHT OF--
NO.
AUDREY, I SWEAR TO YOU-- I WILL NEVER LET THIS TOUCH OUR SON.
I PROMISE.

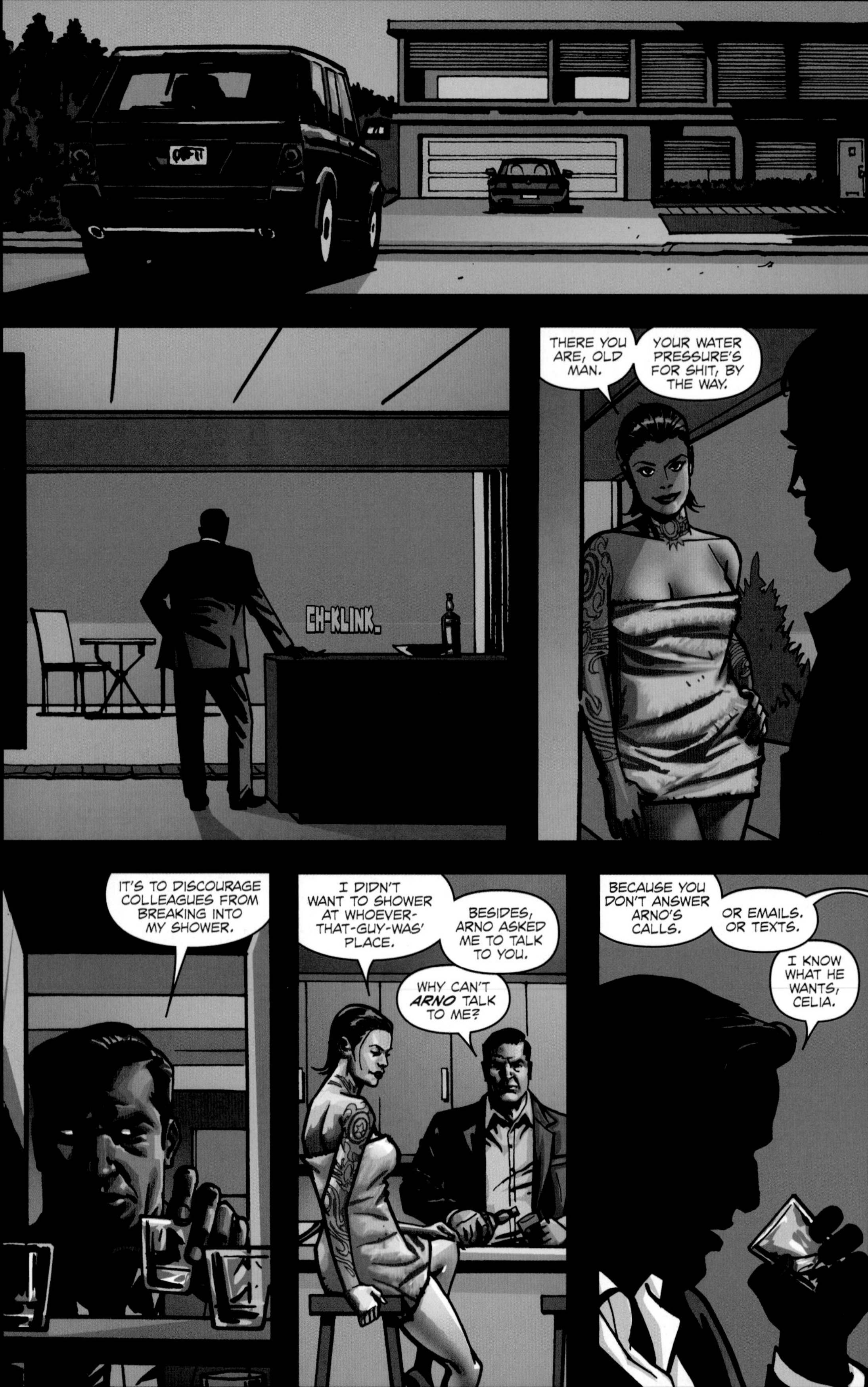
CH-KLINK.
THERE YOU ARE, OLD MAN.
YOUR WATER PRESSURE'S FOR SHIT, BY THE WAY.
IT'S TO DISCOURAGE COLLEAGUES FROM BREAKING INTO MY SHOWER.
I DIDN'T WANT TO SHOWER AT WHOEVER-THAT-GUY-WAS' PLACE.
BESIDES, ARNO ASKED ME TO TALK TO YOU.
WHY CAN'T ARNO TALK TO ME?
BECAUSE YOU DON'T ANSWER ARNO'S CALLS.
OR EMAILS. OR TEXTS.
I KNOW WHAT HE WANTS, CELIA.

YEAH. HE WANTS WHAT YOU OWE HIM. WHAT YOU OWE ALL OF US--

FINE. I CAN PAY EVERYONE THAT HELPED CLEAR AUGUSTUS.

YOU KNOW I'VE GOT THE MONEY.

BUT THE FEDS ARE STILL WATCHING MY ACCOUNTS, SO--

SCREW YOUR MONEY.

SOME OF US STILL NEED TO *WORK*.

ARNO NEEDS GOODS TO SELL-- OR HE'LL LOSE HIS PLACE IN THE BUSINESS!

AND THE REST OF US ARE PRETTY SICK OF SITTIN' ON OUR FUCKING HANDS BECAUSE YOU WANT TO JOIN THE AARP.

YOU *OWE* US.

AND I KNOW YOU.

YOU LOVE THIS JOB AS MUCH AS ANY OF US.

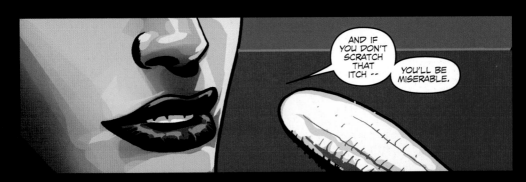

AND IF YOU DON'T SCRATCH THAT ITCH --

YOU'LL BE MISERABLE.

PUT SOME FUCKING CLOTHES ON.

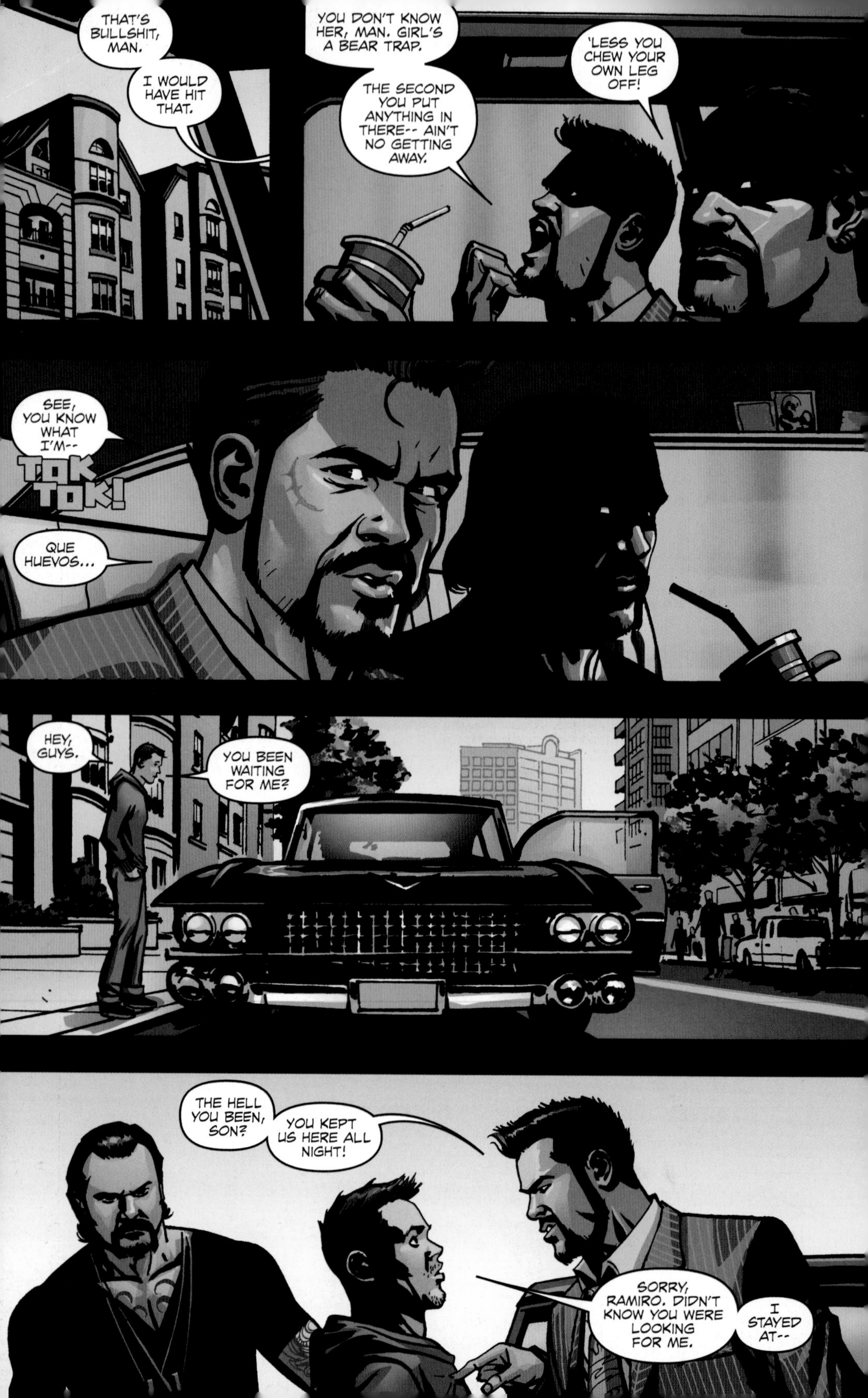
THAT'S BULLSHIT, MAN.
I WOULD HAVE HIT THAT.
YOU DON'T KNOW HER, MAN. GIRL'S A BEAR TRAP.
THE SECOND YOU PUT ANYTHING IN THERE-- AIN'T NO GETTING AWAY.
'LESS YOU CHEW YOUR OWN LEG OFF!
SEE, YOU KNOW WHAT I'M--
TOK TOK!
QUE HUEVOS...
HEY, GUYS.
YOU BEEN WAITING FOR ME?
THE HELL YOU BEEN, SON?
YOU KEPT US HERE ALL NIGHT!
SORRY, RAMIRO. DIDN'T KNOW YOU WERE LOOKING FOR ME.
I STAYED AT--

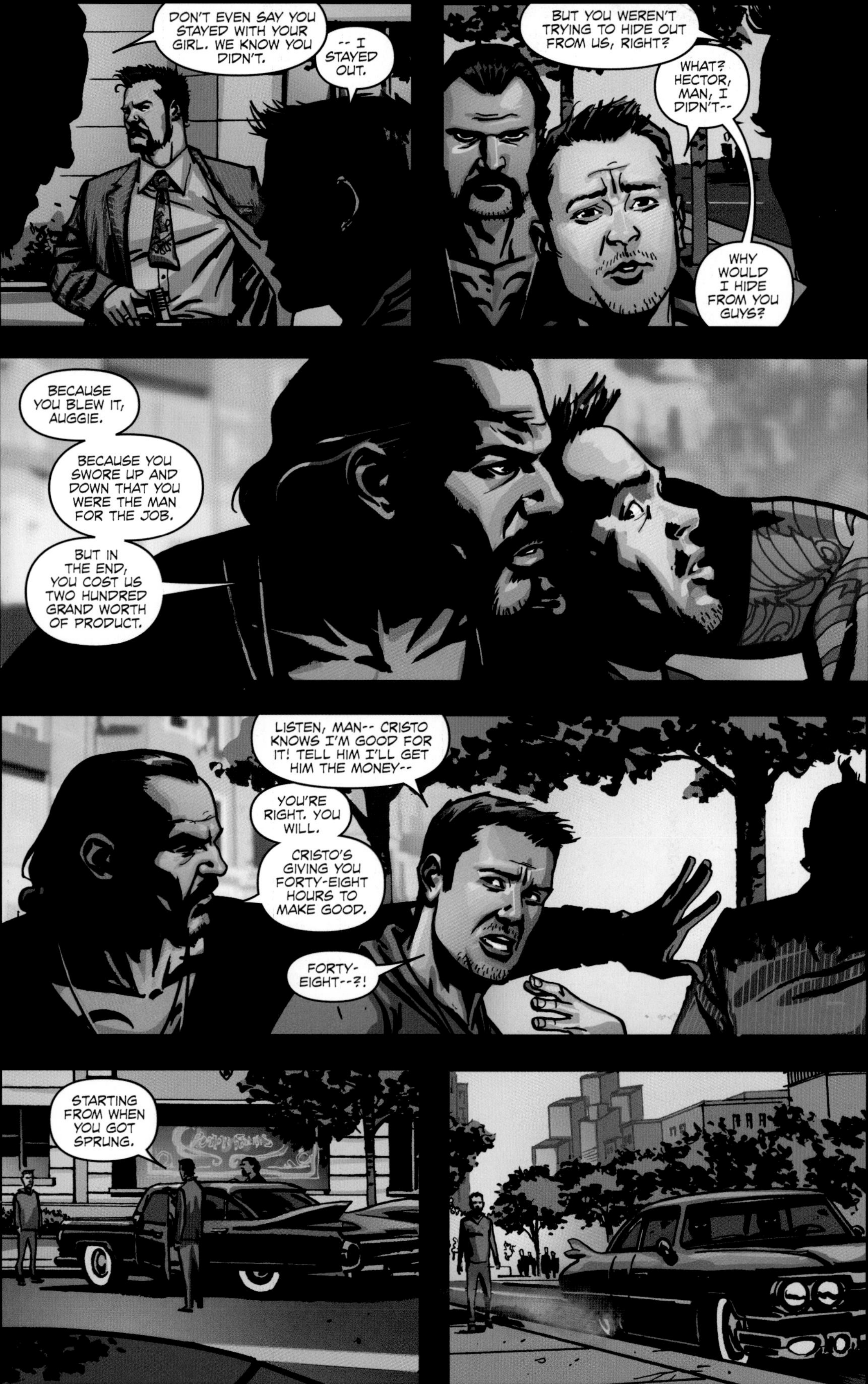
DON'T EVEN SAY YOU STAYED WITH YOUR GIRL. WE KNOW YOU DIDN'T.
-- I STAYED OUT.
BUT YOU WEREN'T TRYING TO HIDE OUT FROM US, RIGHT?
WHAT? HECTOR, MAN, I DIDN'T--
WHY WOULD I HIDE FROM YOU GUYS?
BECAUSE YOU BLEW IT, AUGGIE.
BECAUSE YOU SWORE UP AND DOWN THAT YOU WERE THE MAN FOR THE JOB.
BUT IN THE END, YOU COST US TWO HUNDRED GRAND WORTH OF PRODUCT.
LISTEN, MAN-- CRISTO KNOWS I'M GOOD FOR IT! TELL HIM I'LL GET HIM THE MONEY--
YOU'RE RIGHT. YOU WILL.
CRISTO'S GIVING YOU FORTY-EIGHT HOURS TO MAKE GOOD.
FORTY-EIGHT--?!
STARTING FROM WHEN YOU GOT SPRUNG.

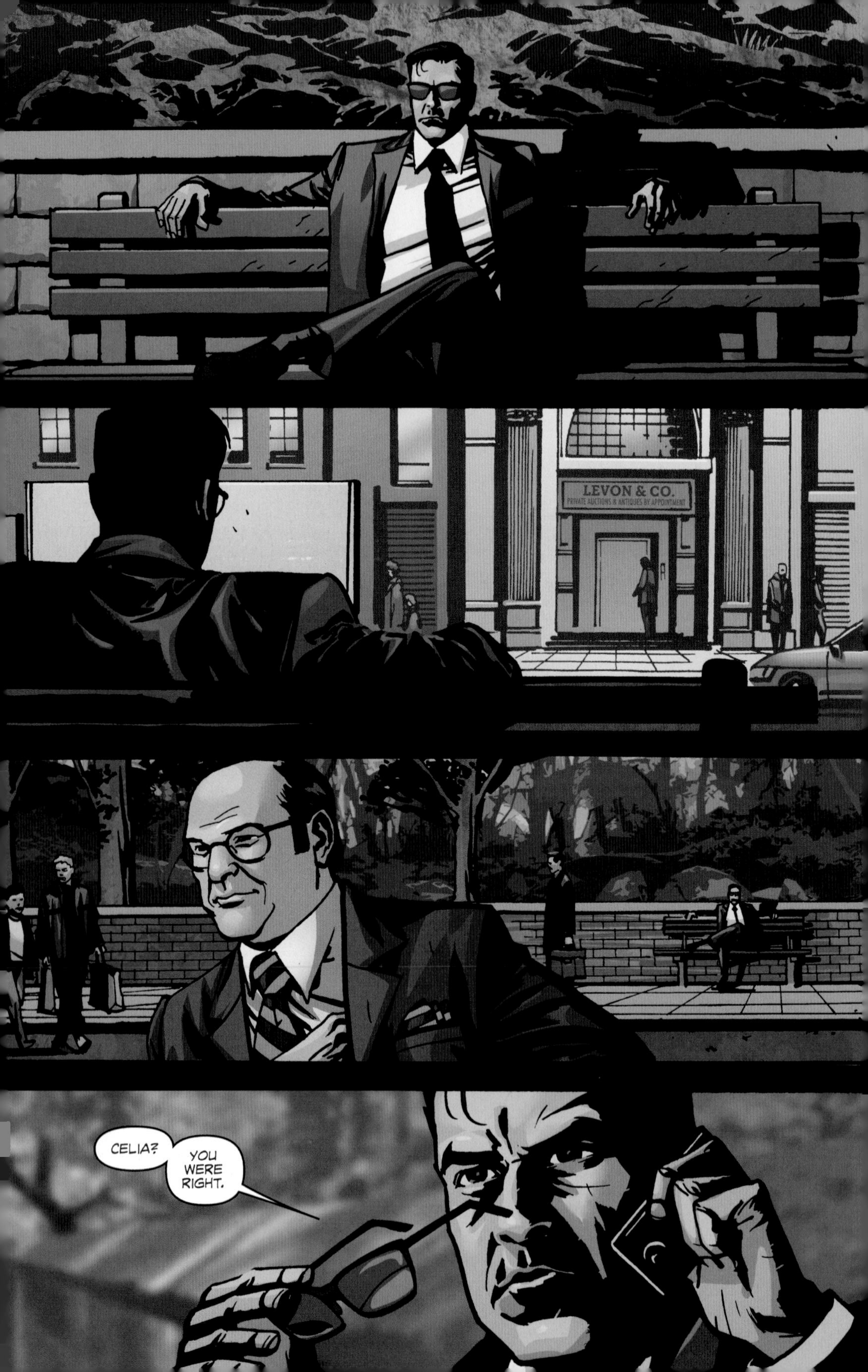
LEVON & CO.
PRIVATE AUCTIONS & ANTIQUES BY APPOINTMENT
CELIA?
YOU WERE RIGHT.

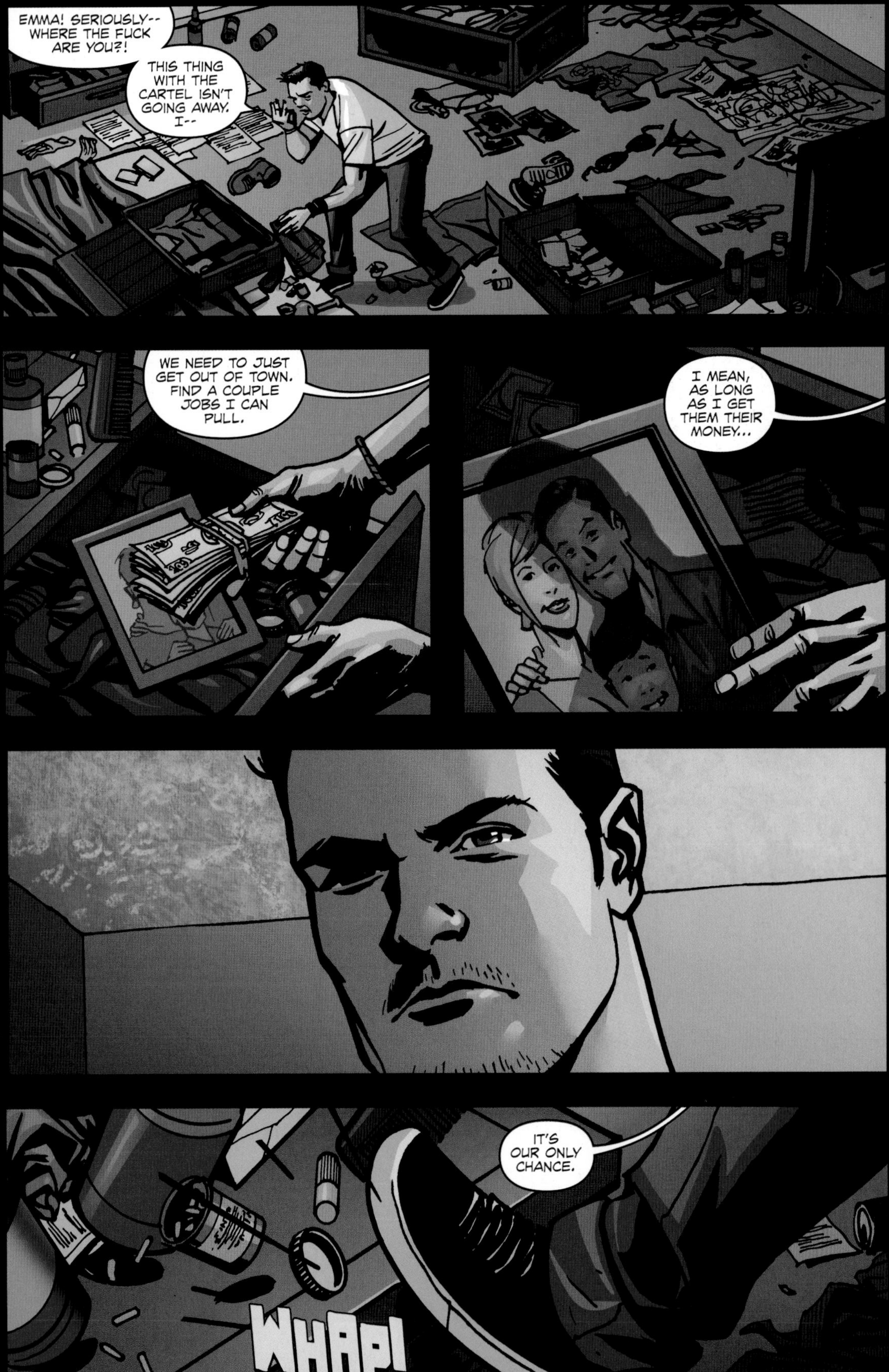
EMMA! SERIOUSLY--
WHERE THE FUCK
ARE YOU?!
THIS THING WITH THE CARTEL ISN'T GOING AWAY. I--
WE NEED TO JUST GET OUT OF TOWN. FIND A COUPLE JOBS I CAN PULL.
I MEAN, AS LONG AS I GET THEM THEIR MONEY...
IT'S OUR ONLY CHANCE.
WHAP!

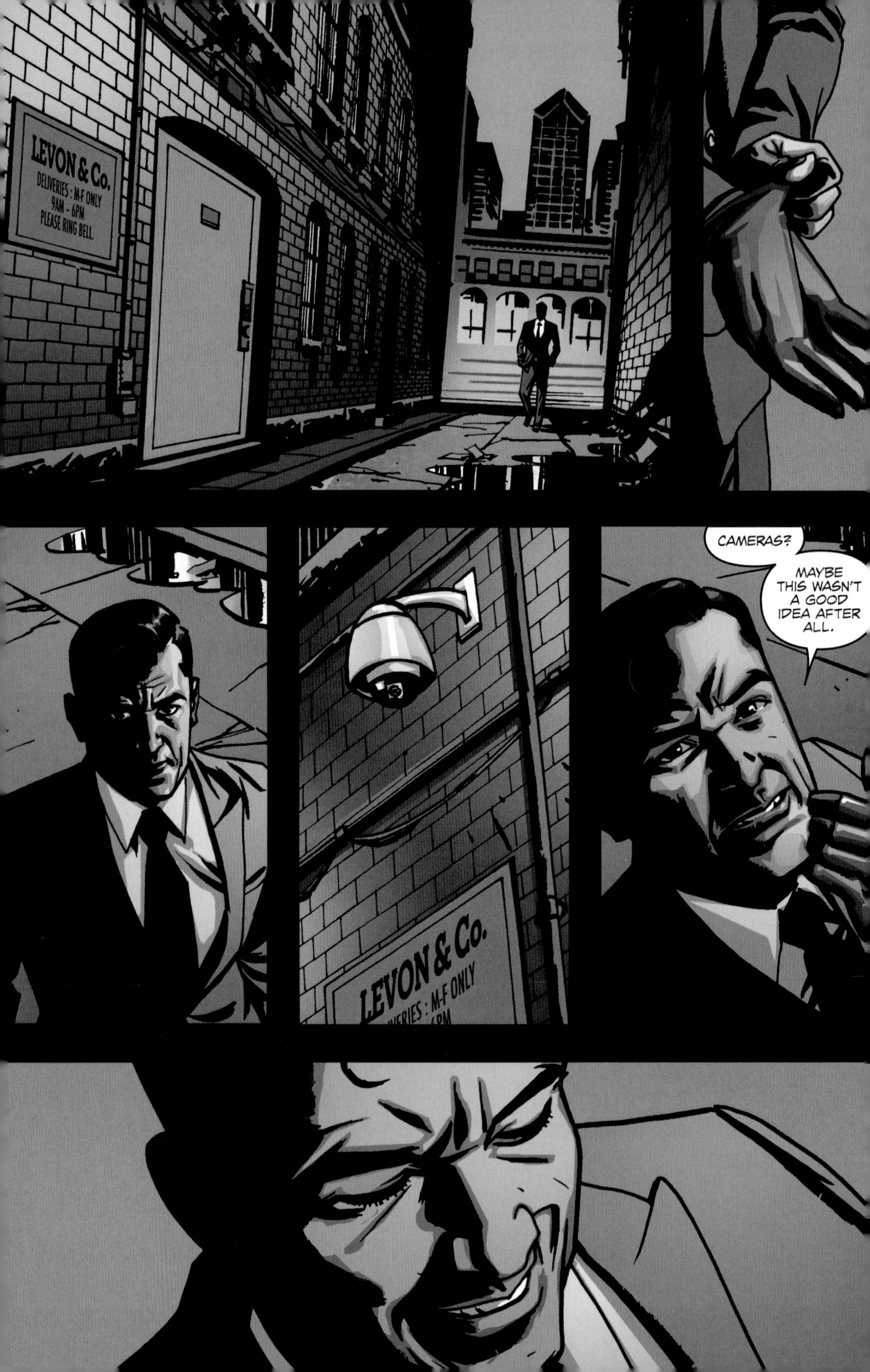
LEVON & Co.
DELIVERIES : M-F ONLY
9AM - 6PM
PLEASE RING BELL.
LEVON & Co.
CAMERAS?
MAYBE THIS WASN'T A GOOD IDEA AFTER ALL.

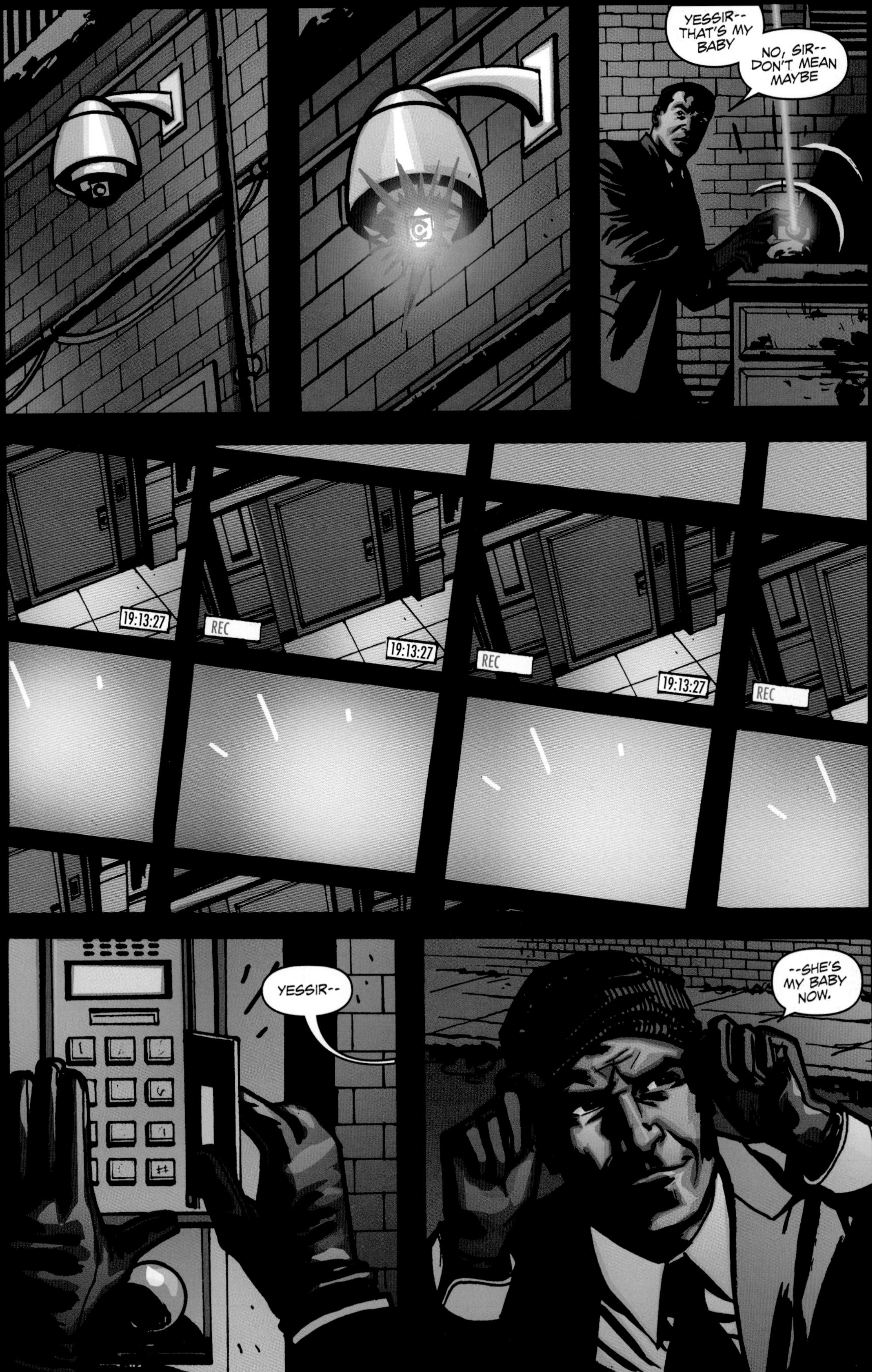
YESSIR--
THAT'S MY
BABY
NO, SIR--
DON'T MEAN
MAYBE
19:13:27
REC
19:13:27
REC
19:13:27
REC
YESSIR--
--SHE'S
MY BABY
NOW.

EET
EET
EET

THAT'S ADORABLE.

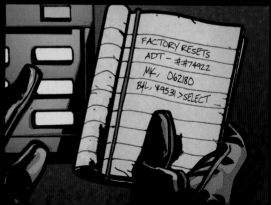

FACTORY RESETS
ADT - #\#74922
MK, 062180
B4L, ¥9531 >SELECT

ITEM 42 OF 83
S.P. $26,000.00

WELL, THAT'S MORE THAN I WOULD PAY FOR IT...

J. FREEHLING
Item 117 of 197
S.P. $49,000.00

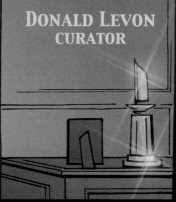

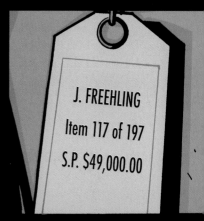

J. FREEHLING

Item 117 of 197

S.P. $49,000.00

DONALD LEVON
CURATOR

YOU'RE RIGHT, DONNY. YOUR WINNER'S CUP DOES LOOK LONELY...

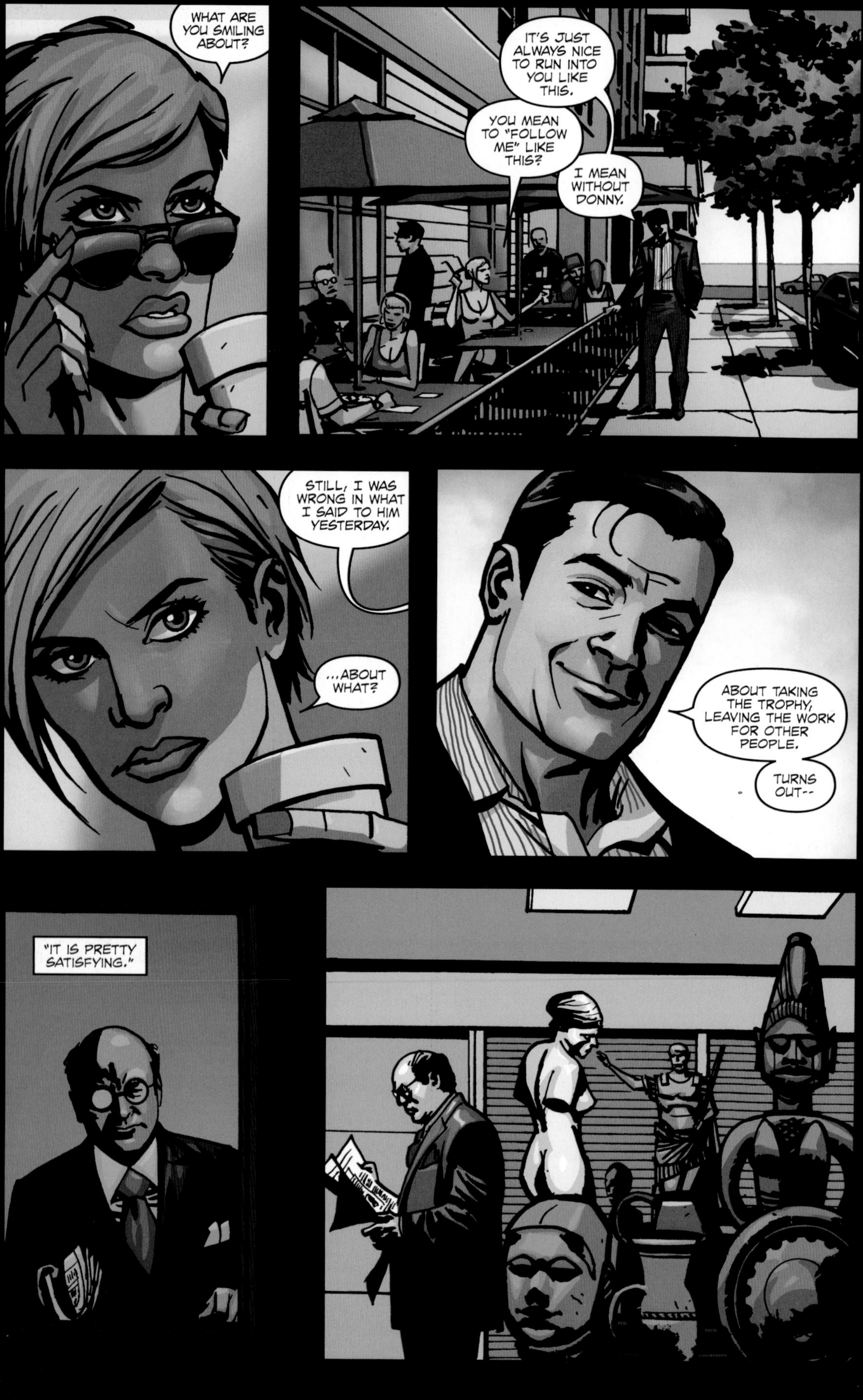
WHAT ARE YOU SMILING ABOUT?
IT'S JUST ALWAYS NICE TO RUN INTO YOU LIKE THIS.
YOU MEAN TO "FOLLOW ME" LIKE THIS?
I MEAN WITHOUT DONNY.
STILL, I WAS WRONG IN WHAT I SAID TO HIM YESTERDAY.
...ABOUT WHAT?
ABOUT TAKING THE TROPHY, LEAVING THE WORK FOR OTHER PEOPLE.
TURNS OUT--
"IT IS PRETTY SATISFYING."

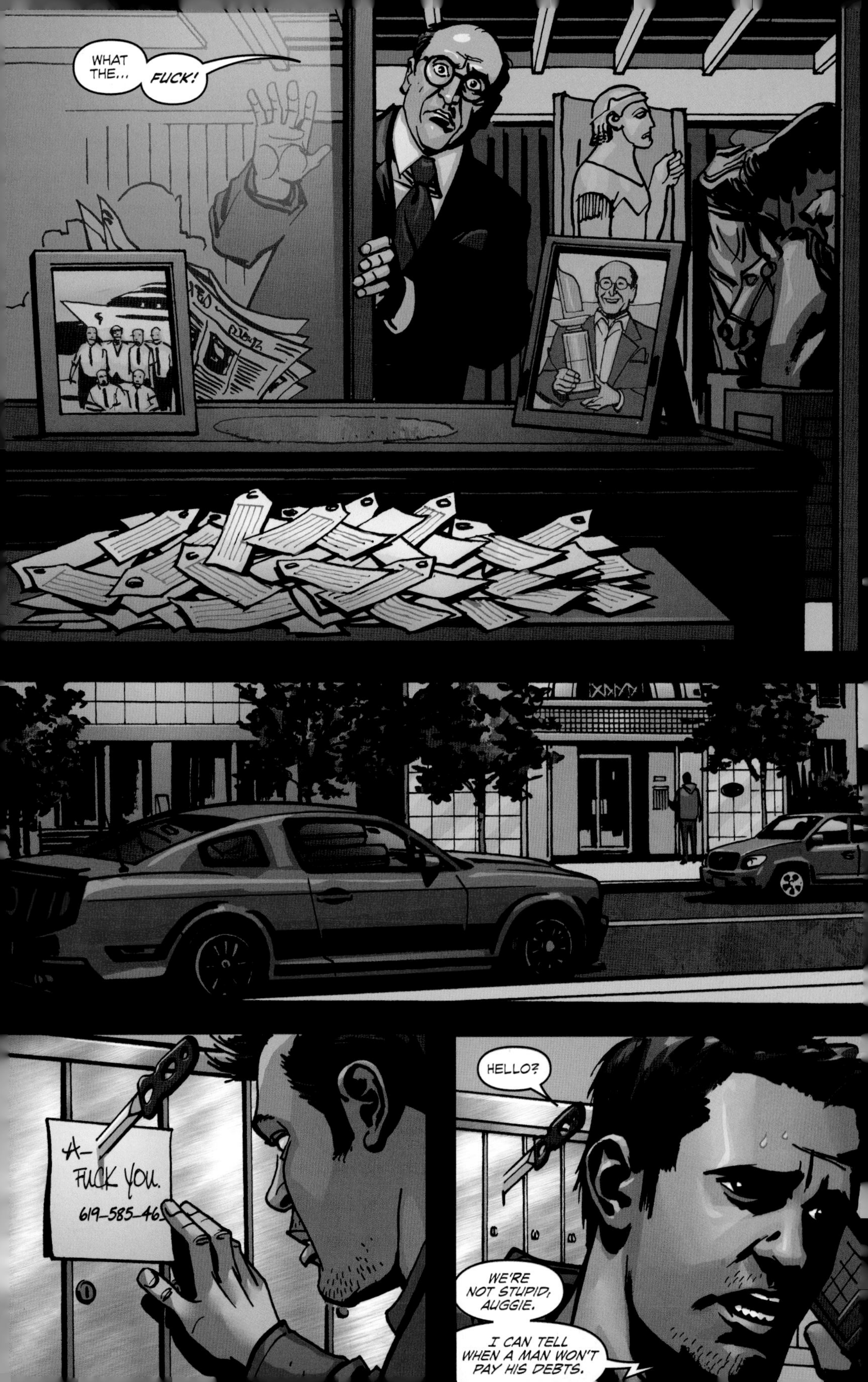

WHAT THE... FUCK!
A- FUCK YOU. 619-585-46
HELLO?
WE'RE NOT STUPID, AUGGIE.
I CAN TELL WHEN A MAN WON'T PAY HIS DEBTS.

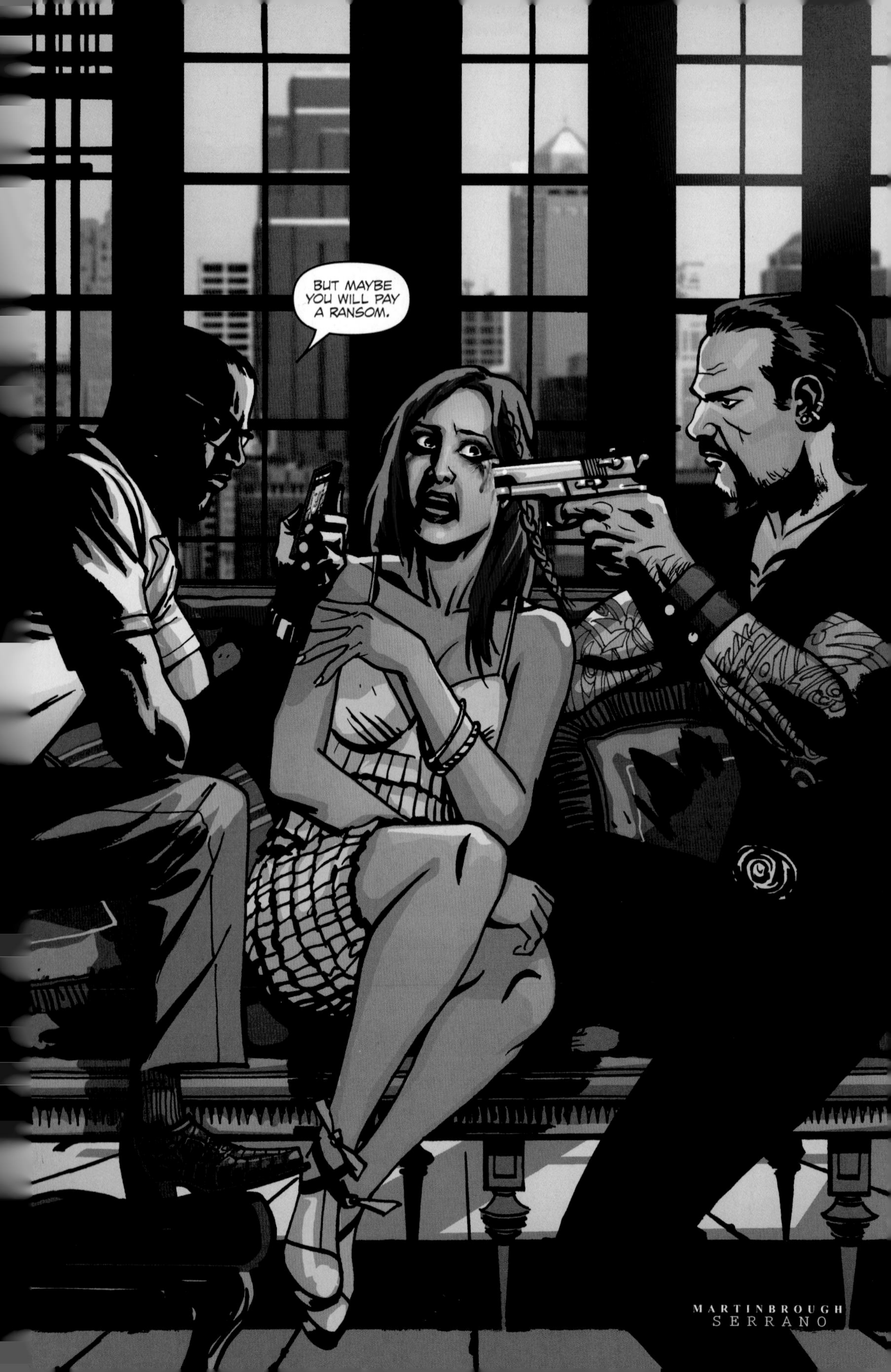
BUT MAYBE YOU WILL PAY A RANSOM.
MARTINBROUGH
SERRANO

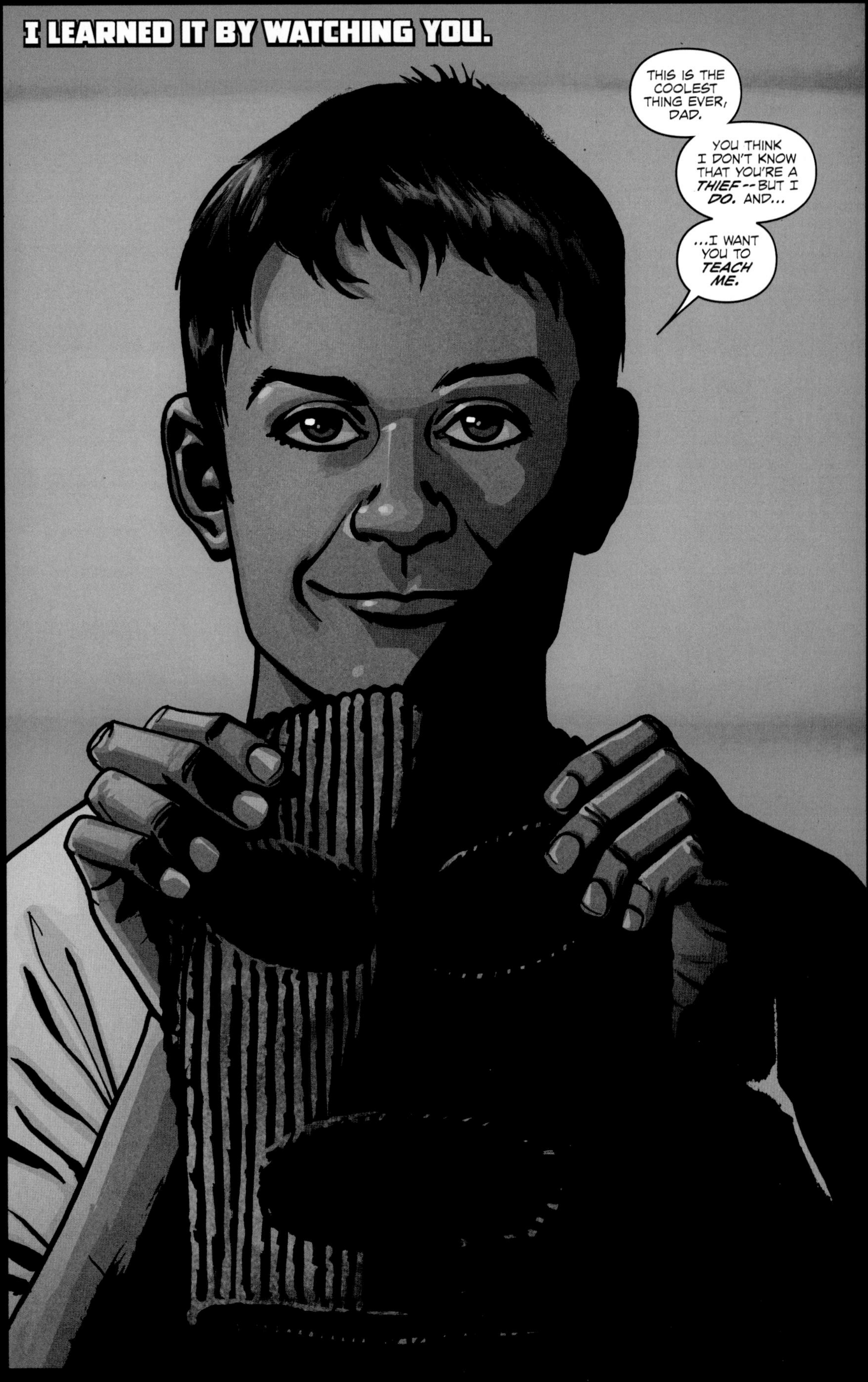
I LEARNED IT BY WATCHING YOU.
THIS IS THE COOLEST THING EVER, DAD.
YOU THINK I DON'T KNOW THAT YOU'RE A *THIEF*--BUT I *DO.* AND...
...I WANT YOU TO *TEACH ME.*

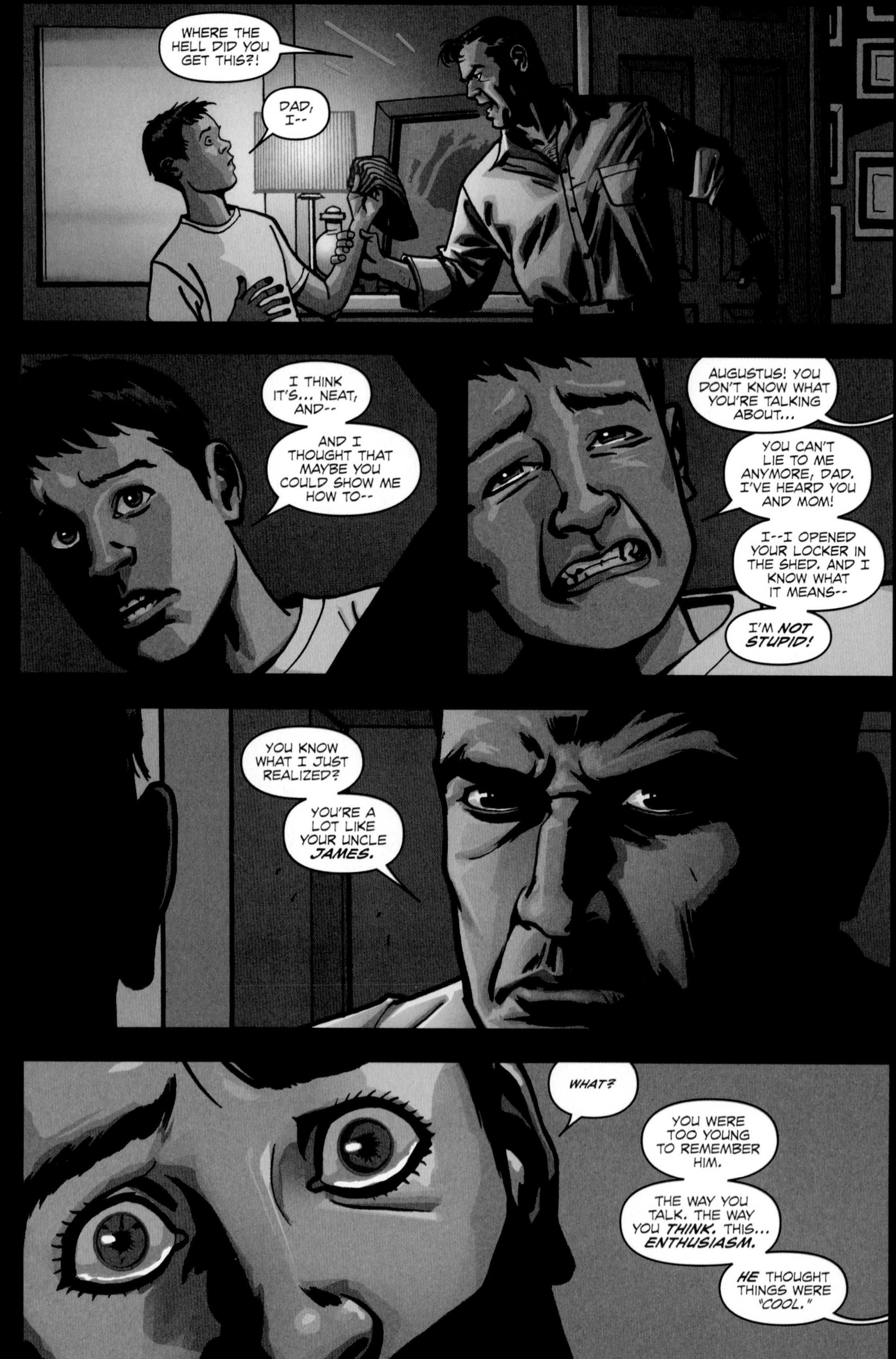
WHERE THE HELL DID YOU GET THIS?!
DAD, I--
I THINK IT'S... NEAT, AND--
AND I THOUGHT THAT MAYBE YOU COULD SHOW ME HOW TO--
AUGUSTUS! YOU DON'T KNOW WHAT YOU'RE TALKING ABOUT...
YOU CAN'T LIE TO ME ANYMORE, DAD. I'VE HEARD YOU AND MOM!
I--I OPENED YOUR LOCKER IN THE SHED. AND I KNOW WHAT IT MEANS--
I'M NOT STUPID!
YOU KNOW WHAT I JUST REALIZED?
YOU'RE A LOT LIKE YOUR UNCLE JAMES.
WHAT?
YOU WERE TOO YOUNG TO REMEMBER HIM.
THE WAY YOU TALK. THE WAY YOU THINK. THIS... ENTHUSIASM.
HE THOUGHT THINGS WERE "COOL."

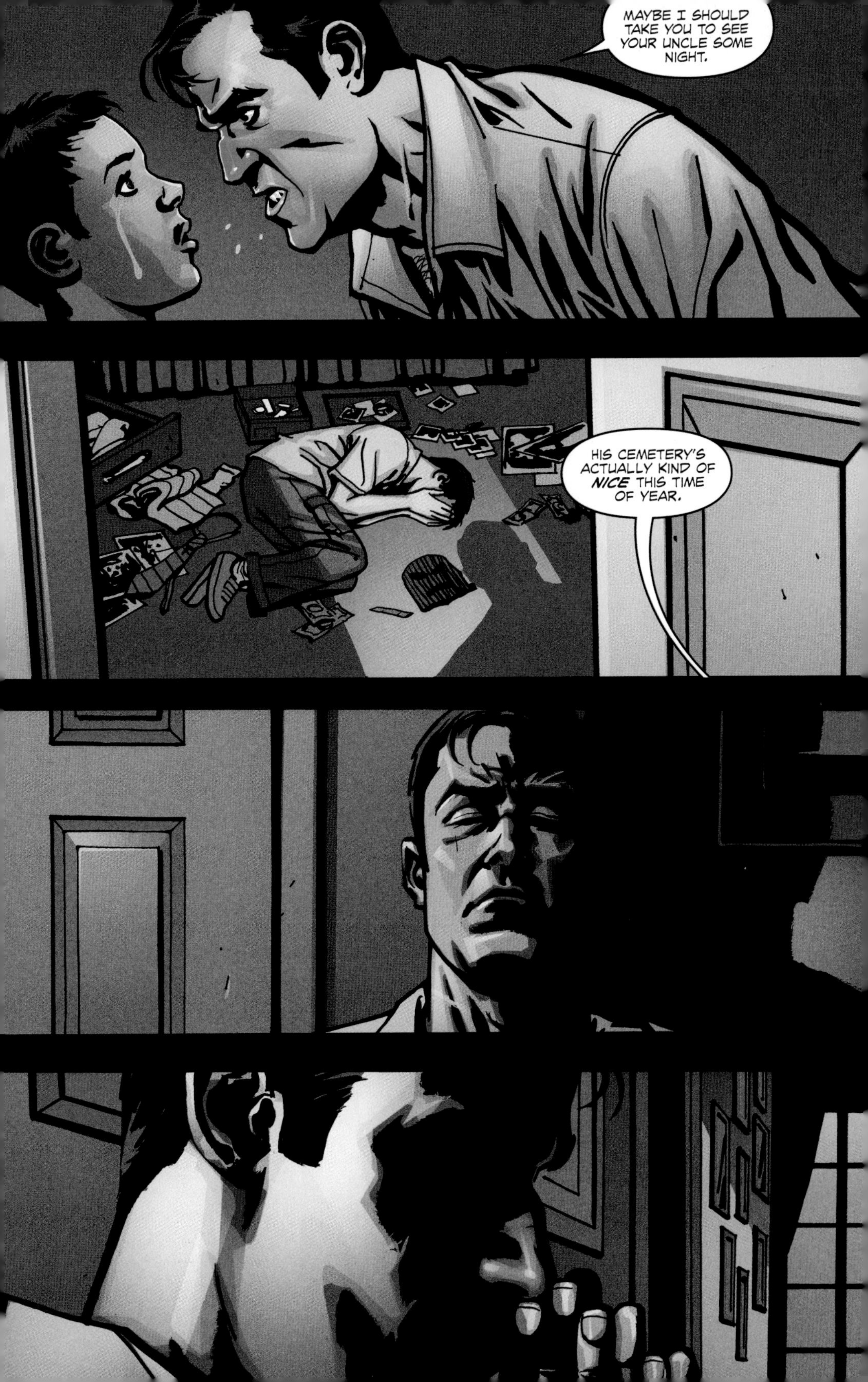
MAYBE I SHOULD TAKE YOU TO SEE YOUR UNCLE SOME NIGHT.
HIS CEMETERY'S ACTUALLY KIND OF *NICE* THIS TIME OF YEAR.

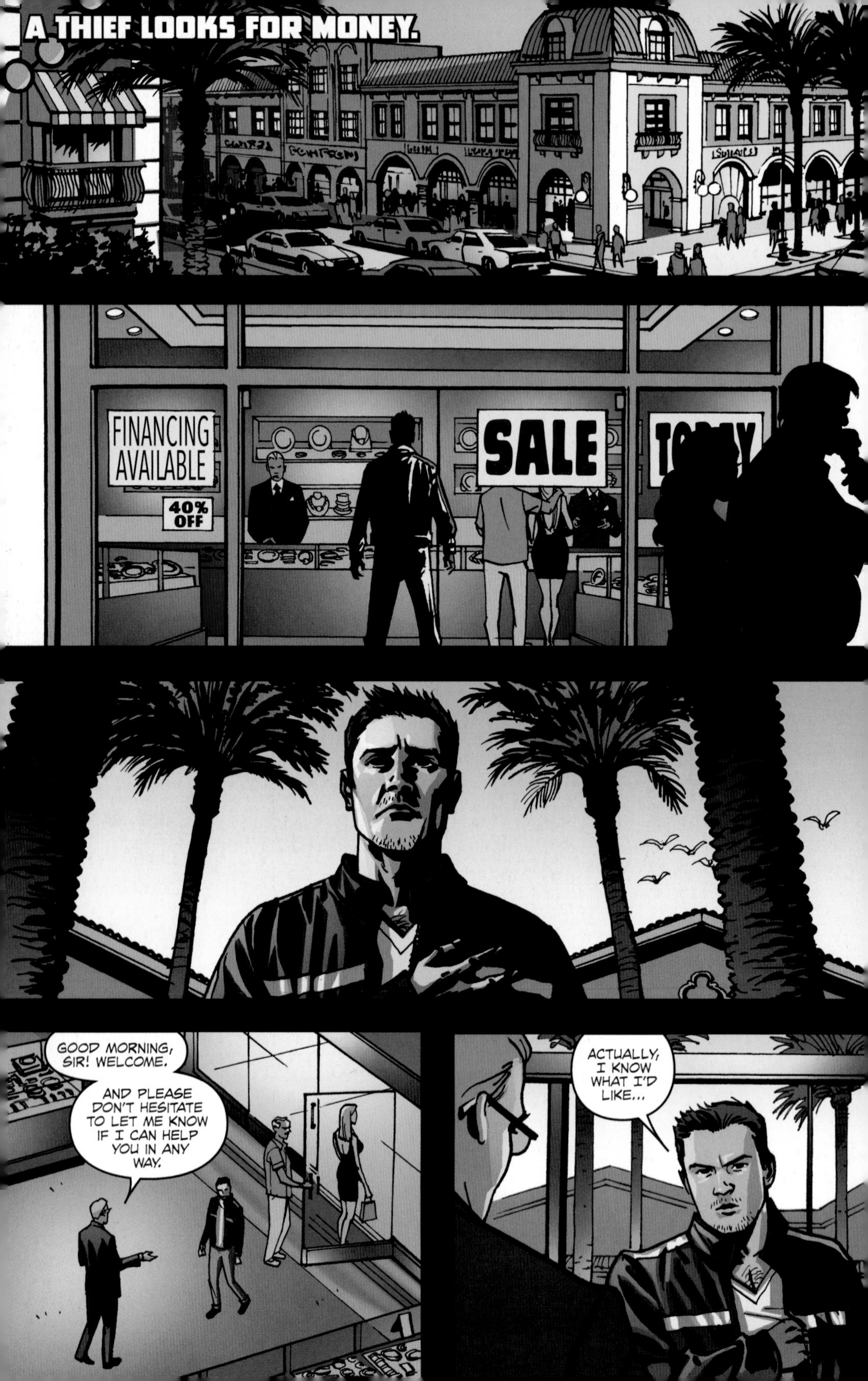
A THIEF LOOKS FOR MONEY.
FINANCING AVAILABLE
40% OFF
SALE
GOOD MORNING, SIR! WELCOME.
AND PLEASE DON'T HESITATE TO LET ME KNOW IF I CAN HELP YOU IN ANY WAY.
ACTUALLY, I KNOW WHAT I'D LIKE...

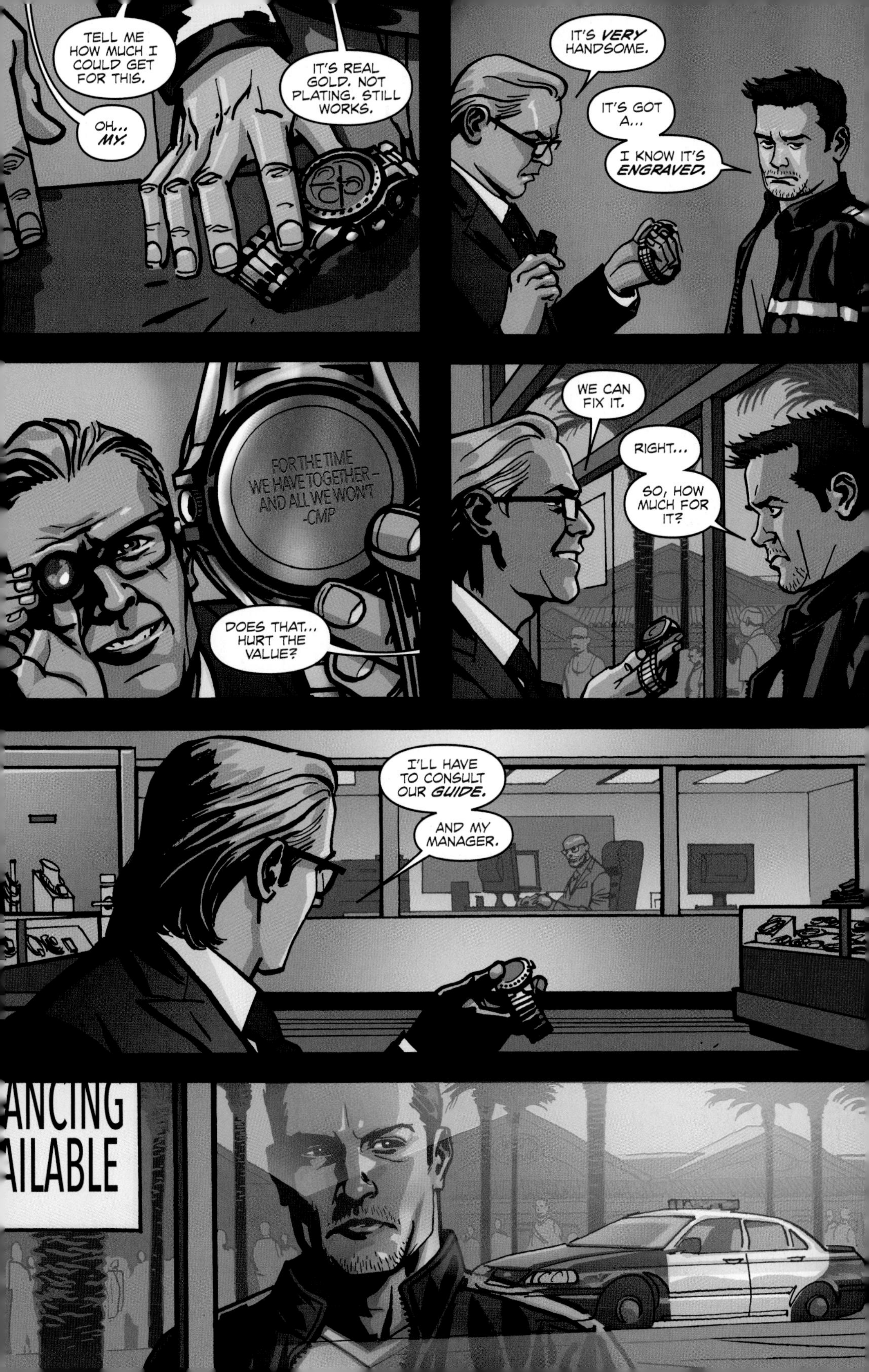
TELL ME HOW MUCH I COULD GET FOR THIS.
OH... MY.
IT'S REAL GOLD. NOT PLATING. STILL WORKS.
IT'S VERY HANDSOME.
IT'S GOT A...
I KNOW IT'S ENGRAVED.
FOR THE TIME WE HAVE TOGETHER — AND ALL WE WON'T -CMP
DOES THAT... HURT THE VALUE?
WE CAN FIX IT.
RIGHT...
SO, HOW MUCH FOR IT?
I'LL HAVE TO CONSULT OUR GUIDE.
AND MY MANAGER.
ANCING
AILABLE

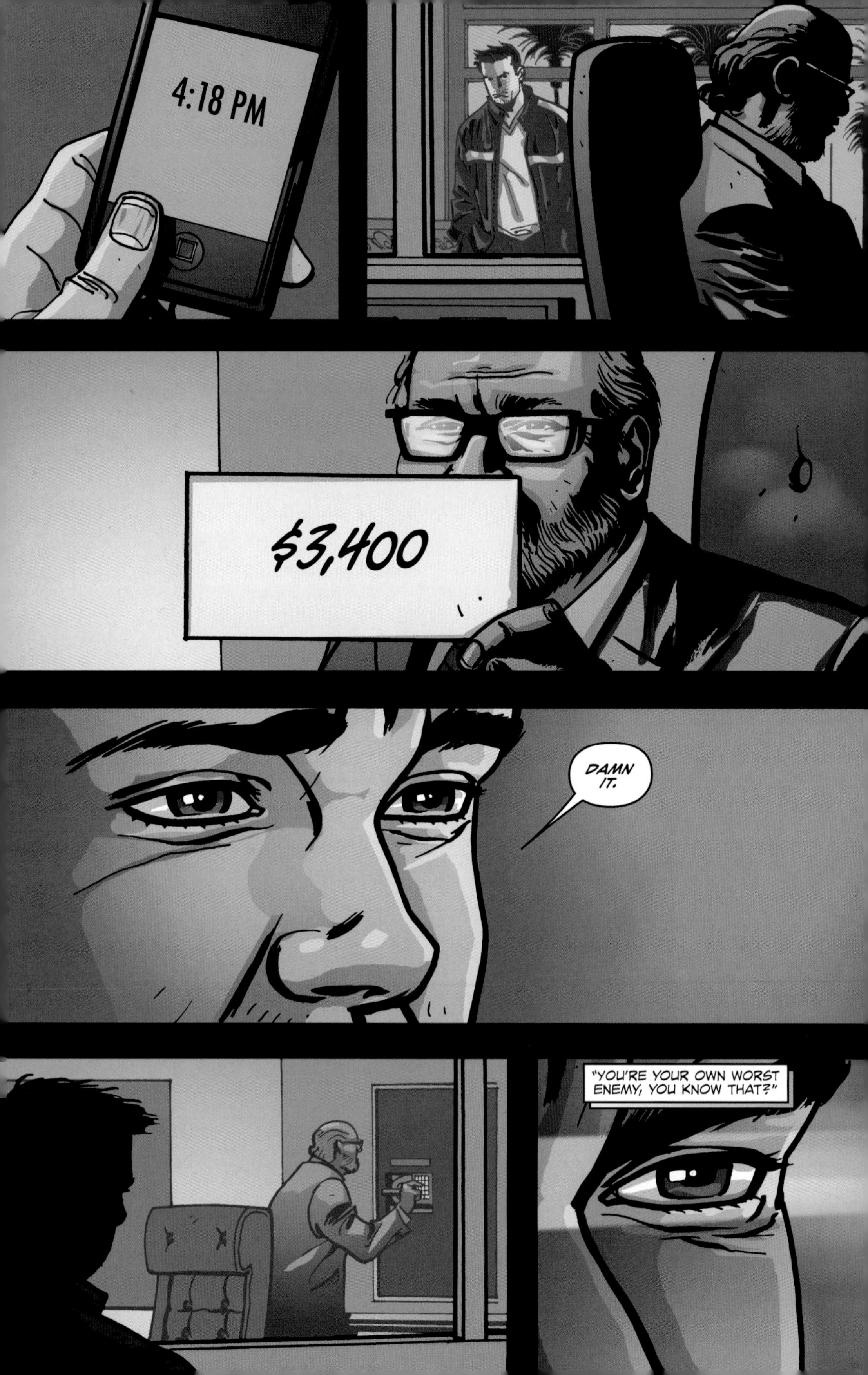
4:18 PM
$3,400
DAMN IT.
"YOU'RE YOUR OWN WORST ENEMY, YOU KNOW THAT?"

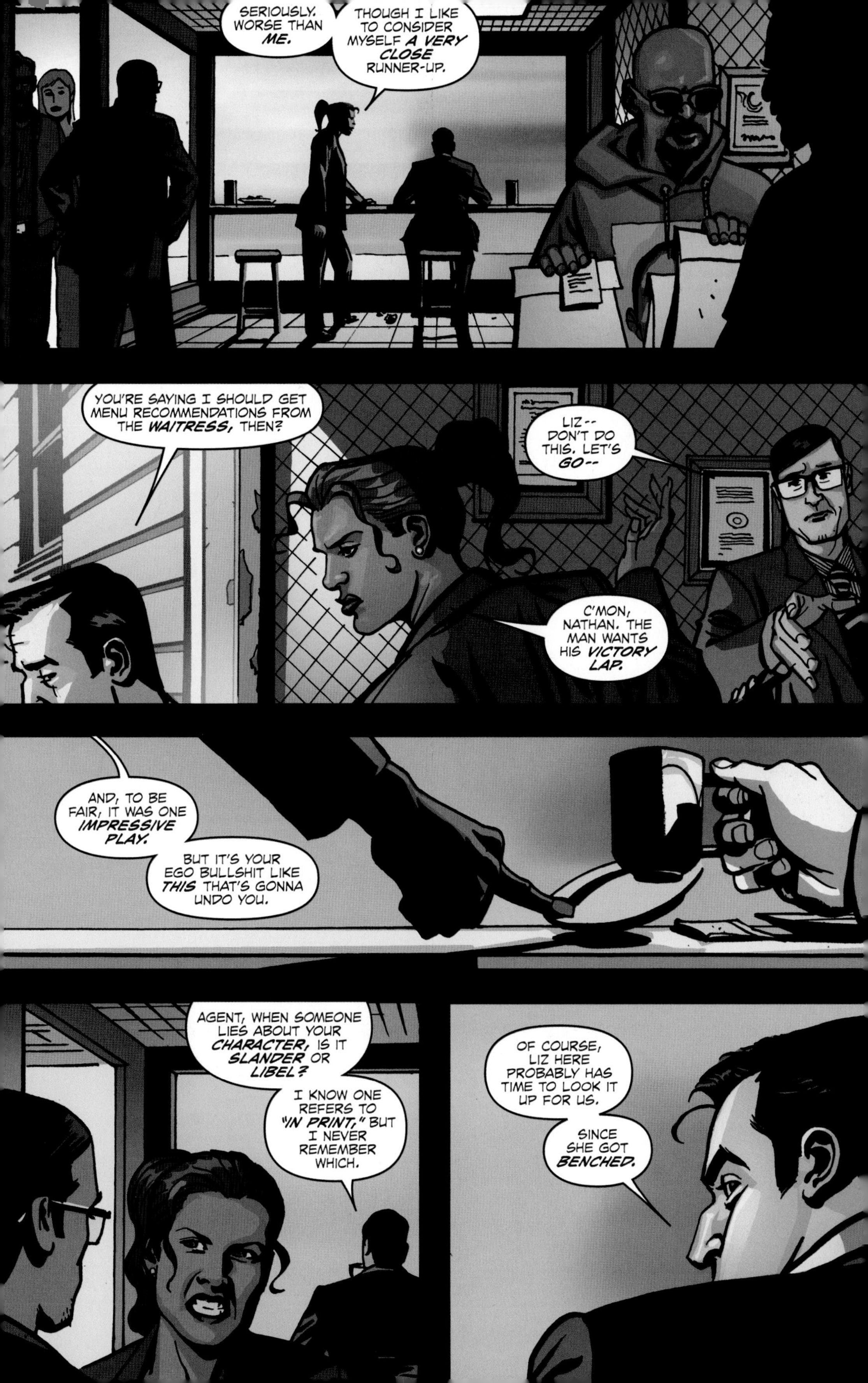
SERIOUSLY. WORSE THAN ME.
THOUGH I LIKE TO CONSIDER MYSELF A VERY CLOSE RUNNER-UP.
YOU'RE SAYING I SHOULD GET MENU RECOMMENDATIONS FROM THE WAITRESS, THEN?
LIZ-- DON'T DO THIS. LET'S GO--
C'MON, NATHAN. THE MAN WANTS HIS VICTORY LAP.
AND, TO BE FAIR, IT WAS ONE IMPRESSIVE PLAY.
BUT IT'S YOUR EGO BULLSHIT LIKE THIS THAT'S GONNA UNDO YOU.
AGENT, WHEN SOMEONE LIES ABOUT YOUR CHARACTER, IS IT SLANDER OR LIBEL?
I KNOW ONE REFERS TO "IN PRINT," BUT I NEVER REMEMBER WHICH.
OF COURSE, LIZ HERE PROBABLY HAS TIME TO LOOK IT UP FOR US.
SINCE SHE GOT BENCHED.

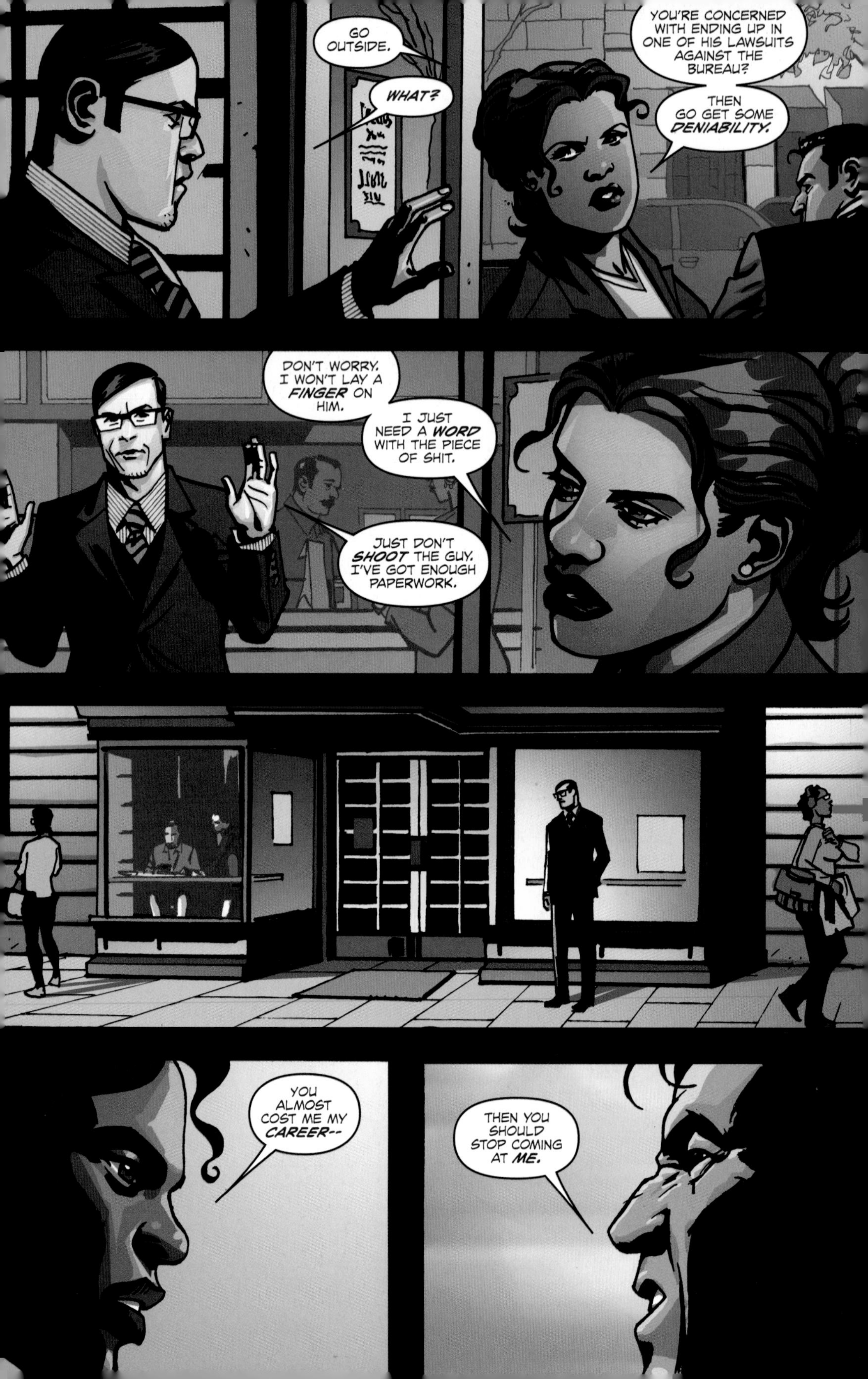
GO OUTSIDE.
WHAT?
YOU'RE CONCERNED WITH ENDING UP IN ONE OF HIS LAWSUITS AGAINST THE BUREAU?
THEN GO GET SOME DENIABILITY.
DON'T WORRY. I WON'T LAY A FINGER ON HIM.
I JUST NEED A WORD WITH THE PIECE OF SHIT.
JUST DON'T SHOOT THE GUY. I'VE GOT ENOUGH PAPERWORK.
YOU ALMOST COST ME MY CAREER--
THEN YOU SHOULD STOP COMING AT ME.

REALLY?

WELL YOU'RE IN *LUCK.*

BECAUSE I WON'T BE *AFTER YOU* NOW.

YOU MEAN "GOOD OL' RELIABLE *NATHAN"?*

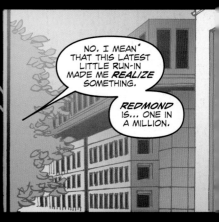

NO. I MEAN THAT THIS LATEST LITTLE RUN-IN MADE ME *REALIZE* SOMETHING.

REDMOND IS... ONE IN A MILLION.

AND MAYBE I SHOULD ASSUME HE CAN JUST KEEP ONE STEP AHEAD OF US... *FOREVER.*

JEEZ. YOU'RE STARTING TO MAKE ME WISH I *WAS* REDMOND.

YEAH, WELL-- I REALIZED SOMETHING *ELSE,* TOO.

YOUR SON IS DEFINITELY *NO REDMOND.*

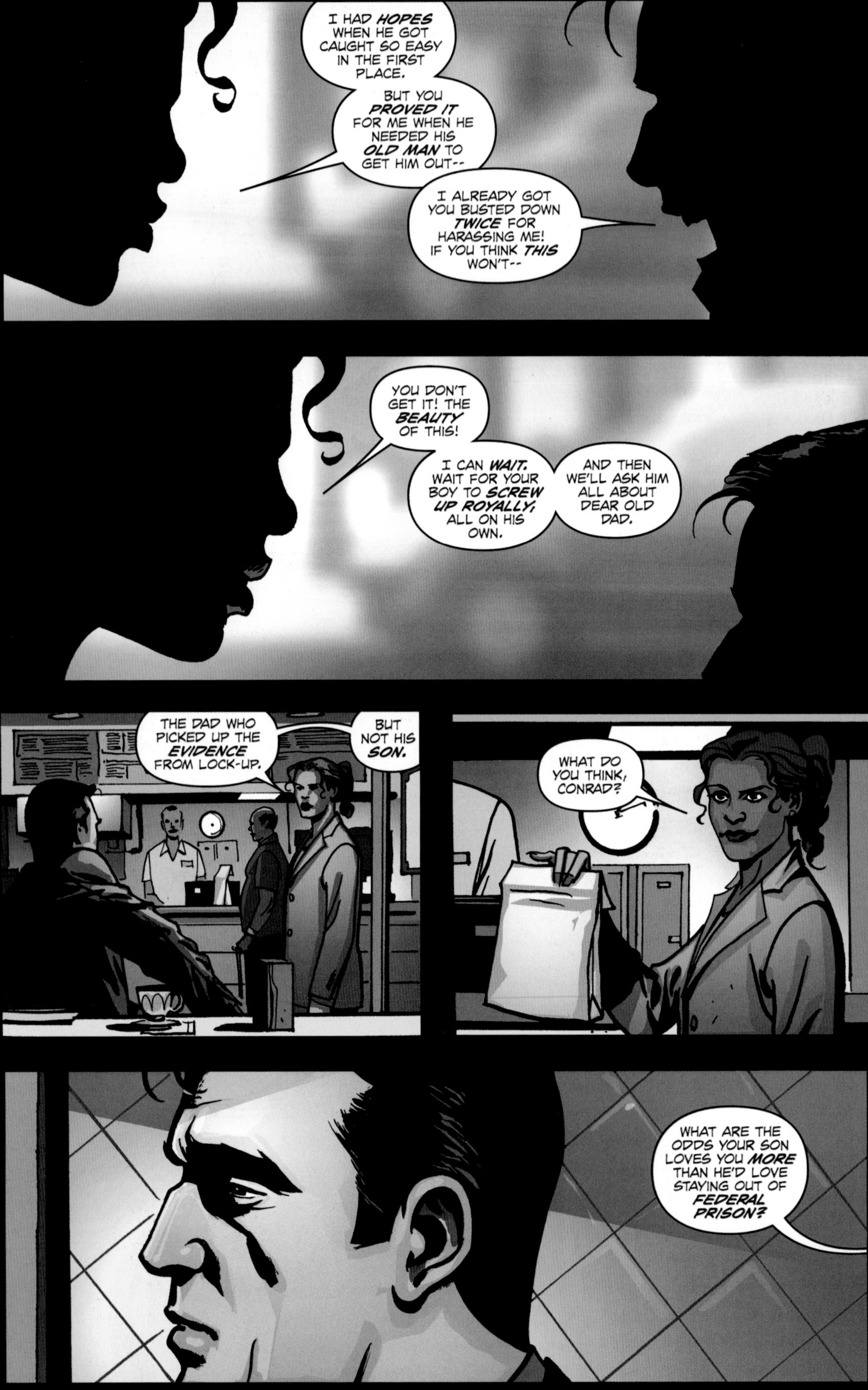
I HAD HOPES WHEN HE GOT CAUGHT SO EASY IN THE FIRST PLACE.
BUT YOU PROVED IT FOR ME WHEN HE NEEDED HIS OLD MAN TO GET HIM OUT--
I ALREADY GOT YOU BUSTED DOWN TWICE FOR HARASSING ME! IF YOU THINK THIS WON'T--
YOU DON'T GET IT! THE BEAUTY OF THIS!
I CAN WAIT. WAIT FOR YOUR BOY TO SCREW UP ROYALLY, ALL ON HIS OWN.
AND THEN WE'LL ASK HIM ALL ABOUT DEAR OLD DAD.
THE DAD WHO PICKED UP THE EVIDENCE FROM LOCK-UP.
BUT NOT HIS SON.
WHAT DO YOU THINK, CONRAD?
WHAT ARE THE ODDS YOUR SON LOVES YOU MORE THAN HE'D LOVE STAYING OUT OF FEDERAL PRISON?

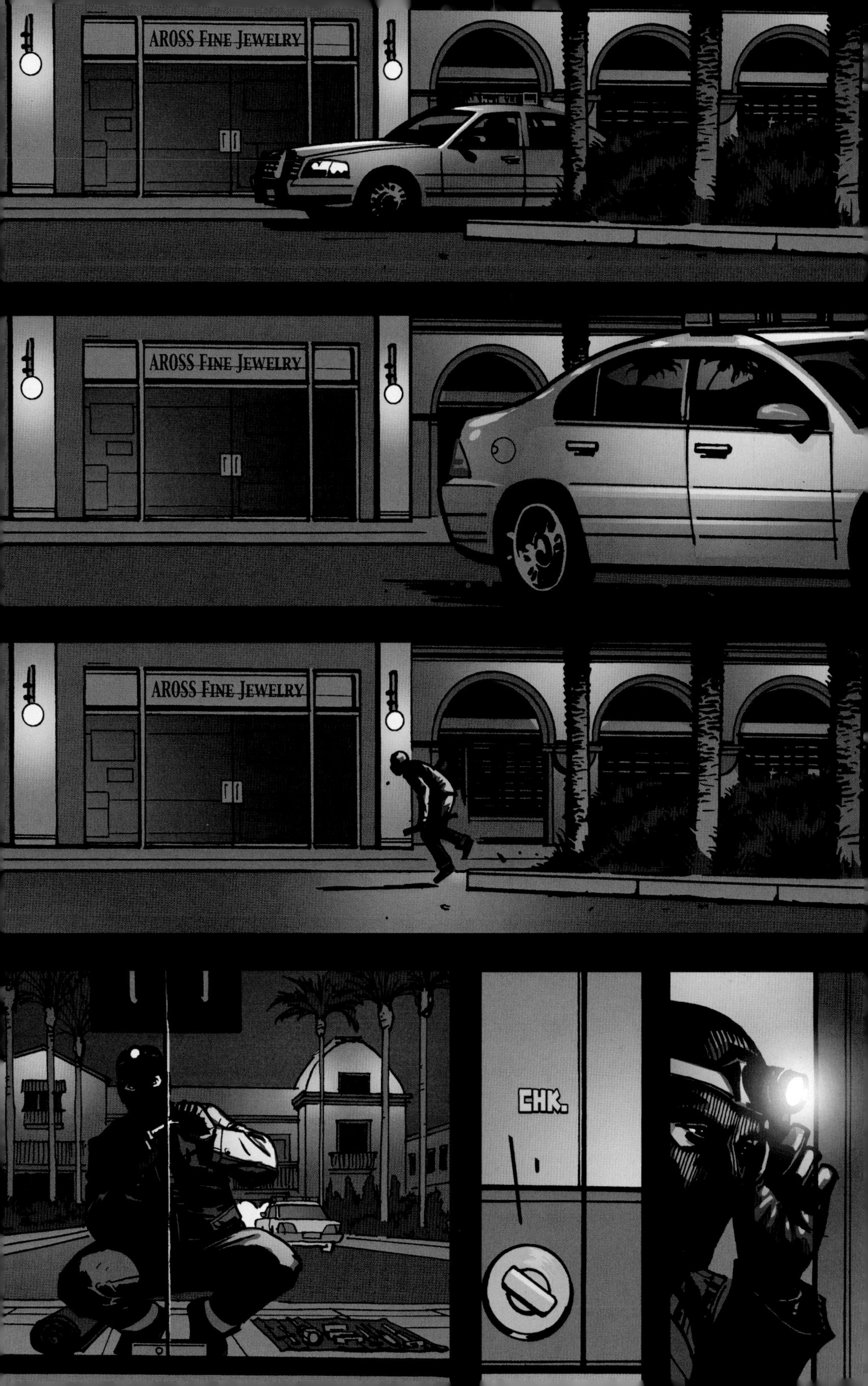
AROSS FINE JEWELRY
AROSS FINE JEWELRY
AROSS FINE JEWELRY
CHK.

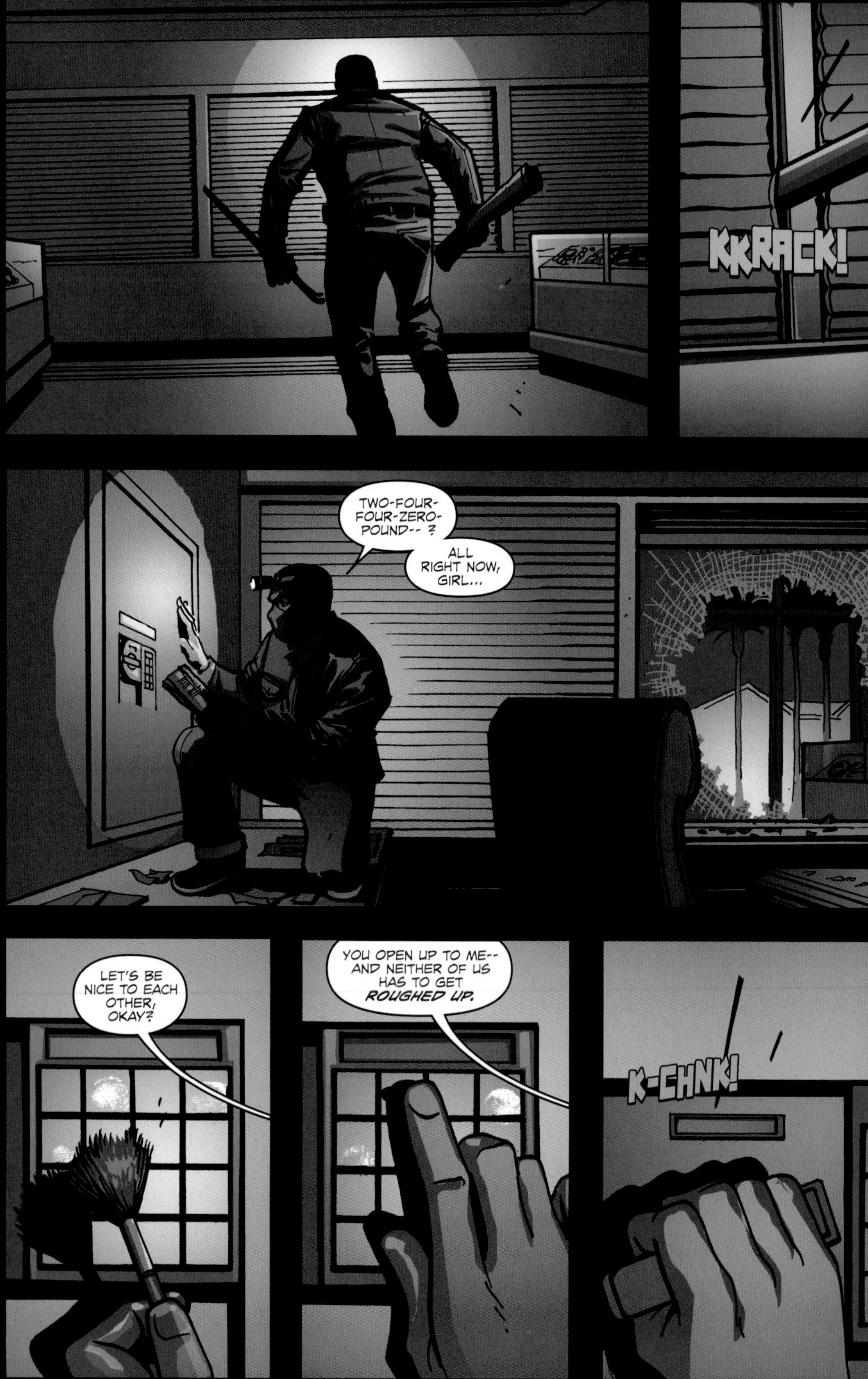
KKRACK!
TWO-FOUR-FOUR-ZERO-POUND-- ?
ALL RIGHT NOW, GIRL...
LET'S BE NICE TO EACH OTHER, OKAY?
YOU OPEN UP TO ME-- AND NEITHER OF US HAS TO GET *ROUGHED UP.*
K-CHNK!

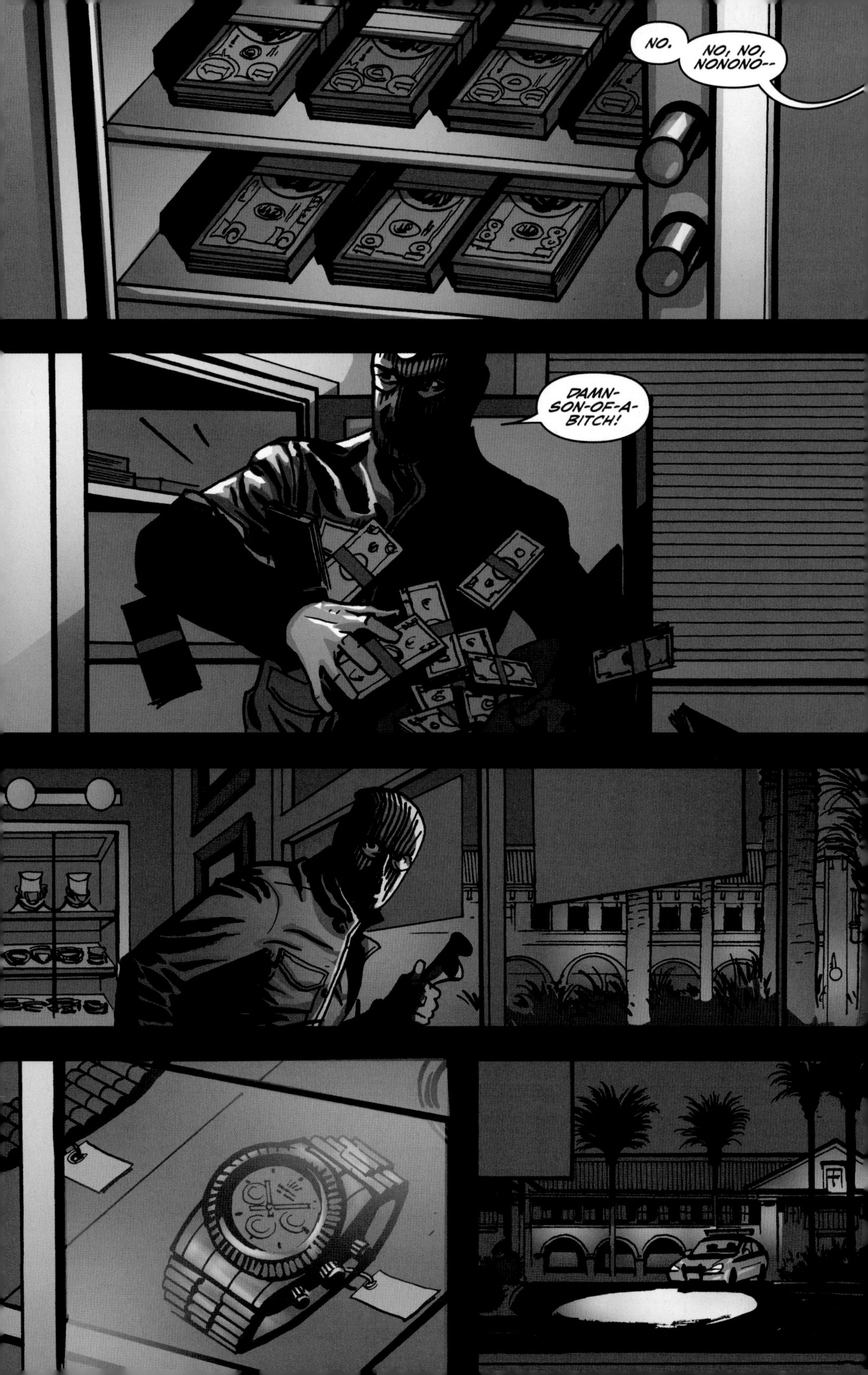
NO.
NO, NO, NONONO--
DAMN-SON-OF-A-BITCH!

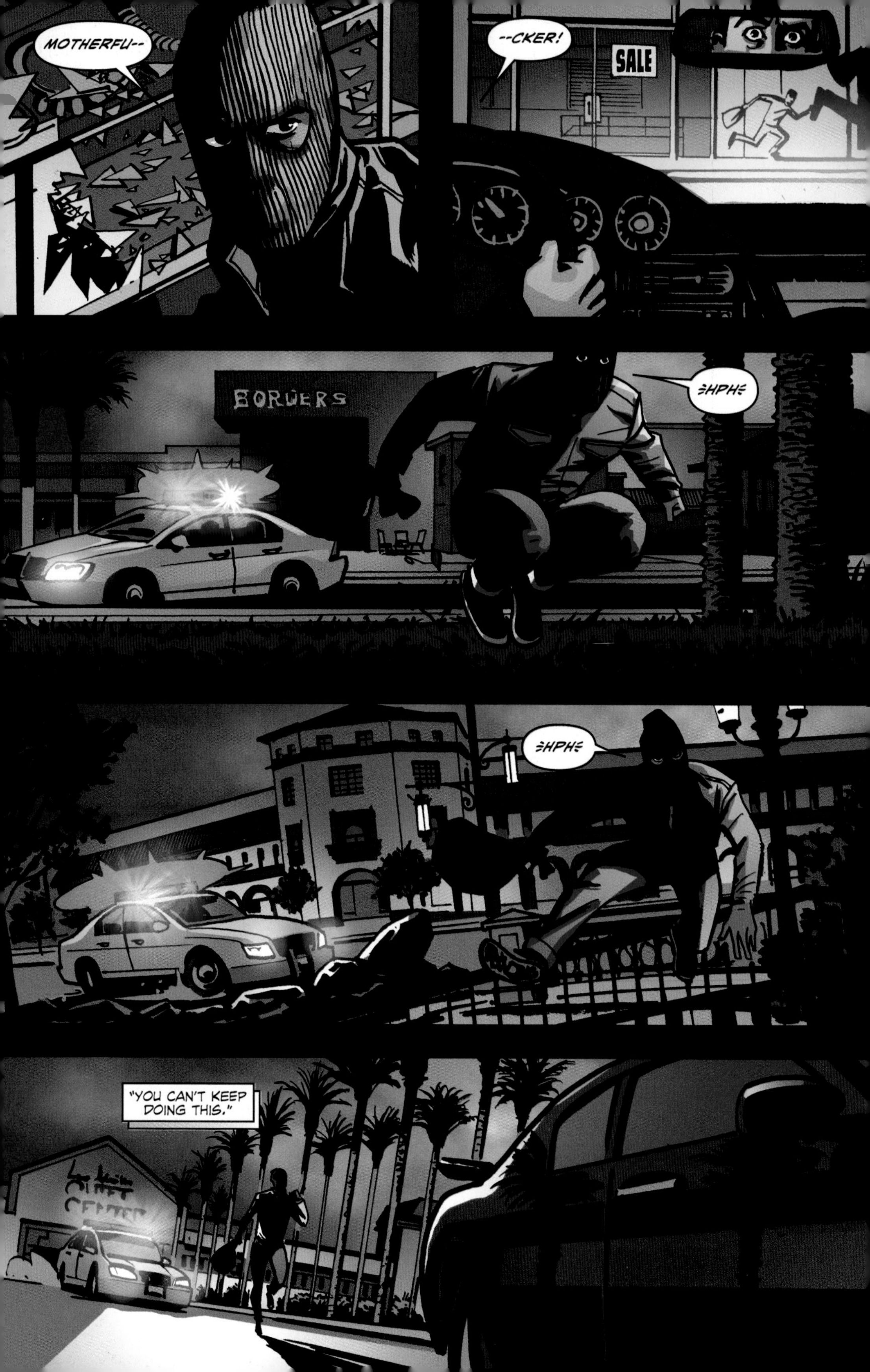
MOTHERFU--
--CKER!
SALE
BORDERS
HPH
HPH
"YOU CAN'T KEEP DOING THIS."

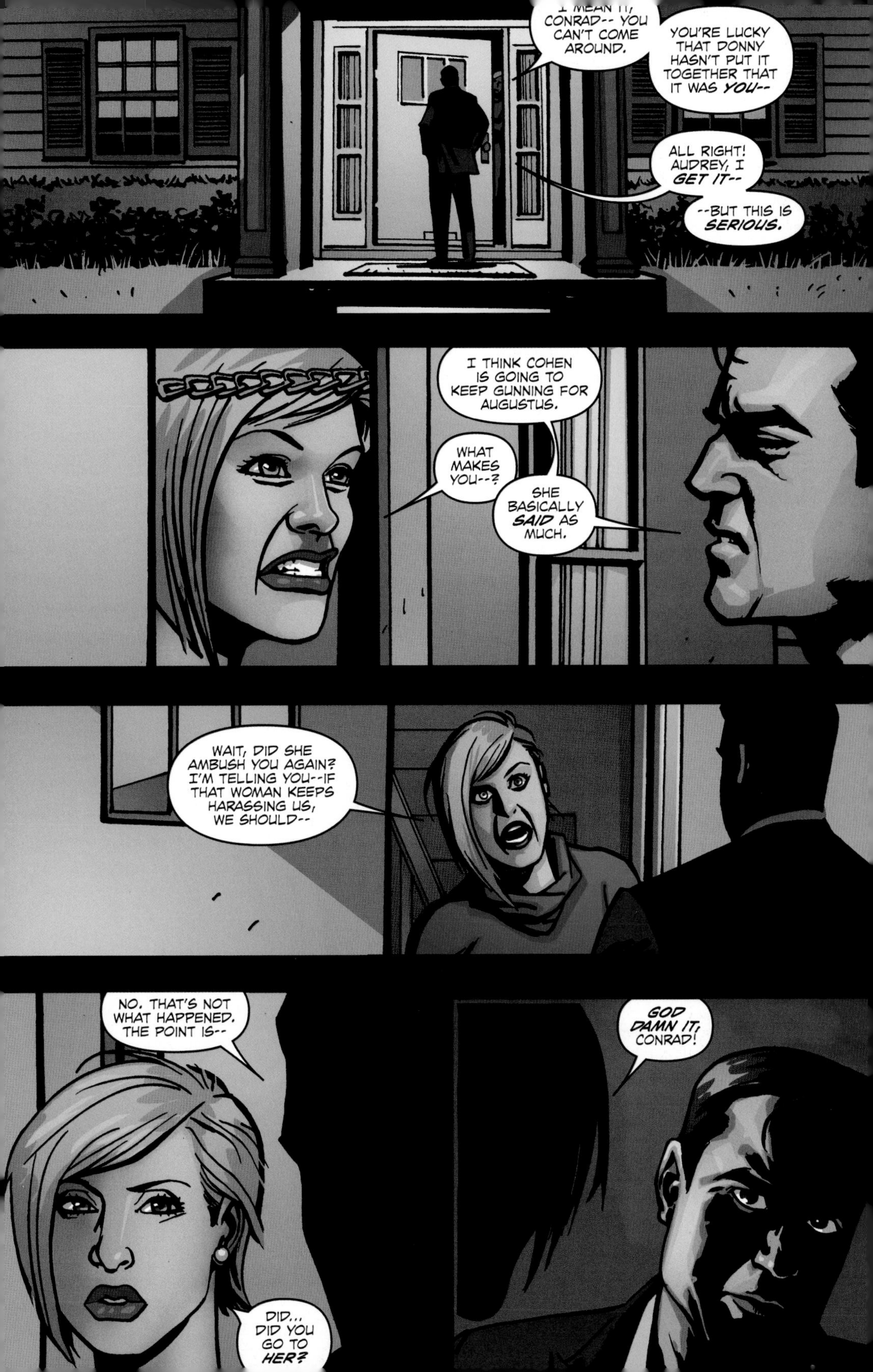
I MEAN IT, CONRAD-- YOU CAN'T COME AROUND.
YOU'RE LUCKY THAT DONNY HASN'T PUT IT TOGETHER THAT IT WAS YOU--
ALL RIGHT! AUDREY, I GET IT--
--BUT THIS IS SERIOUS.
I THINK COHEN IS GOING TO KEEP GUNNING FOR AUGUSTUS.
WHAT MAKES YOU--?
SHE BASICALLY SAID AS MUCH.
WAIT, DID SHE AMBUSH YOU AGAIN? I'M TELLING YOU--IF THAT WOMAN KEEPS HARASSING US, WE SHOULD--
NO. THAT'S NOT WHAT HAPPENED. THE POINT IS--
GOD DAMN IT, CONRAD!
DID... DID YOU GO TO HER?

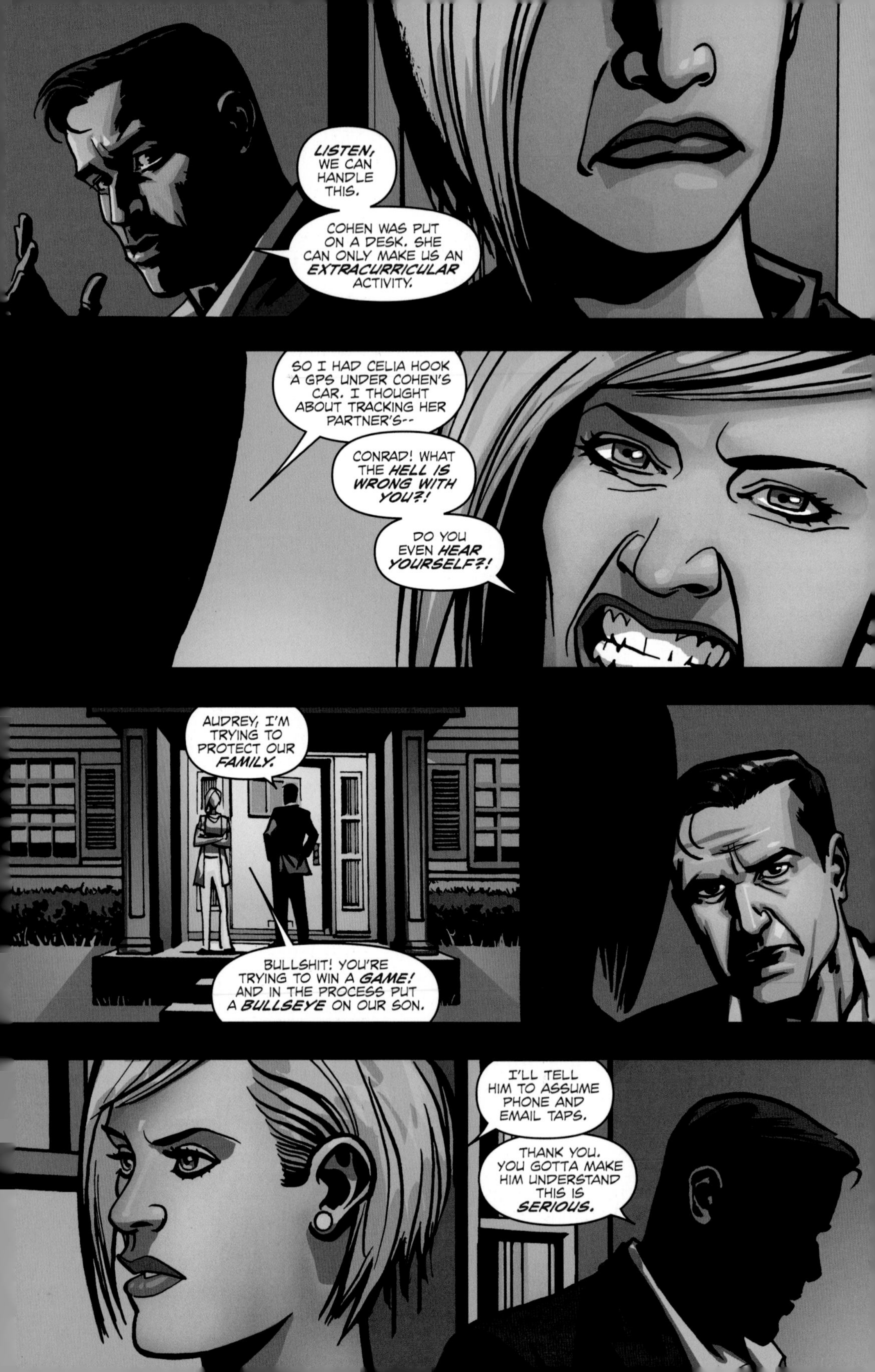
LISTEN, WE CAN HANDLE THIS.
COHEN WAS PUT ON A DESK. SHE CAN ONLY MAKE US AN EXTRACURRICULAR ACTIVITY.
SO I HAD CELIA HOOK A GPS UNDER COHEN'S CAR. I THOUGHT ABOUT TRACKING HER PARTNER'S--
CONRAD! WHAT THE HELL IS WRONG WITH YOU?!
DO YOU EVEN HEAR YOURSELF?!
AUDREY, I'M TRYING TO PROTECT OUR FAMILY.
BULLSHIT! YOU'RE TRYING TO WIN A GAME! AND IN THE PROCESS PUT A BULLSEYE ON OUR SON.
I'LL TELL HIM TO ASSUME PHONE AND EMAIL TAPS.
THANK YOU. YOU GOTTA MAKE HIM UNDERSTAND THIS IS SERIOUS.

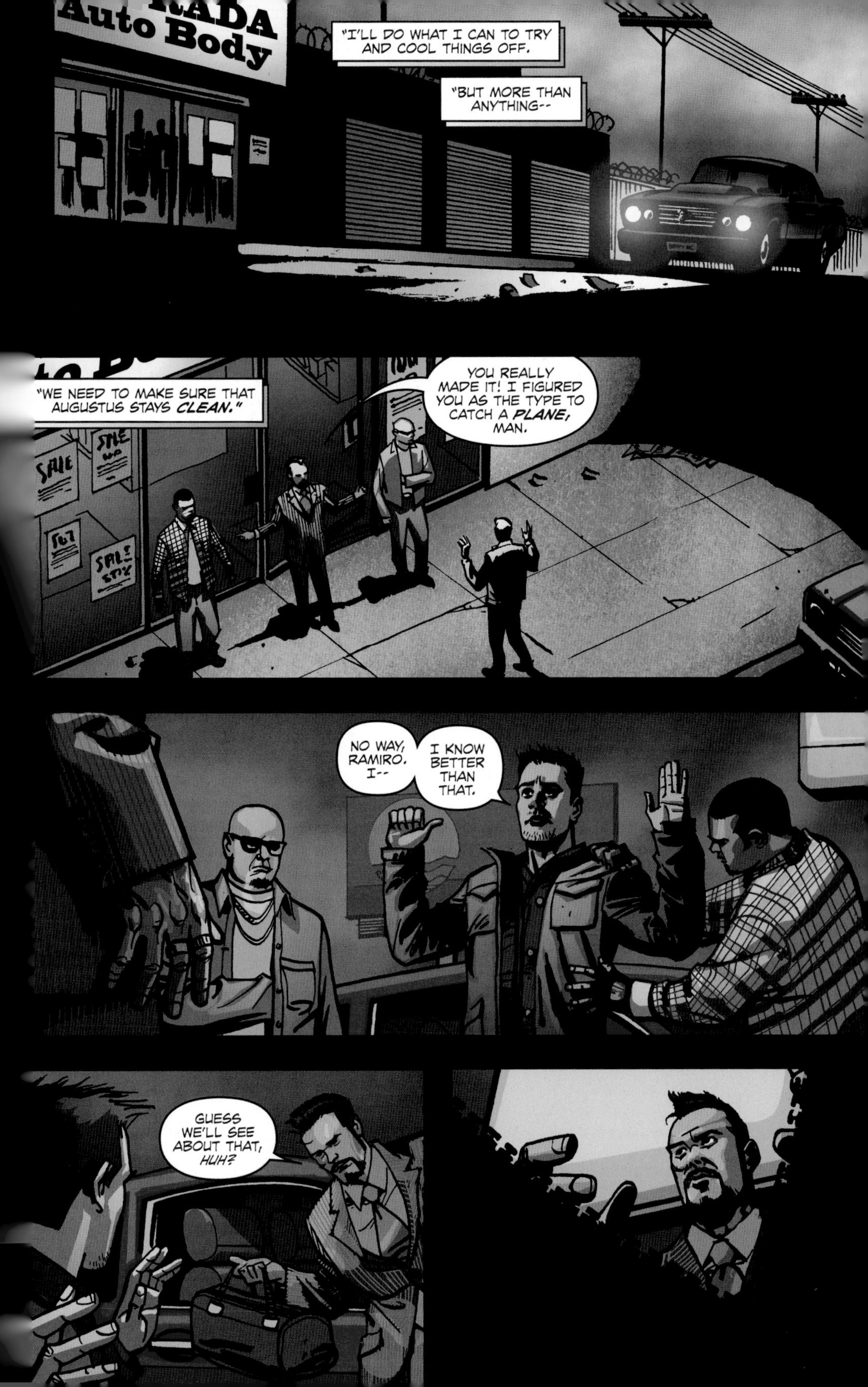

RADA
Auto Body
"I'LL DO WHAT I CAN TO TRY AND COOL THINGS OFF.
"BUT MORE THAN ANYTHING--
"WE NEED TO MAKE SURE THAT AUGUSTUS STAYS CLEAN."
YOU REALLY MADE IT! I FIGURED YOU AS THE TYPE TO CATCH A PLANE, MAN.
NO WAY, RAMIRO. I--
I KNOW BETTER THAN THAT.
GUESS WE'LL SEE ABOUT THAT, HUH?

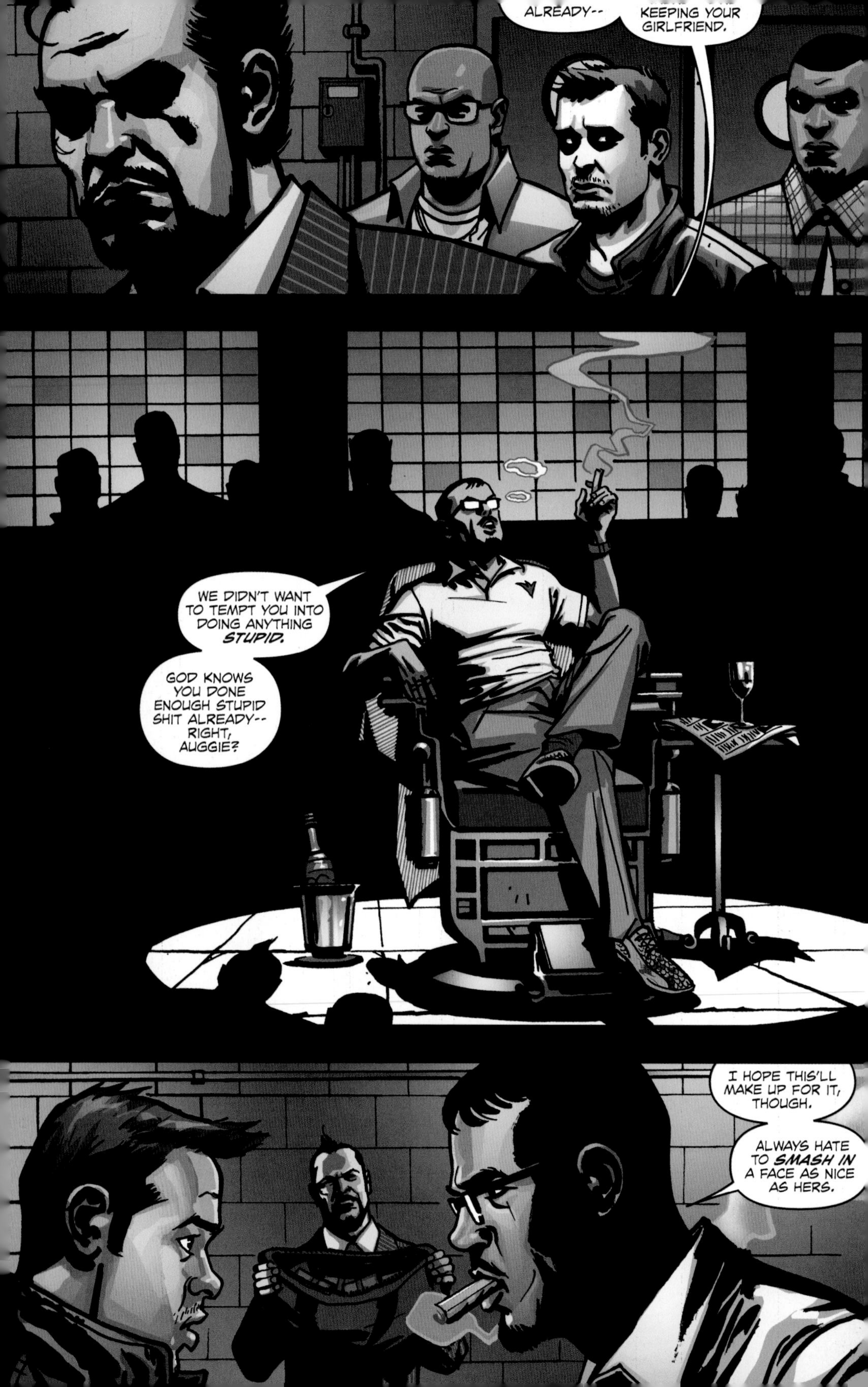
ALREADY--
KEEPING YOUR GIRLFRIEND.
WE DIDN'T WANT TO TEMPT YOU INTO DOING ANYTHING STUPID.
GOD KNOWS YOU DONE ENOUGH STUPID SHIT ALREADY-- RIGHT, AUGGIE?
I HOPE THIS'LL MAKE UP FOR IT, THOUGH.
ALWAYS HATE TO SMASH IN A FACE AS NICE AS HERS.

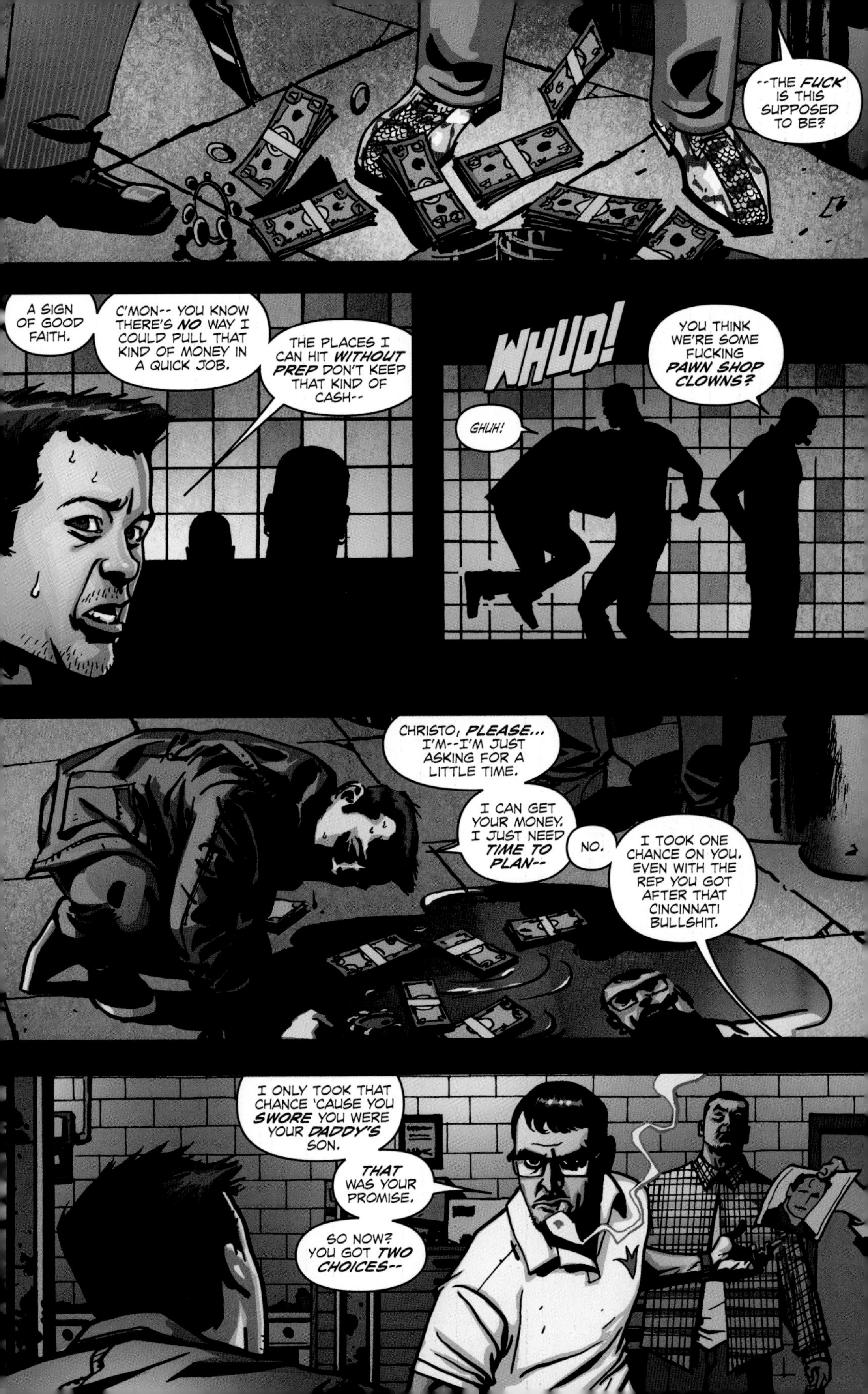
--THE FUCK IS THIS SUPPOSED TO BE?
A SIGN OF GOOD FAITH.
C'MON-- YOU KNOW THERE'S NO WAY I COULD PULL THAT KIND OF MONEY IN A QUICK JOB.
THE PLACES I CAN HIT WITHOUT PREP DON'T KEEP THAT KIND OF CASH--
WHUD!
GHUH!
YOU THINK WE'RE SOME FUCKING PAWN SHOP CLOWNS?
CHRISTO, PLEASE... I'M--I'M JUST ASKING FOR A LITTLE TIME.
I CAN GET YOUR MONEY. I JUST NEED TIME TO PLAN--
NO.
I TOOK ONE CHANCE ON YOU. EVEN WITH THE REP YOU GOT AFTER THAT CINCINNATI BULLSHIT.
I ONLY TOOK THAT CHANCE 'CAUSE YOU SWORE YOU WERE YOUR DADDY'S SON.
THAT WAS YOUR PROMISE.
SO NOW? YOU GOT TWO CHOICES--

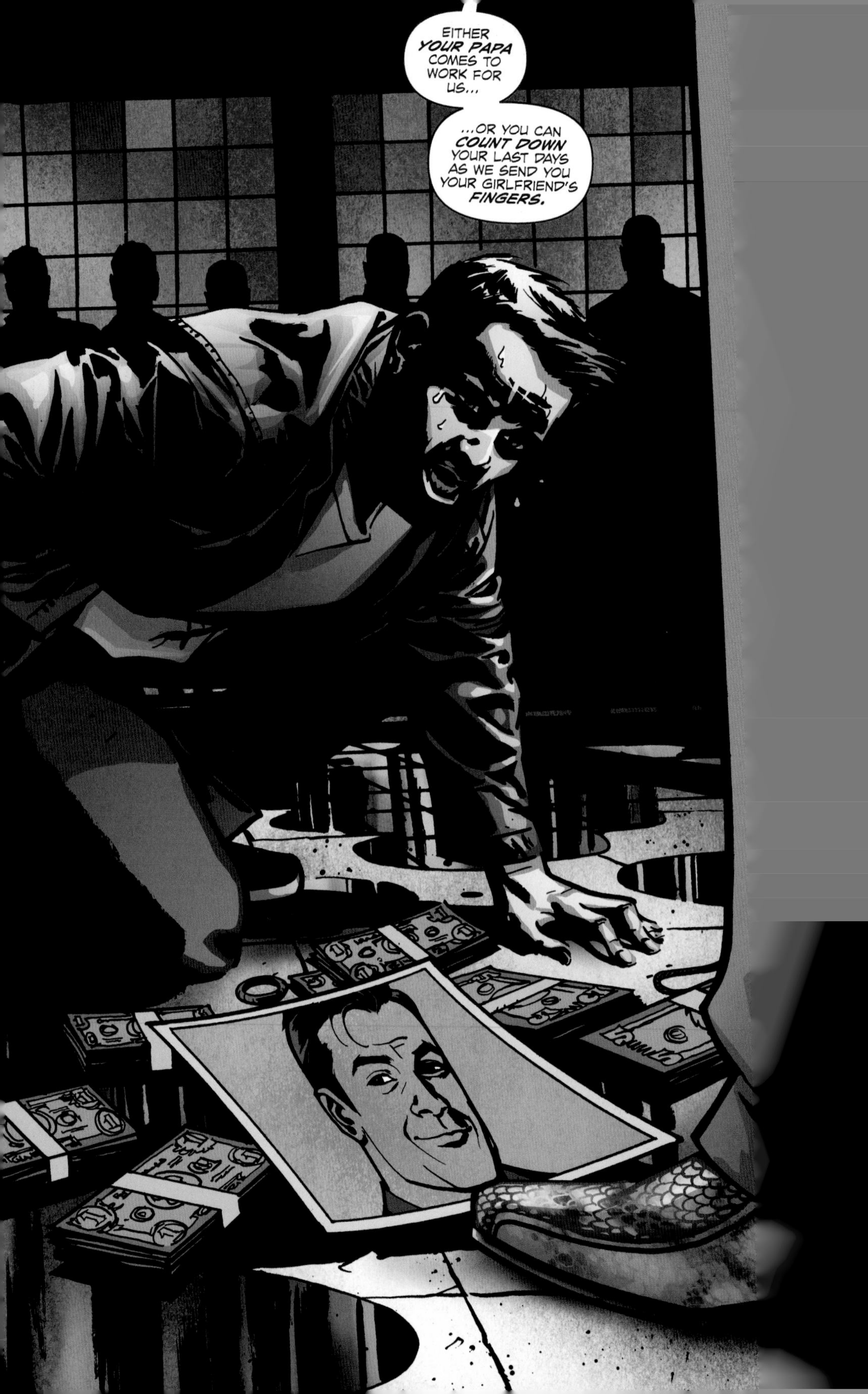
EITHER YOUR PAPA COMES TO WORK FOR US...
...OR YOU CAN COUNT DOWN YOUR LAST DAYS AS WE SEND YOU YOUR GIRLFRIEND'S FINGERS.

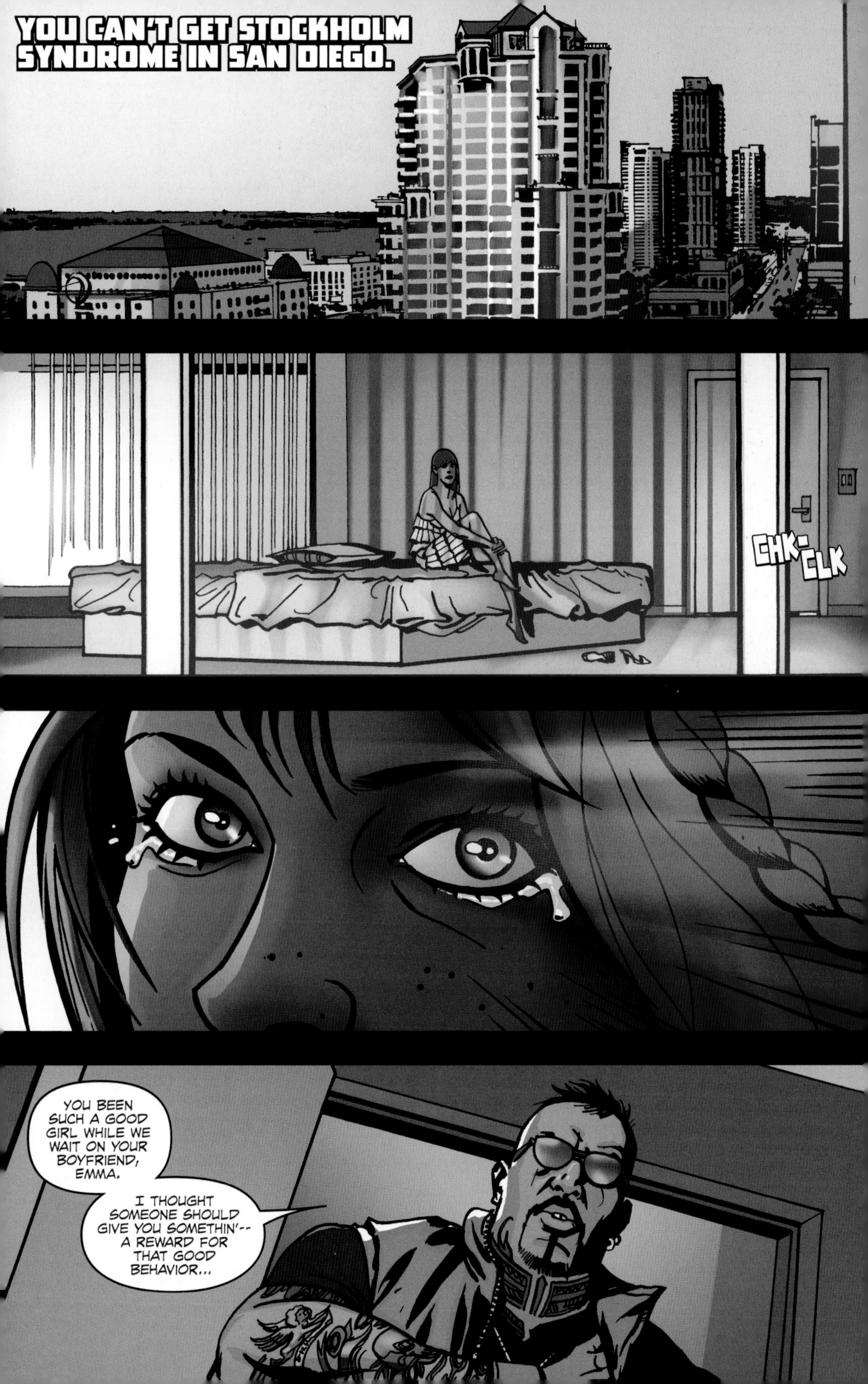
YOU CAN'T GET STOCKHOLM SYNDROME IN SAN DIEGO.
CHK-CLK
YOU BEEN SUCH A GOOD GIRL WHILE WE WAIT ON YOUR BOYFRIEND, EMMA.
I THOUGHT SOMEONE SHOULD GIVE YOU SOMETHIN'-- A REWARD FOR THAT GOOD BEHAVIOR...

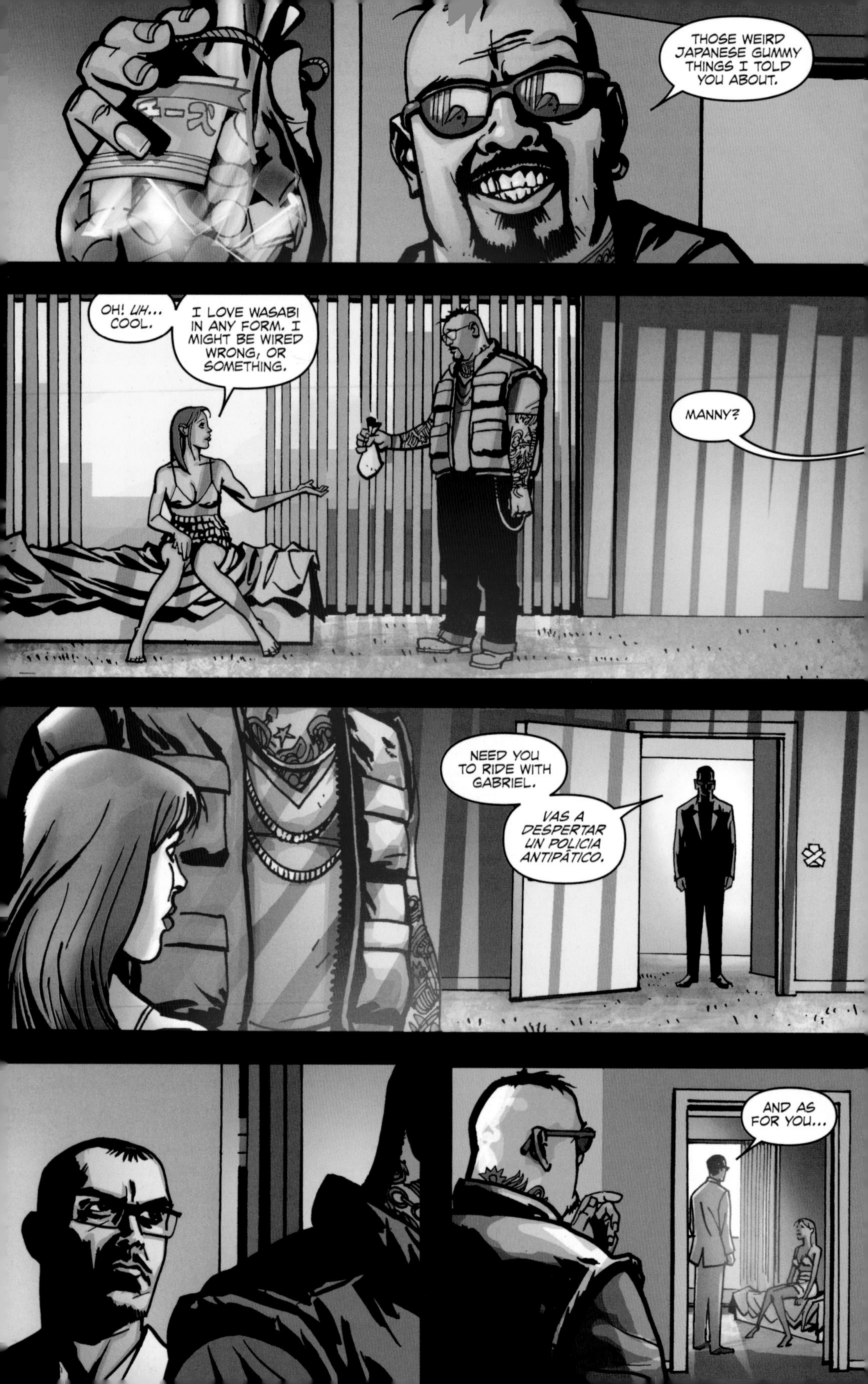
THOSE WEIRD JAPANESE GUMMY THINGS I TOLD YOU ABOUT.
OH! *UH...* COOL.
I LOVE WASABI IN ANY FORM. I MIGHT BE WIRED WRONG, OR SOMETHING.
MANNY?
NEED YOU TO RIDE WITH GABRIEL.
VAS A DESPERTAR UN POLICIA ANTIPÁTICO.
AND AS FOR YOU...

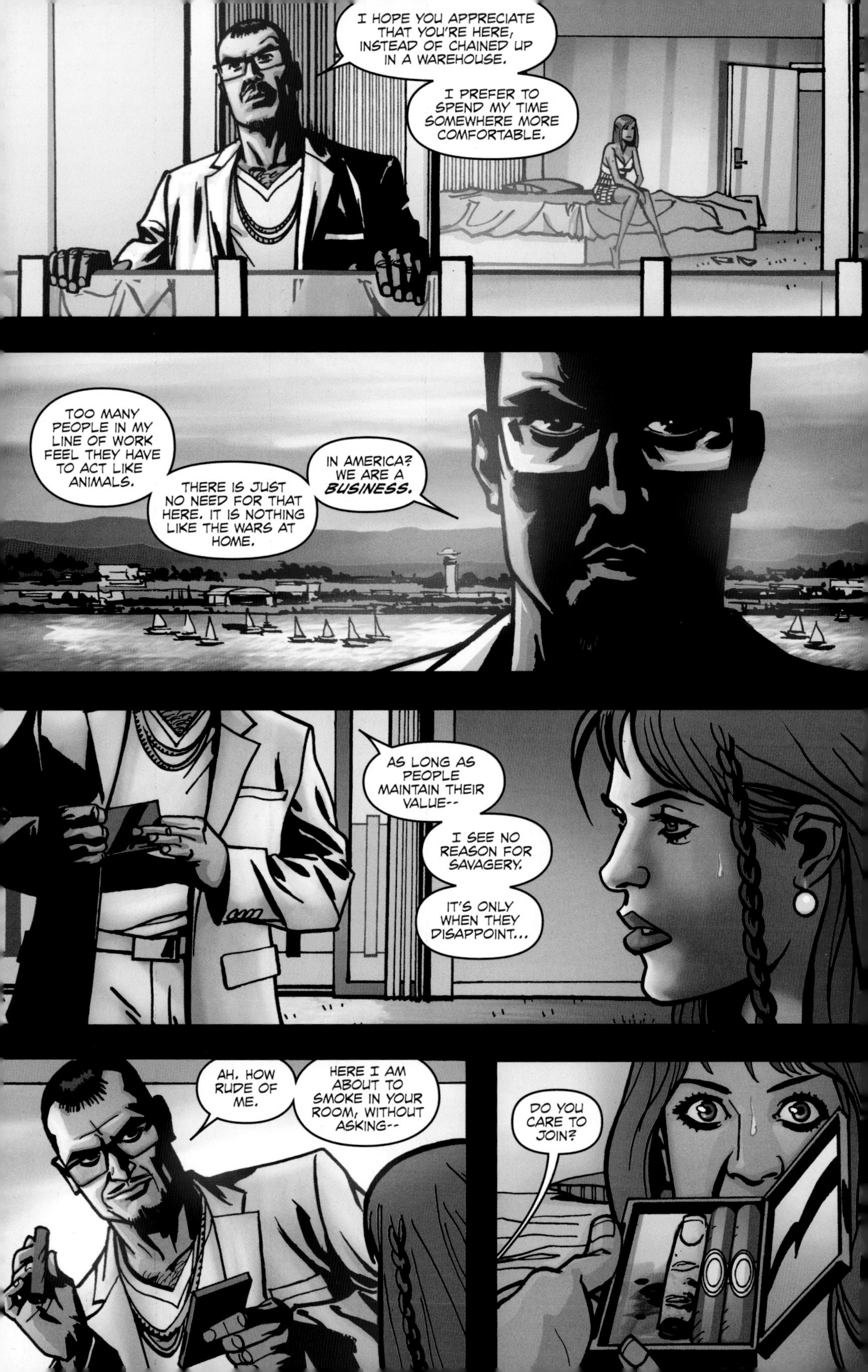
I HOPE YOU APPRECIATE THAT YOU'RE HERE, INSTEAD OF CHAINED UP IN A WAREHOUSE.
I PREFER TO SPEND MY TIME SOMEWHERE MORE COMFORTABLE.
TOO MANY PEOPLE IN MY LINE OF WORK FEEL THEY HAVE TO ACT LIKE ANIMALS.
THERE IS JUST NO NEED FOR THAT HERE. IT IS NOTHING LIKE THE WARS AT HOME.
IN AMERICA? WE ARE A BUSINESS.
AS LONG AS PEOPLE MAINTAIN THEIR VALUE--
I SEE NO REASON FOR SAVAGERY.
IT'S ONLY WHEN THEY DISAPPOINT...
AH. HOW RUDE OF ME.
HERE I AM ABOUT TO SMOKE IN YOUR ROOM, WITHOUT ASKING--
DO YOU CARE TO JOIN?

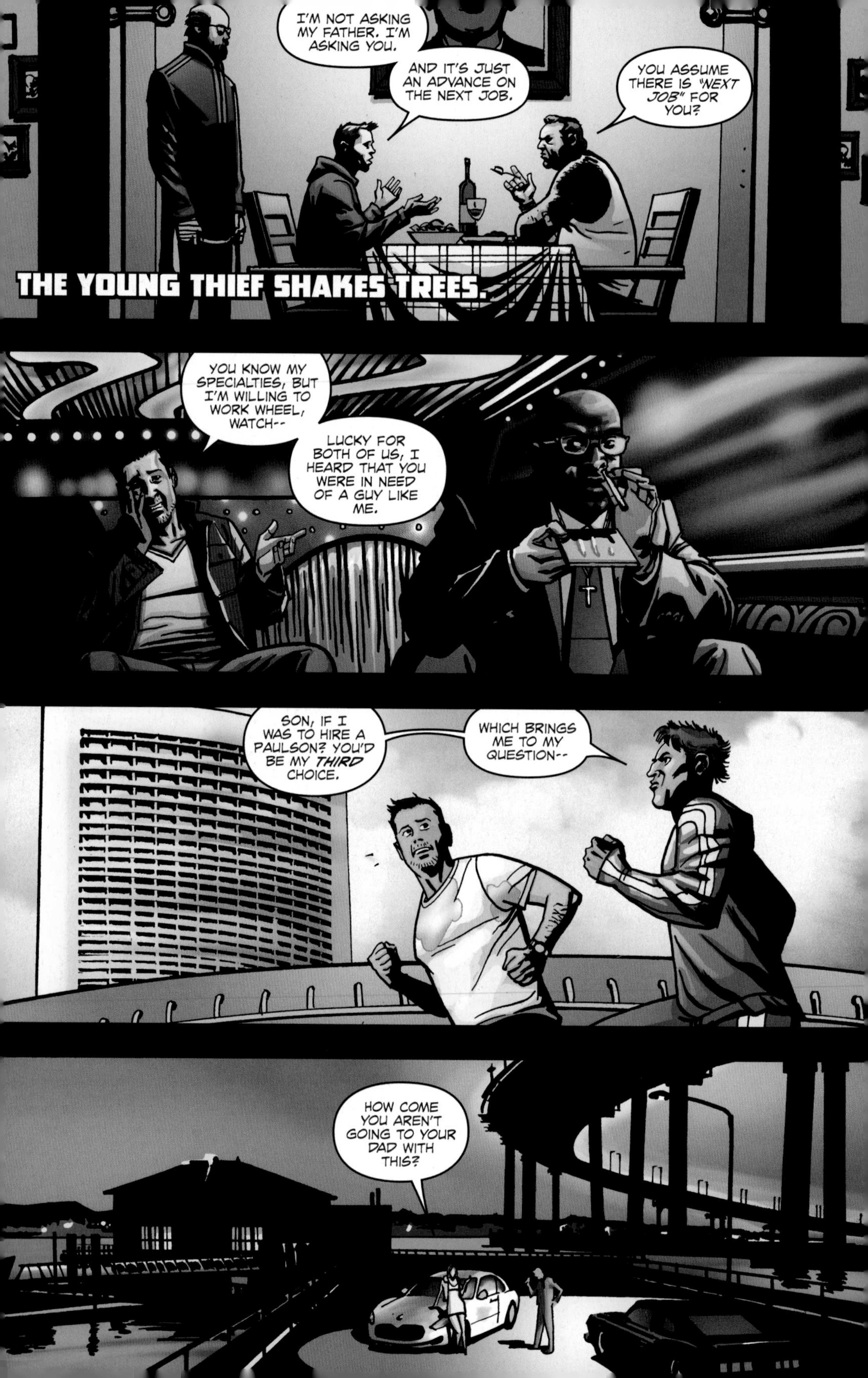
I'M NOT ASKING MY FATHER. I'M ASKING YOU.
AND IT'S JUST AN ADVANCE ON THE NEXT JOB.
YOU ASSUME THERE IS "NEXT JOB" FOR YOU?
THE YOUNG THIEF SHAKES TREES.
YOU KNOW MY SPECIALTIES, BUT I'M WILLING TO WORK WHEEL, WATCH--
LUCKY FOR BOTH OF US, I HEARD THAT YOU WERE IN NEED OF A GUY LIKE ME.
SON, IF I WAS TO HIRE A PAULSON? YOU'D BE MY THIRD CHOICE.
WHICH BRINGS ME TO MY QUESTION--
HOW COME YOU AREN'T GOING TO YOUR DAD WITH THIS?

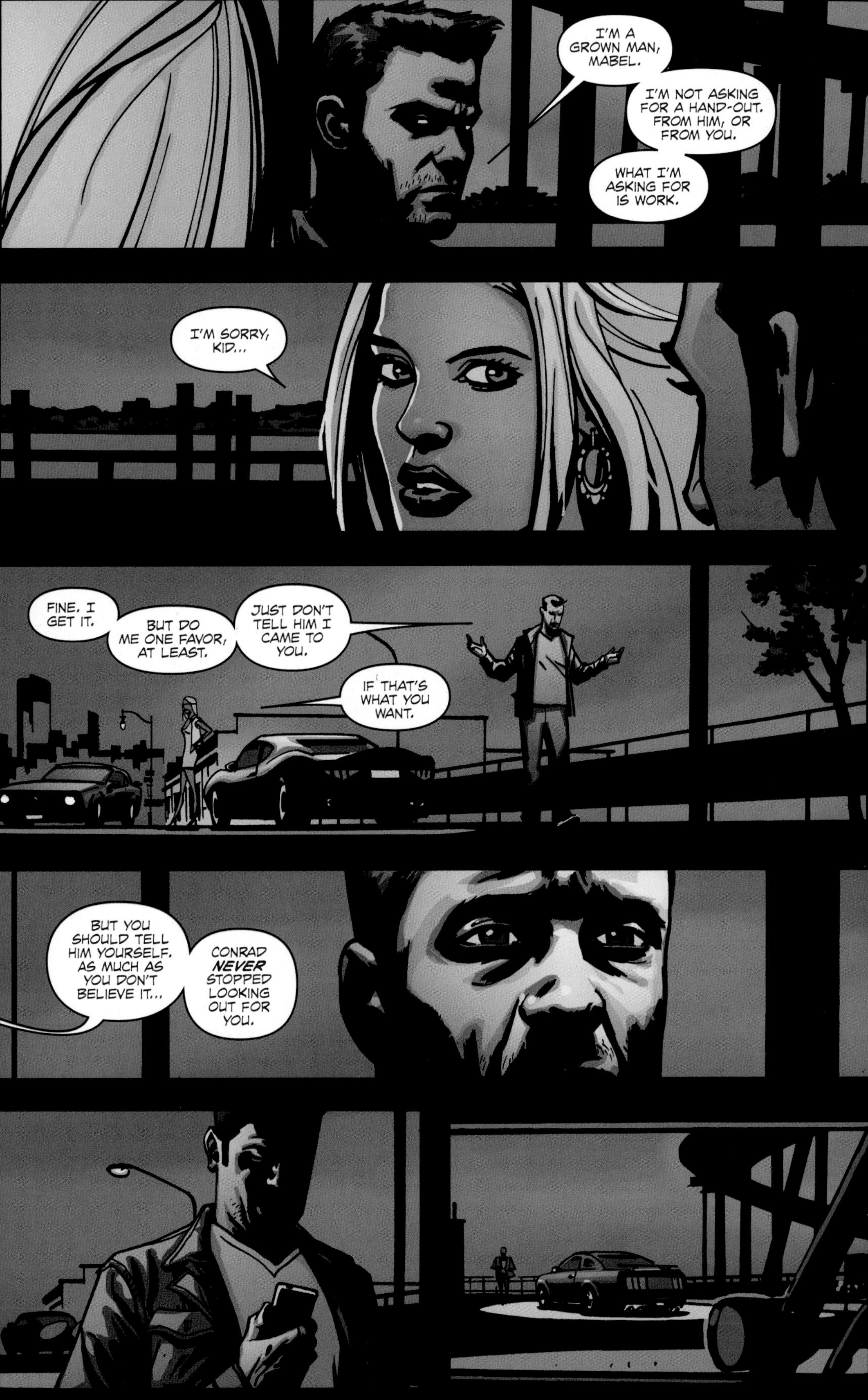

I'M A GROWN MAN, MABEL.
I'M NOT ASKING FOR A HAND-OUT. FROM HIM, OR FROM YOU.
WHAT I'M ASKING FOR IS WORK.
I'M SORRY, KID...
FINE. I GET IT.
BUT DO ME ONE FAVOR, AT LEAST.
JUST DON'T TELL HIM I CAME TO YOU.
IF THAT'S WHAT YOU WANT.
BUT YOU SHOULD TELL HIM YOURSELF. AS MUCH AS YOU DON'T BELIEVE IT...
CONRAD NEVER STOPPED LOOKING OUT FOR YOU.

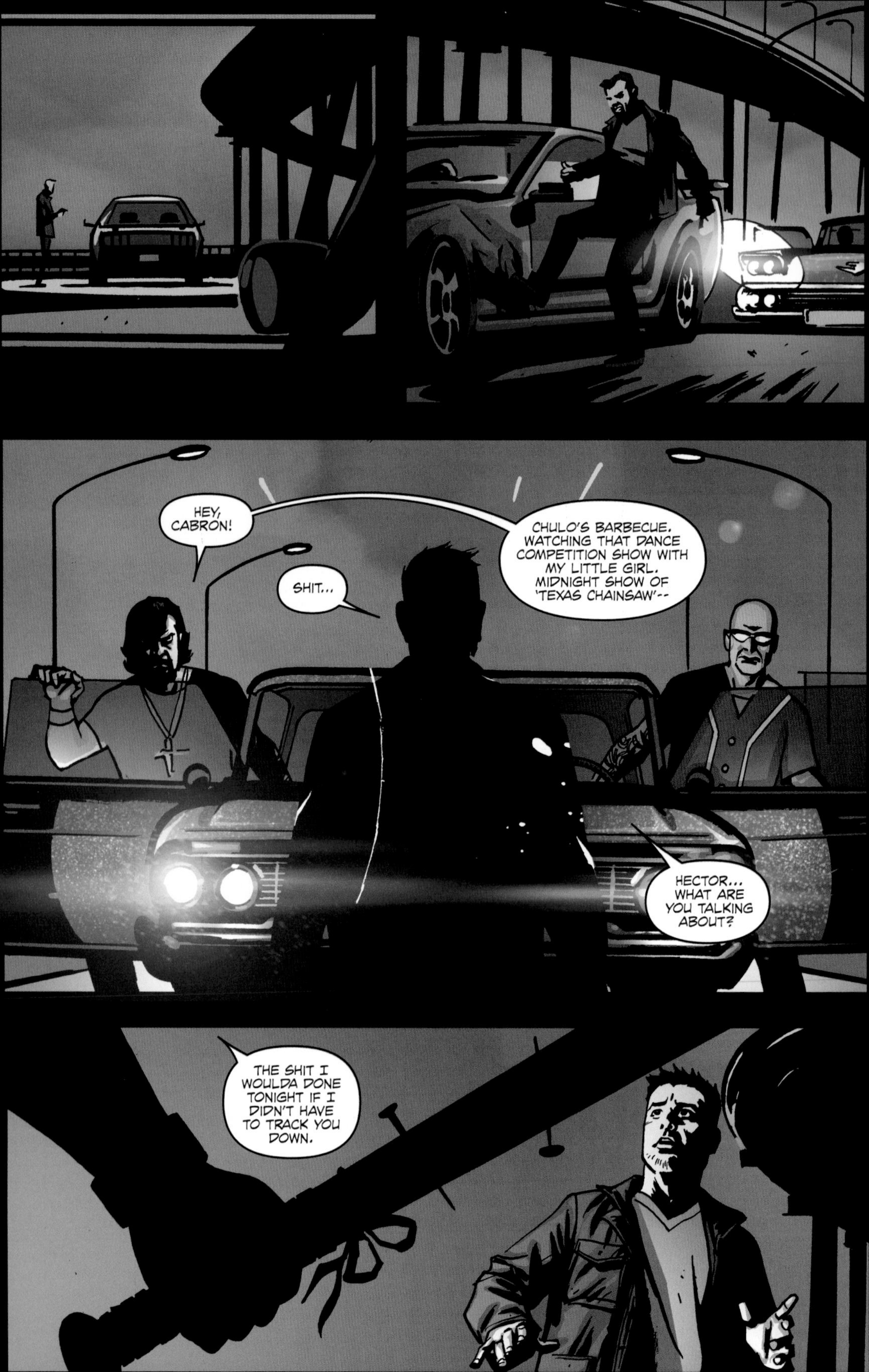
HEY, CABRON!
SHIT...
CHULO'S BARBECUE. WATCHING THAT DANCE COMPETITION SHOW WITH MY LITTLE GIRL. MIDNIGHT SHOW OF 'TEXAS CHAINSAW'--
HECTOR... WHAT ARE YOU TALKING ABOUT?
THE SHIT I WOULDA DONE TONIGHT IF I DIDN'T HAVE TO TRACK YOU DOWN.

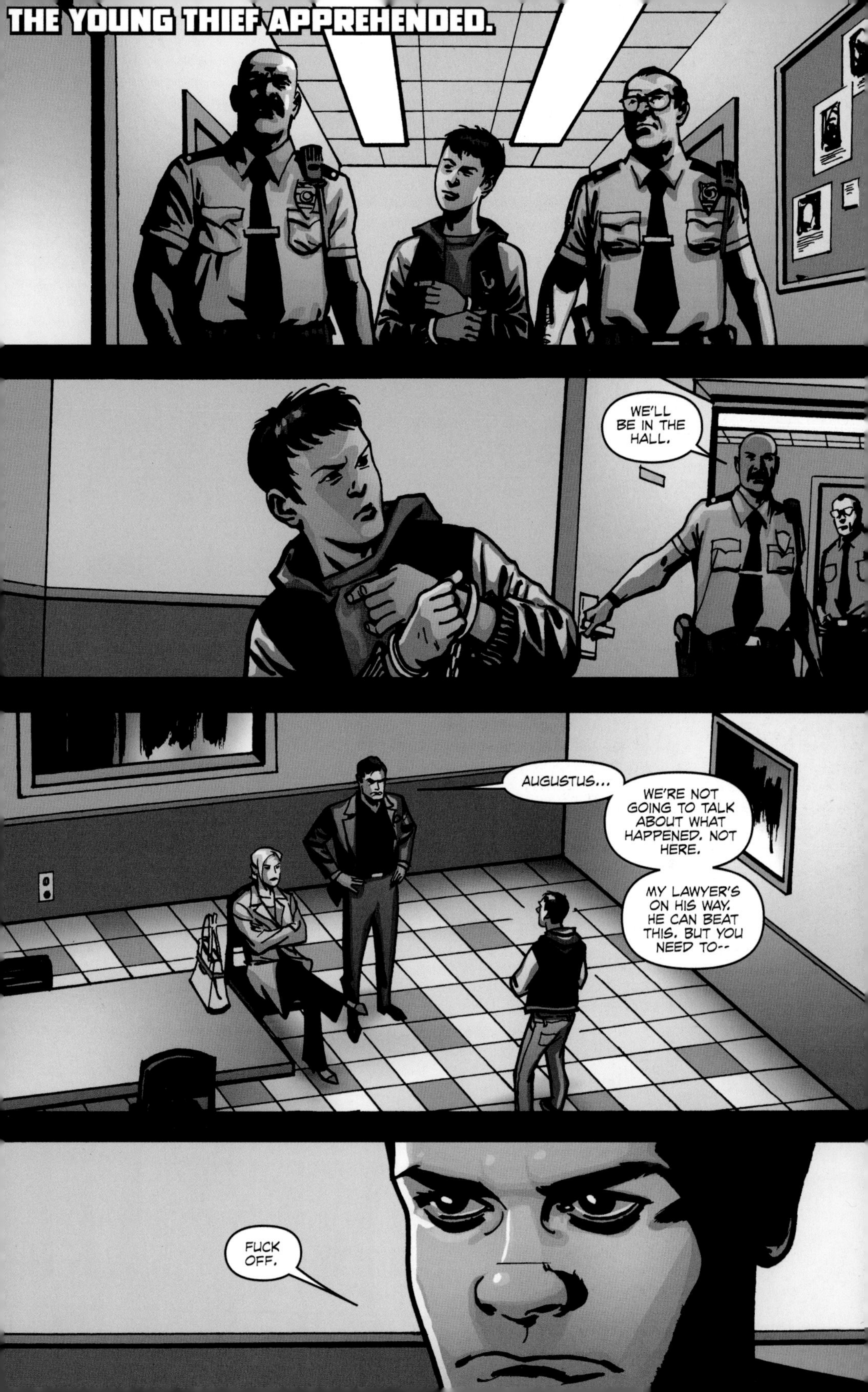
THE YOUNG THIEF APPREHENDED.
WE'LL BE IN THE HALL.
AUGUSTUS...
WE'RE NOT GOING TO TALK ABOUT WHAT HAPPENED. NOT HERE.
MY LAWYER'S ON HIS WAY. HE CAN BEAT THIS. BUT YOU NEED TO--
FUCK OFF.

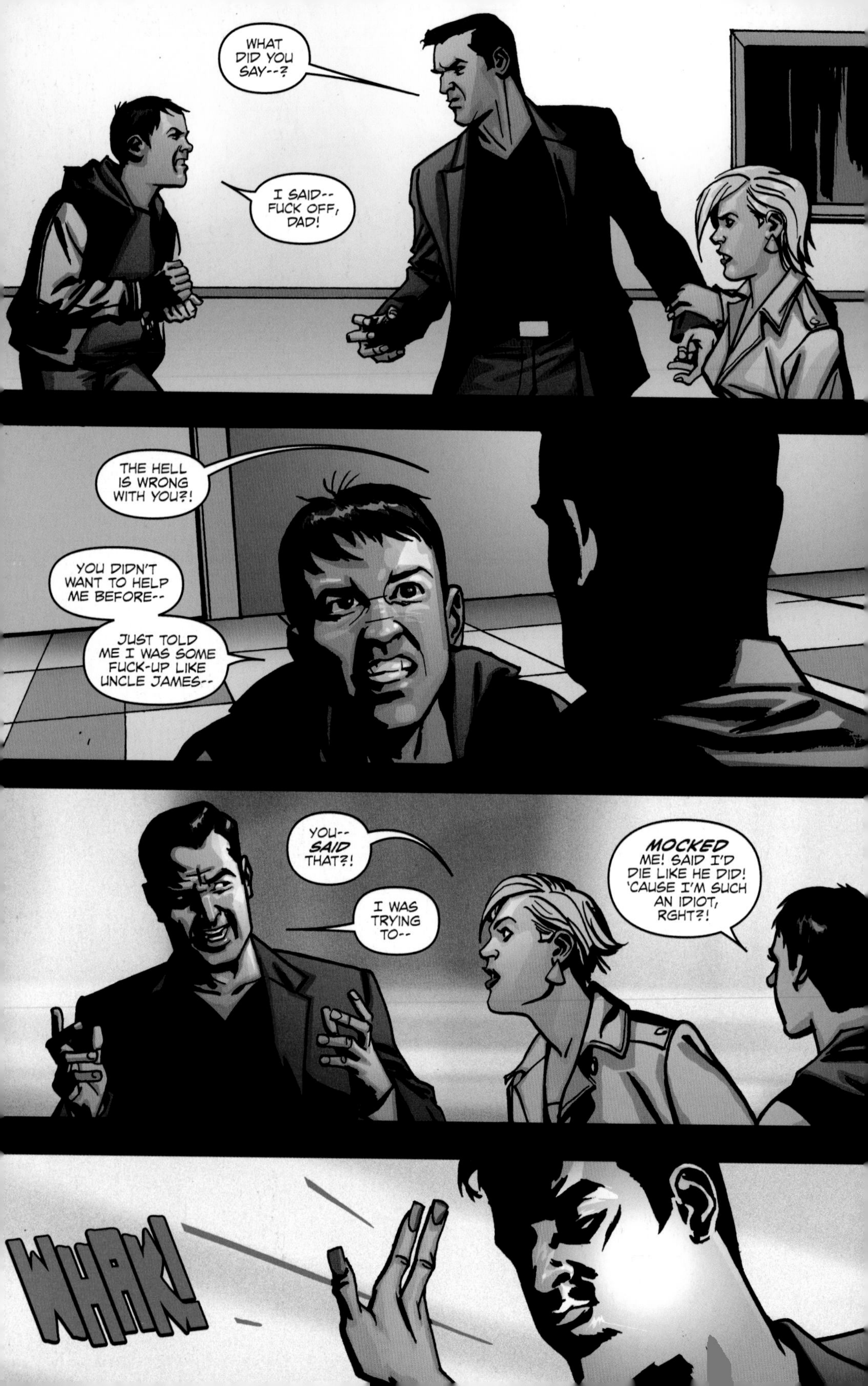
WHAT DID YOU SAY--?
I SAID-- FUCK OFF, DAD!
THE HELL IS WRONG WITH YOU?!
YOU DIDN'T WANT TO HELP ME BEFORE--
JUST TOLD ME I WAS SOME FUCK-UP LIKE UNCLE JAMES--
YOU-- SAID THAT?!
I WAS TRYING TO--
MOCKED ME! SAID I'D DIE LIKE HE DID! 'CAUSE I'M SUCH AN IDIOT, RGHT?!
WHAK!

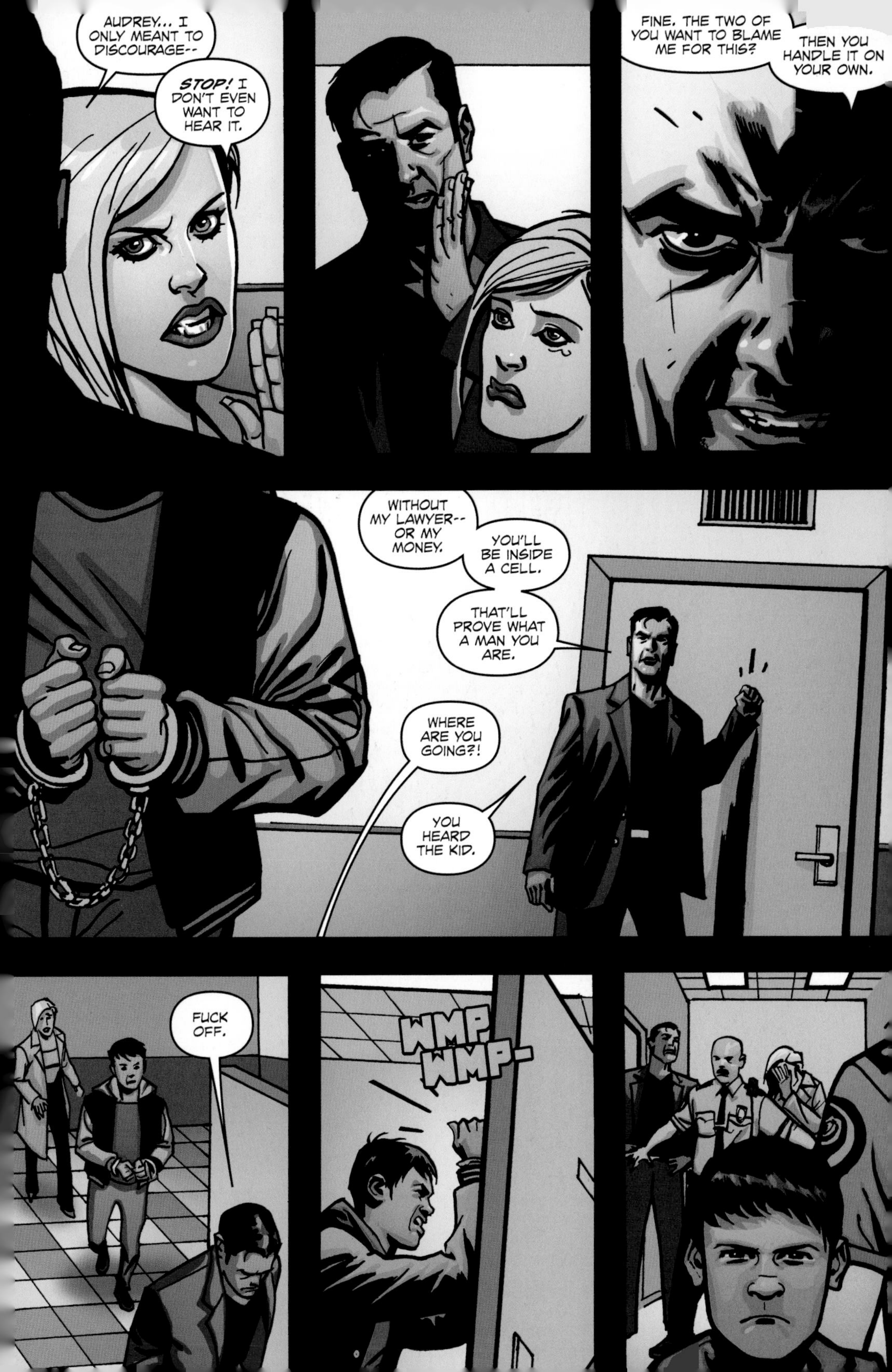
AUDREY... I ONLY MEANT TO DISCOURAGE--
STOP! I DON'T EVEN WANT TO HEAR IT.
FINE. THE TWO OF YOU WANT TO BLAME ME FOR THIS?
THEN YOU HANDLE IT ON YOUR OWN.
WITHOUT MY LAWYER-- OR MY MONEY.
YOU'LL BE INSIDE A CELL.
THAT'LL PROVE WHAT A MAN YOU ARE.
WHERE ARE YOU GOING?!
YOU HEARD THE KID.
FUCK OFF.
WMP WMP-

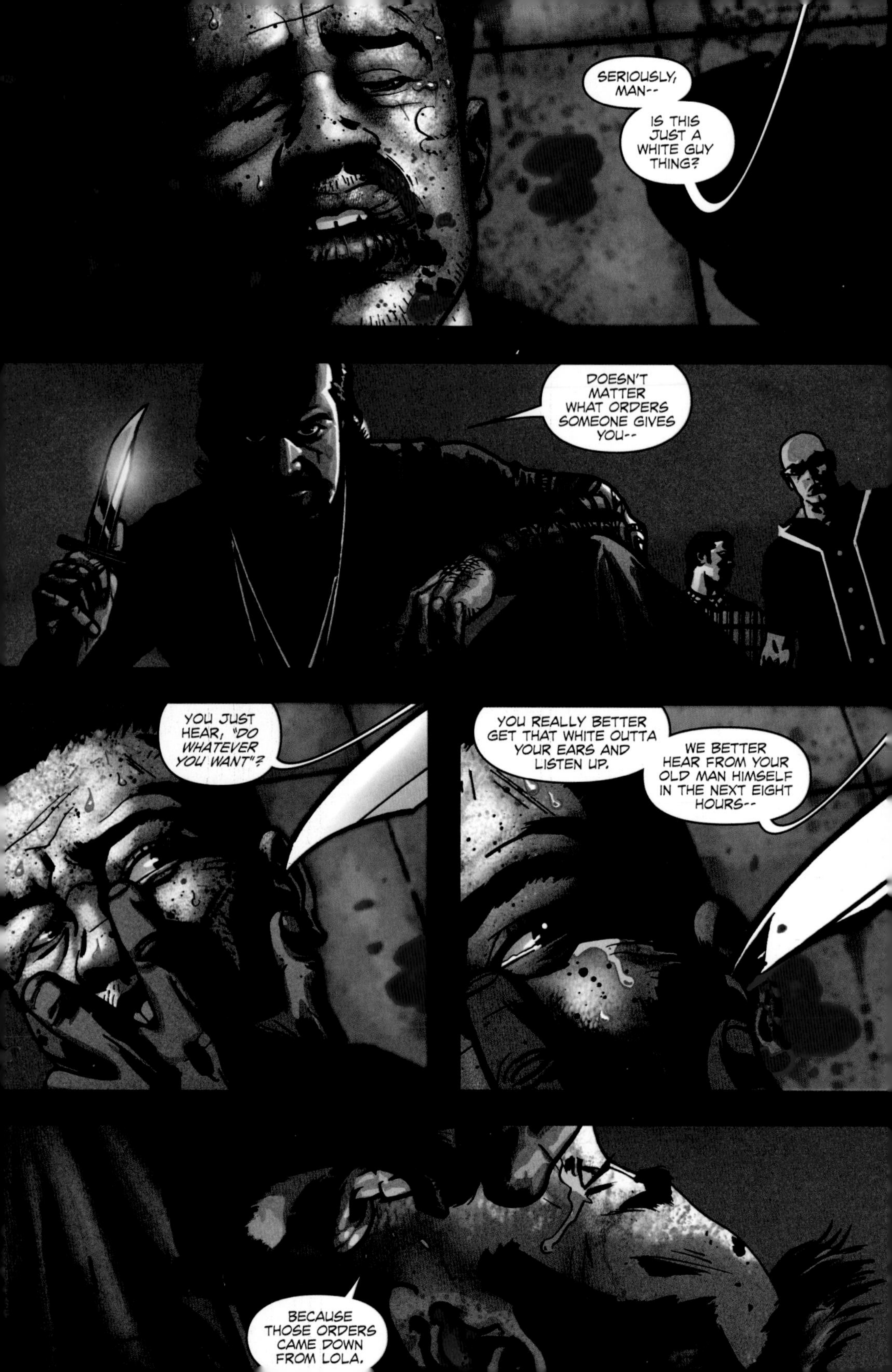
SERIOUSLY, MAN--
IS THIS JUST A WHITE GUY THING?
DOESN'T MATTER WHAT ORDERS SOMEONE GIVES YOU--
YOU JUST HEAR, "DO WHATEVER YOU WANT"?
YOU REALLY BETTER GET THAT WHITE OUTTA YOUR EARS AND LISTEN UP.
WE BETTER HEAR FROM YOUR OLD MAN HIMSELF IN THE NEXT EIGHT HOURS--
BECAUSE THOSE ORDERS CAME DOWN FROM LOLA.

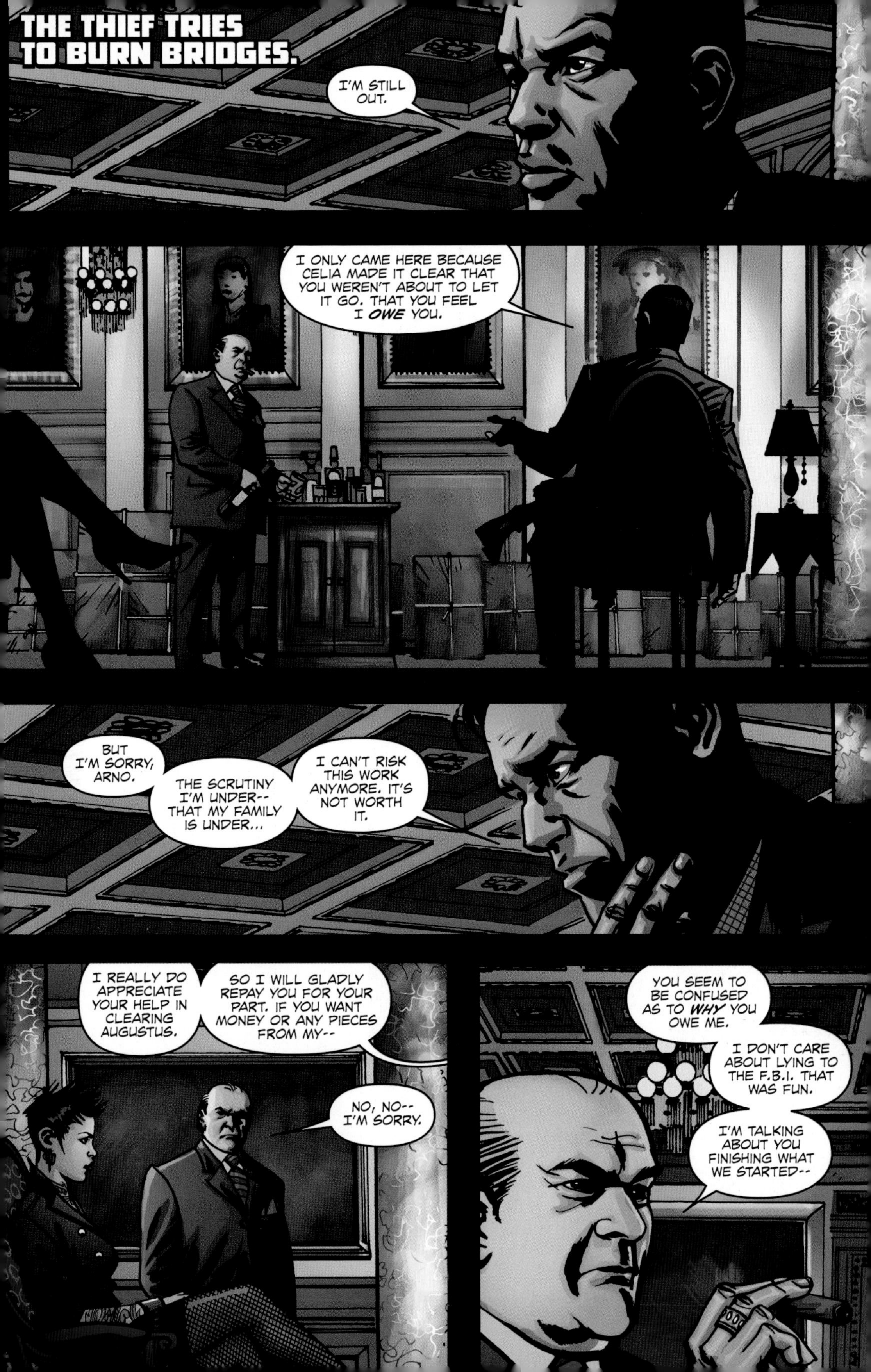
THE THIEF TRIES TO BURN BRIDGES.
I'M STILL OUT.
I ONLY CAME HERE BECAUSE CELIA MADE IT CLEAR THAT YOU WEREN'T ABOUT TO LET IT GO. THAT YOU FEEL I OWE YOU.
BUT I'M SORRY, ARNO.
THE SCRUTINY I'M UNDER-- THAT MY FAMILY IS UNDER...
I CAN'T RISK THIS WORK ANYMORE. IT'S NOT WORTH IT.
I REALLY DO APPRECIATE YOUR HELP IN CLEARING AUGUSTUS.
SO I WILL GLADLY REPAY YOU FOR YOUR PART. IF YOU WANT MONEY OR ANY PIECES FROM MY--
NO, NO-- I'M SORRY.
YOU SEEM TO BE CONFUSED AS TO WHY YOU OWE ME.
I DON'T CARE ABOUT LYING TO THE F.B.I. THAT WAS FUN.
I'M TALKING ABOUT YOU FINISHING WHAT WE STARTED--

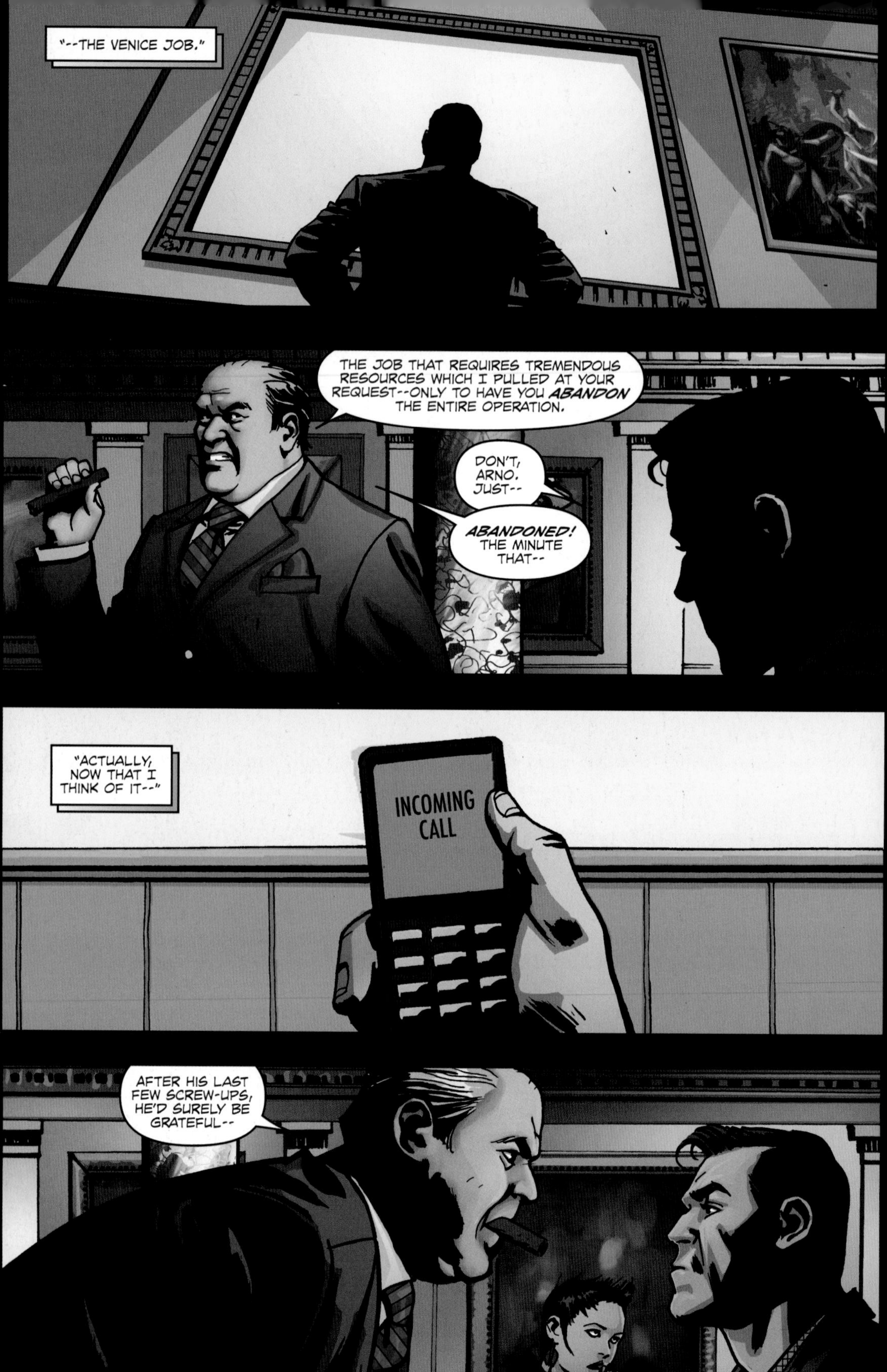
"--THE VENICE JOB."
THE JOB THAT REQUIRES TREMENDOUS RESOURCES WHICH I PULLED AT YOUR REQUEST--ONLY TO HAVE YOU *ABANDON* THE ENTIRE OPERATION.
DON'T, ARNO. JUST--
ABANDONED! THE MINUTE THAT--
"ACTUALLY, NOW THAT I THINK OF IT--"
INCOMING CALL
AFTER HIS LAST FEW SCREW-UPS, HE'D SURELY BE GRATEFUL--

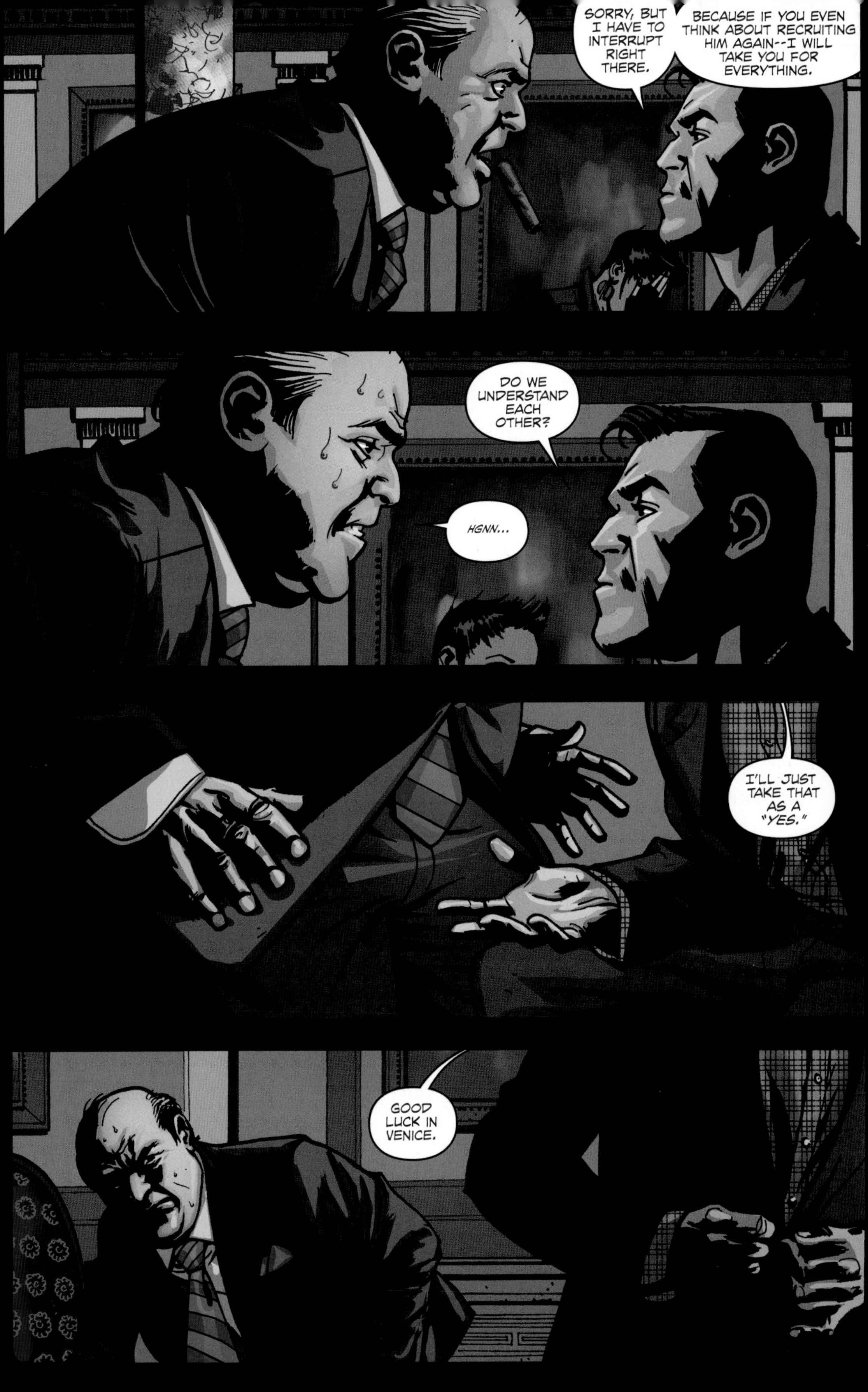
SORRY, BUT I HAVE TO INTERRUPT RIGHT THERE.
BECAUSE IF YOU EVEN THINK ABOUT RECRUITING HIM AGAIN--I WILL TAKE YOU FOR EVERYTHING.
DO WE UNDERSTAND EACH OTHER?
HGNN...
I'LL JUST TAKE THAT AS A "YES."
GOOD LUCK IN VENICE.

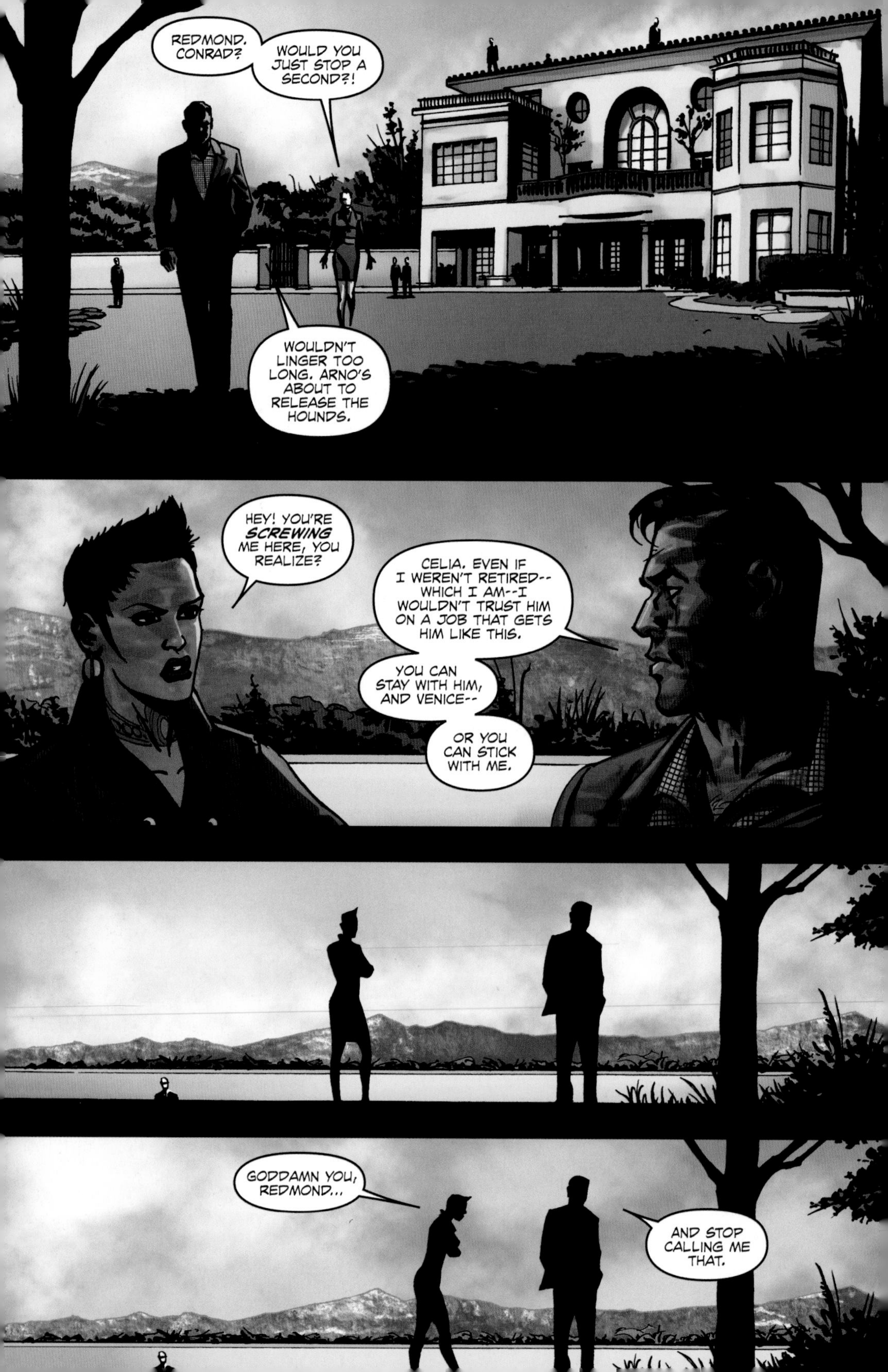
REDMOND. CONRAD?
WOULD YOU JUST STOP A SECOND?!
WOULDN'T LINGER TOO LONG. ARNO'S ABOUT TO RELEASE THE HOUNDS.
HEY! YOU'RE SCREWING ME HERE, YOU REALIZE?
CELIA. EVEN IF I WEREN'T RETIRED--WHICH I AM--I WOULDN'T TRUST HIM ON A JOB THAT GETS HIM LIKE THIS.
YOU CAN STAY WITH HIM, AND VENICE--
OR YOU CAN STICK WITH ME.
GODDAMN YOU, REDMOND...
AND STOP CALLING ME THAT.

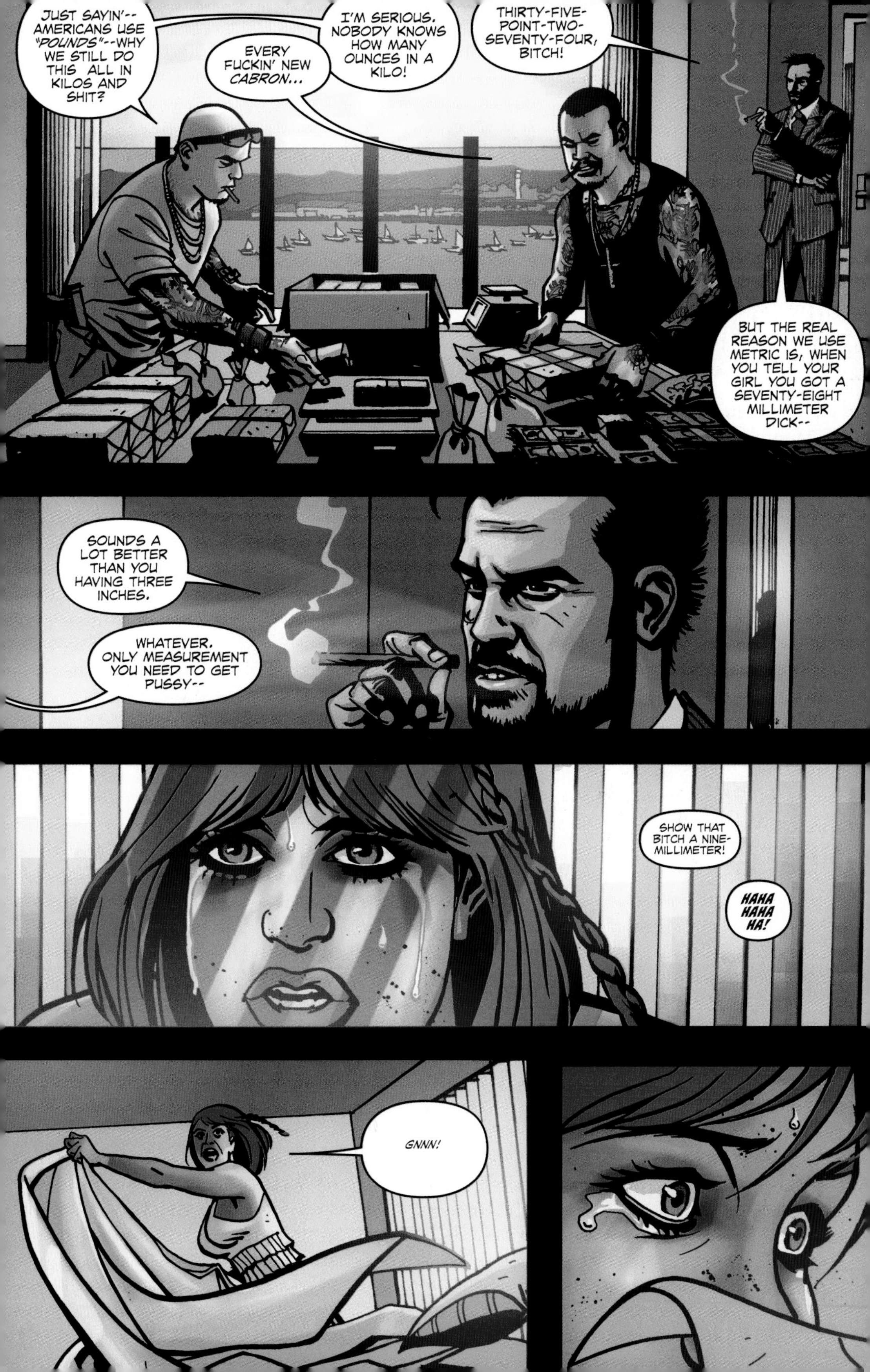
JUST SAYIN'-- AMERICANS USE "POUNDS"--WHY WE STILL DO THIS ALL IN KILOS AND SHIT?
EVERY FUCKIN' NEW CABRON...
I'M SERIOUS. NOBODY KNOWS HOW MANY OUNCES IN A KILO!
THIRTY-FIVE-POINT-TWO-SEVENTY-FOUR, BITCH!
BUT THE REAL REASON WE USE METRIC IS, WHEN YOU TELL YOUR GIRL YOU GOT A SEVENTY-EIGHT MILLIMETER DICK--
SOUNDS A LOT BETTER THAN YOU HAVING THREE INCHES.
WHATEVER. ONLY MEASUREMENT YOU NEED TO GET PUSSY--
SHOW THAT BITCH A NINE-MILLIMETER!
HAHA HAHA HA!
GNNN!

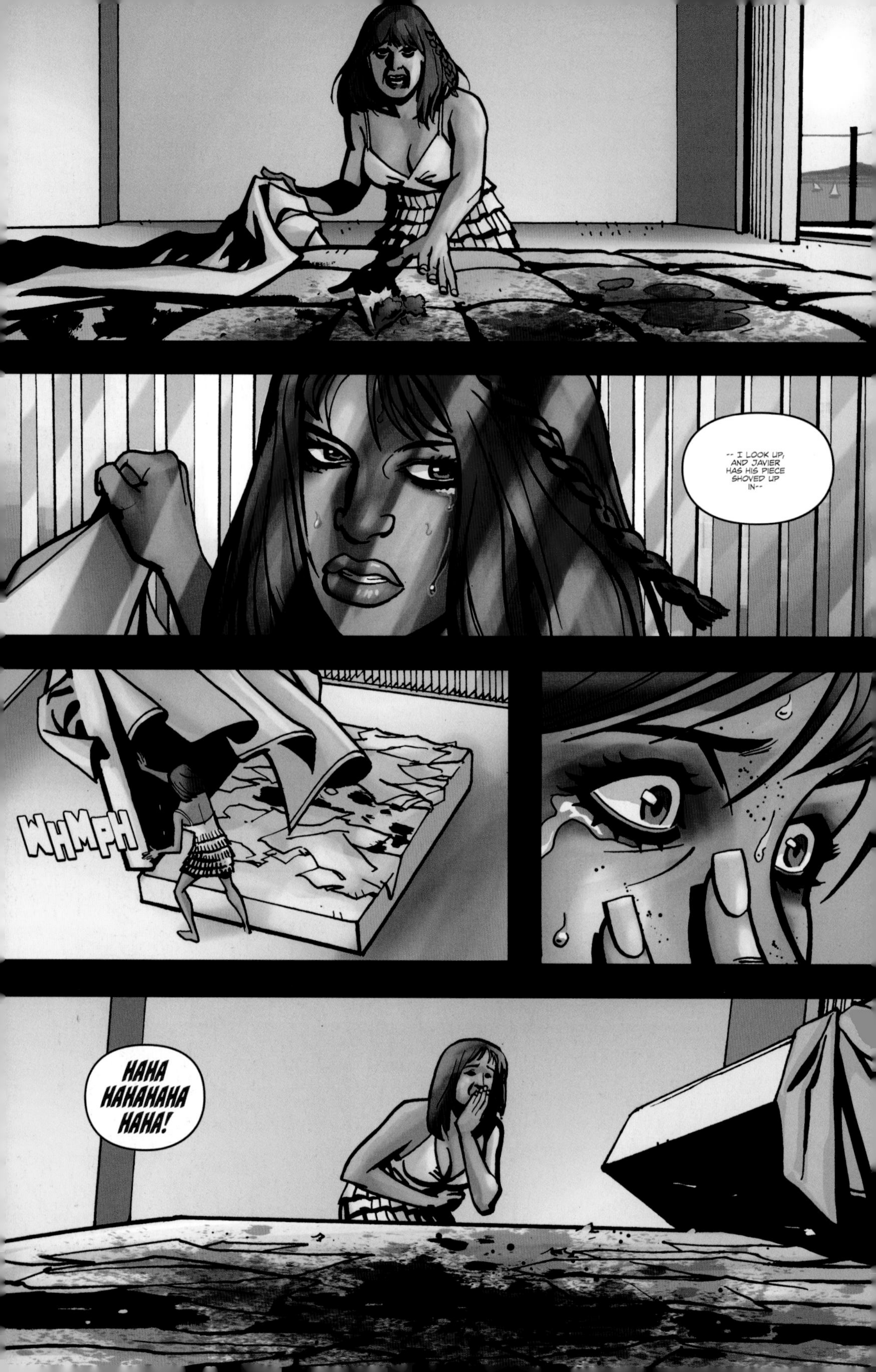
-- I LOOK UP, AND JAVIER HAS HIS PIECE SHOVED UP IN--
WHMPH
HAHA HAHAHAHA HAHA!

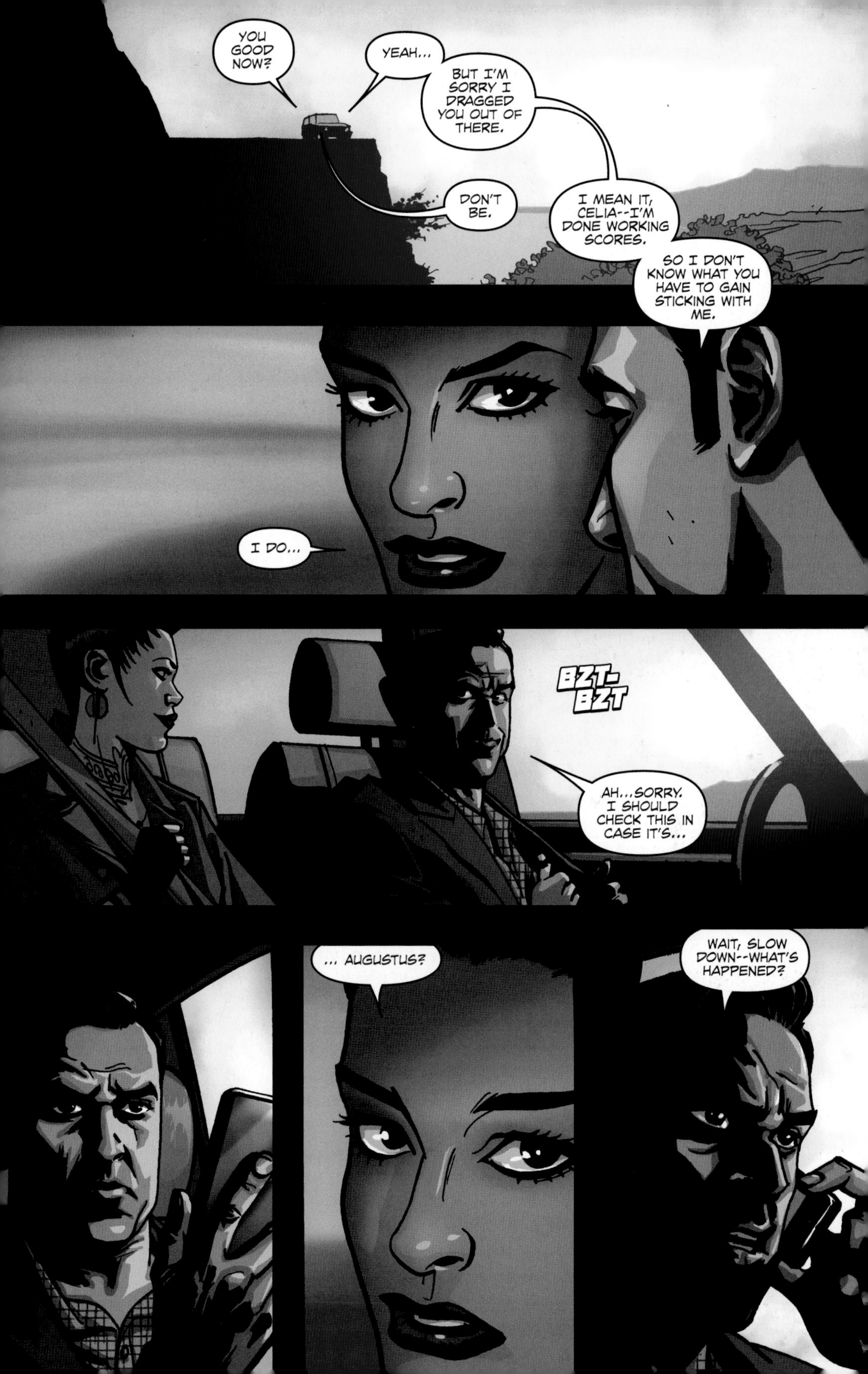
YOU GOOD NOW?
YEAH...
BUT I'M SORRY I DRAGGED YOU OUT OF THERE.
DON'T BE.
I MEAN IT, CELIA--I'M DONE WORKING SCORES.
SO I DON'T KNOW WHAT YOU HAVE TO GAIN STICKING WITH ME.
I DO...
BZT-BZT
AH...SORRY. I SHOULD CHECK THIS IN CASE IT'S...
... AUGUSTUS?
WAIT, SLOW DOWN--WHAT'S HAPPENED?

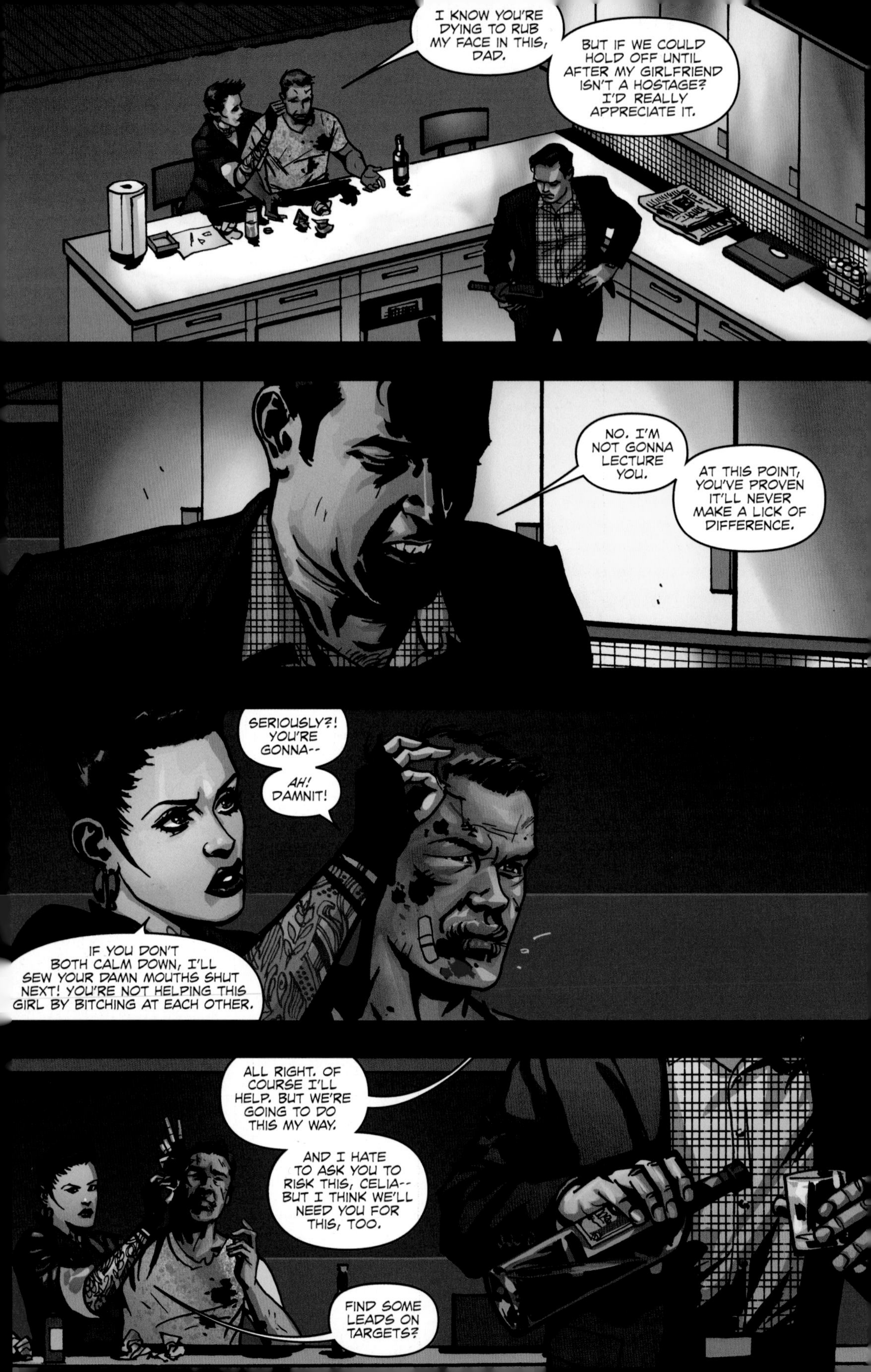
I KNOW YOU'RE DYING TO RUB MY FACE IN THIS, DAD.
BUT IF WE COULD HOLD OFF UNTIL AFTER MY GIRLFRIEND ISN'T A HOSTAGE? I'D REALLY APPRECIATE IT.
NO. I'M NOT GONNA LECTURE YOU.
AT THIS POINT, YOU'VE PROVEN IT'LL NEVER MAKE A LICK OF DIFFERENCE.
SERIOUSLY?! YOU'RE GONNA--
AH! DAMNIT!
IF YOU DON'T BOTH CALM DOWN, I'LL SEW YOUR DAMN MOUTHS SHUT NEXT! YOU'RE NOT HELPING THIS GIRL BY BITCHING AT EACH OTHER.
ALL RIGHT. OF COURSE I'LL HELP. BUT WE'RE GOING TO DO THIS MY WAY.
AND I HATE TO ASK YOU TO RISK THIS, CELIA-- BUT I THINK WE'LL NEED YOU FOR THIS, TOO.
FIND SOME LEADS ON TARGETS?

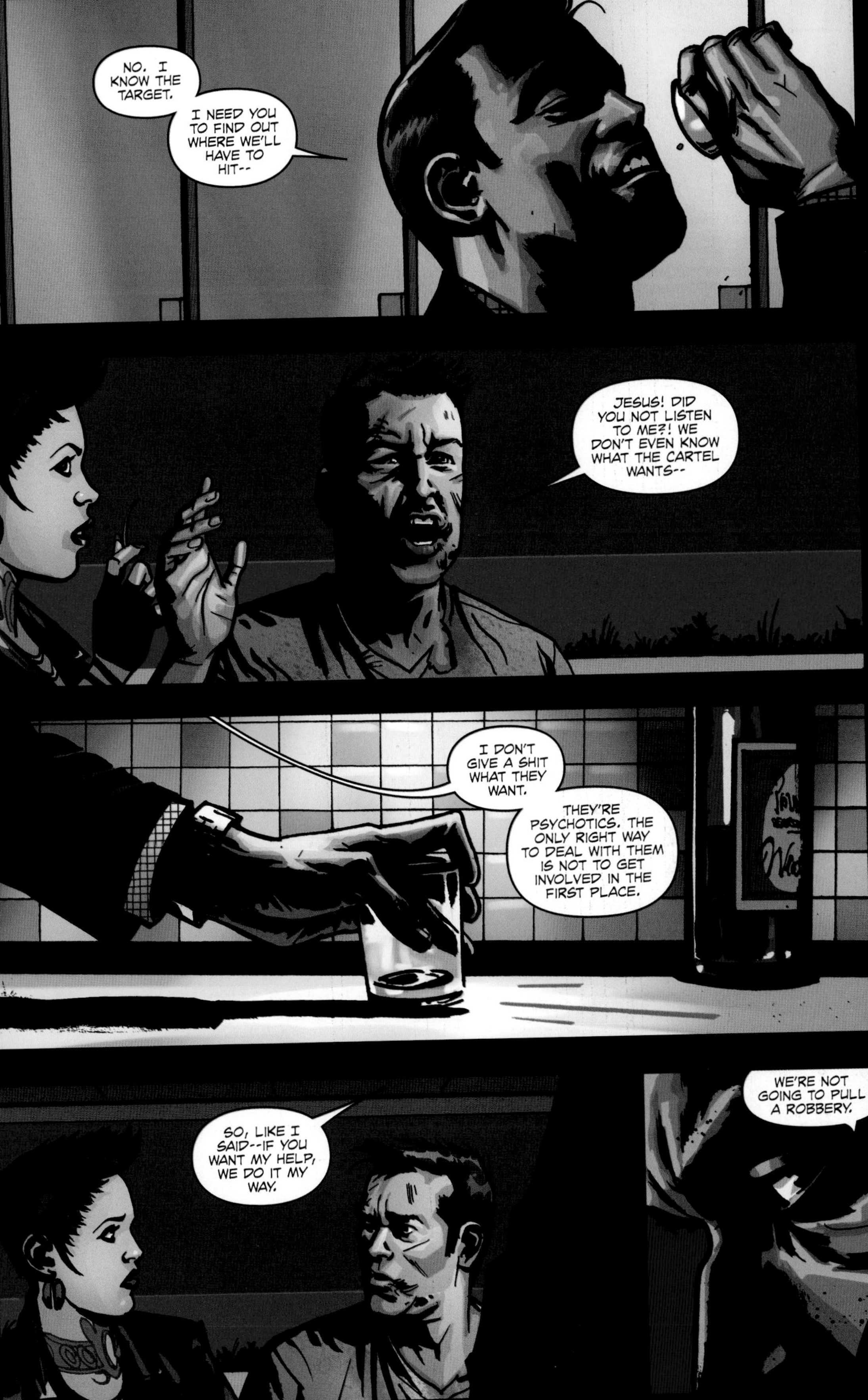
NO. I KNOW THE TARGET.
I NEED YOU TO FIND OUT WHERE WE'LL HAVE TO HIT--
JESUS! DID YOU NOT LISTEN TO ME?! WE DON'T EVEN KNOW WHAT THE CARTEL WANTS--
I DON'T GIVE A SHIT WHAT THEY WANT.
THEY'RE PSYCHOTICS. THE ONLY RIGHT WAY TO DEAL WITH THEM IS NOT TO GET INVOLVED IN THE FIRST PLACE.
SO, LIKE I SAID--IF YOU WANT MY HELP, WE DO IT MY WAY.
WE'RE NOT GOING TO PULL A ROBBERY.

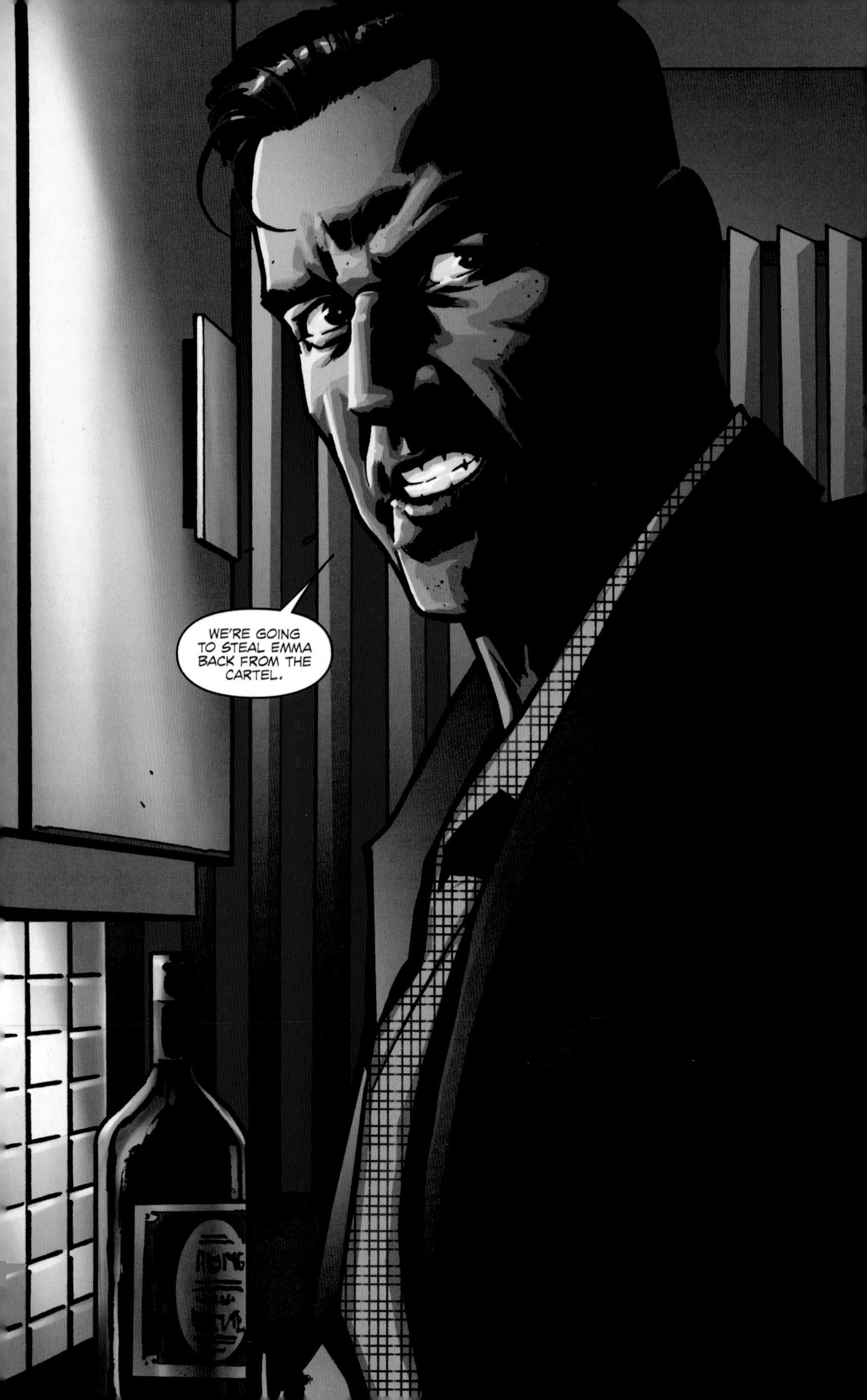
WE'RE GOING TO STEAL EMMA BACK FROM THE CARTEL.

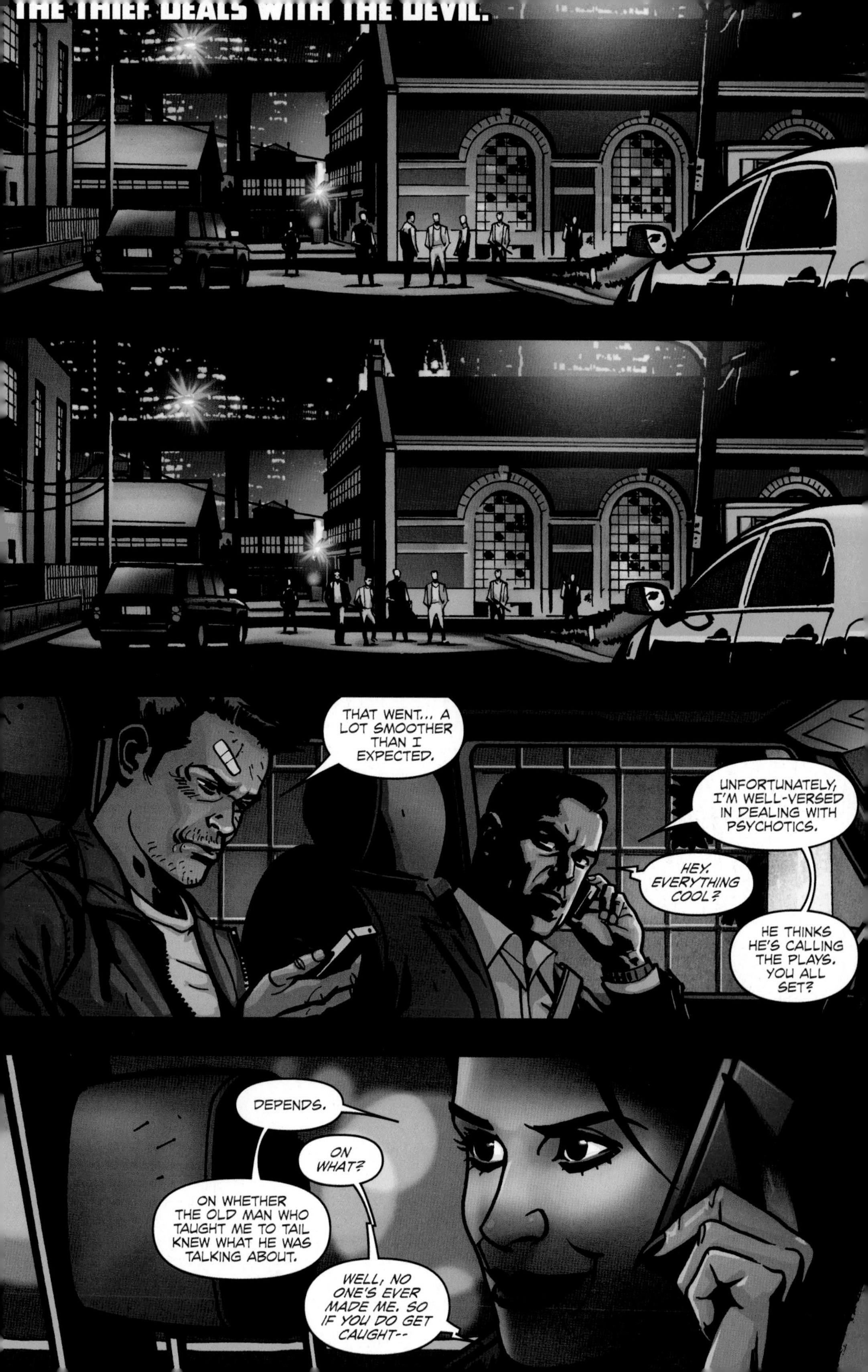
THE THIEF DEALS WITH THE DEVIL.
THAT WENT... A LOT SMOOTHER THAN I EXPECTED.
UNFORTUNATELY, I'M WELL-VERSED IN DEALING WITH PSYCHOTICS.
HEY. EVERYTHING COOL?
HE THINKS HE'S CALLING THE PLAYS. YOU ALL SET?
DEPENDS.
ON WHAT?
ON WHETHER THE OLD MAN WHO TAUGHT ME TO TAIL KNEW WHAT HE WAS TALKING ABOUT.
WELL, NO ONE'S EVER MADE ME. SO IF YOU DO GET CAUGHT--

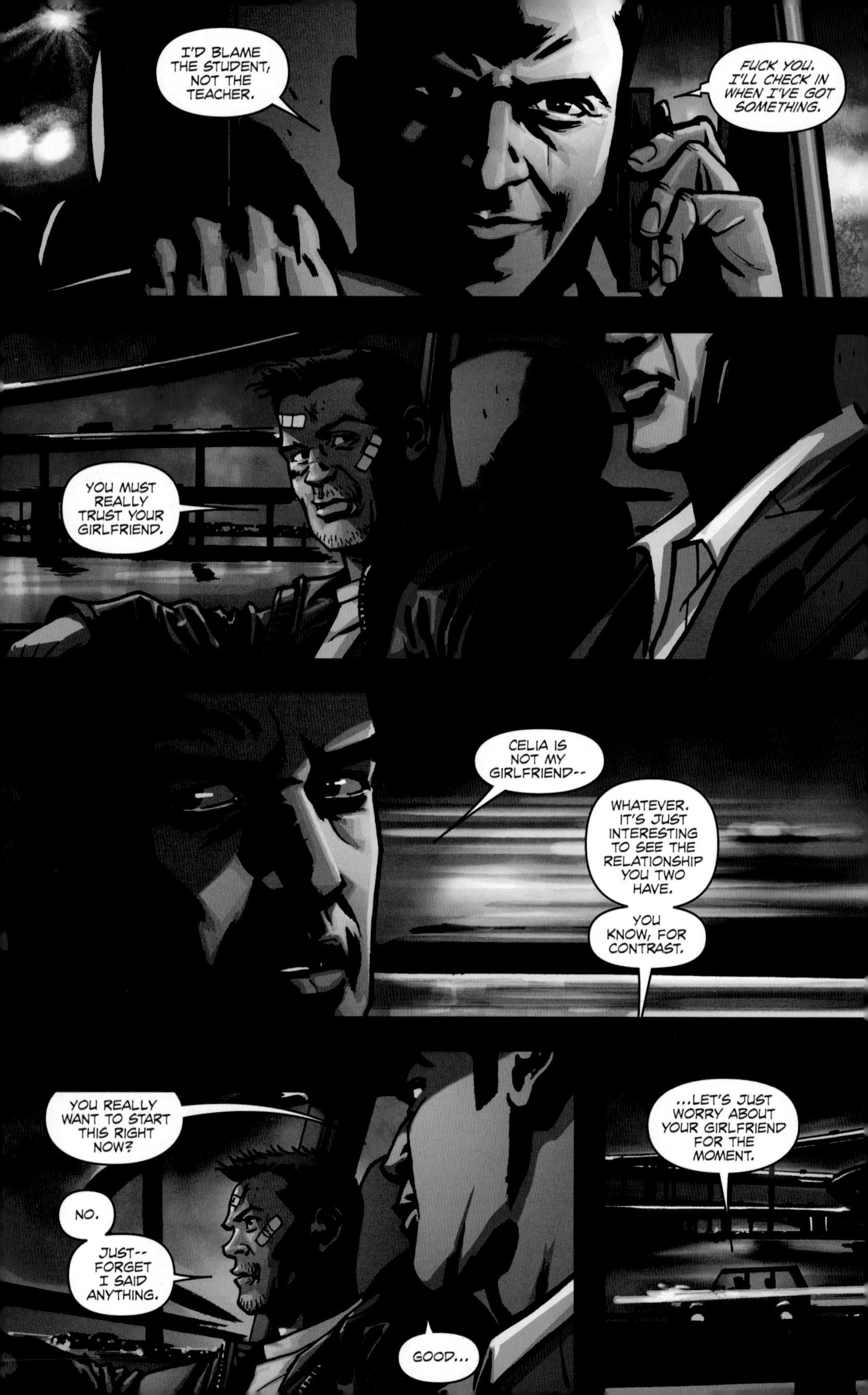
I'D BLAME THE STUDENT, NOT THE TEACHER.
FUCK YOU. I'LL CHECK IN WHEN I'VE GOT SOMETHING.
YOU MUST REALLY TRUST YOUR GIRLFRIEND.
CELIA IS NOT MY GIRLFRIEND--
WHATEVER. IT'S JUST INTERESTING TO SEE THE RELATIONSHIP YOU TWO HAVE.
YOU KNOW, FOR CONTRAST.
YOU REALLY WANT TO START THIS RIGHT NOW?
NO.
JUST-- FORGET I SAID ANYTHING.
GOOD...
...LET'S JUST WORRY ABOUT YOUR GIRLFRIEND FOR THE MOMENT.

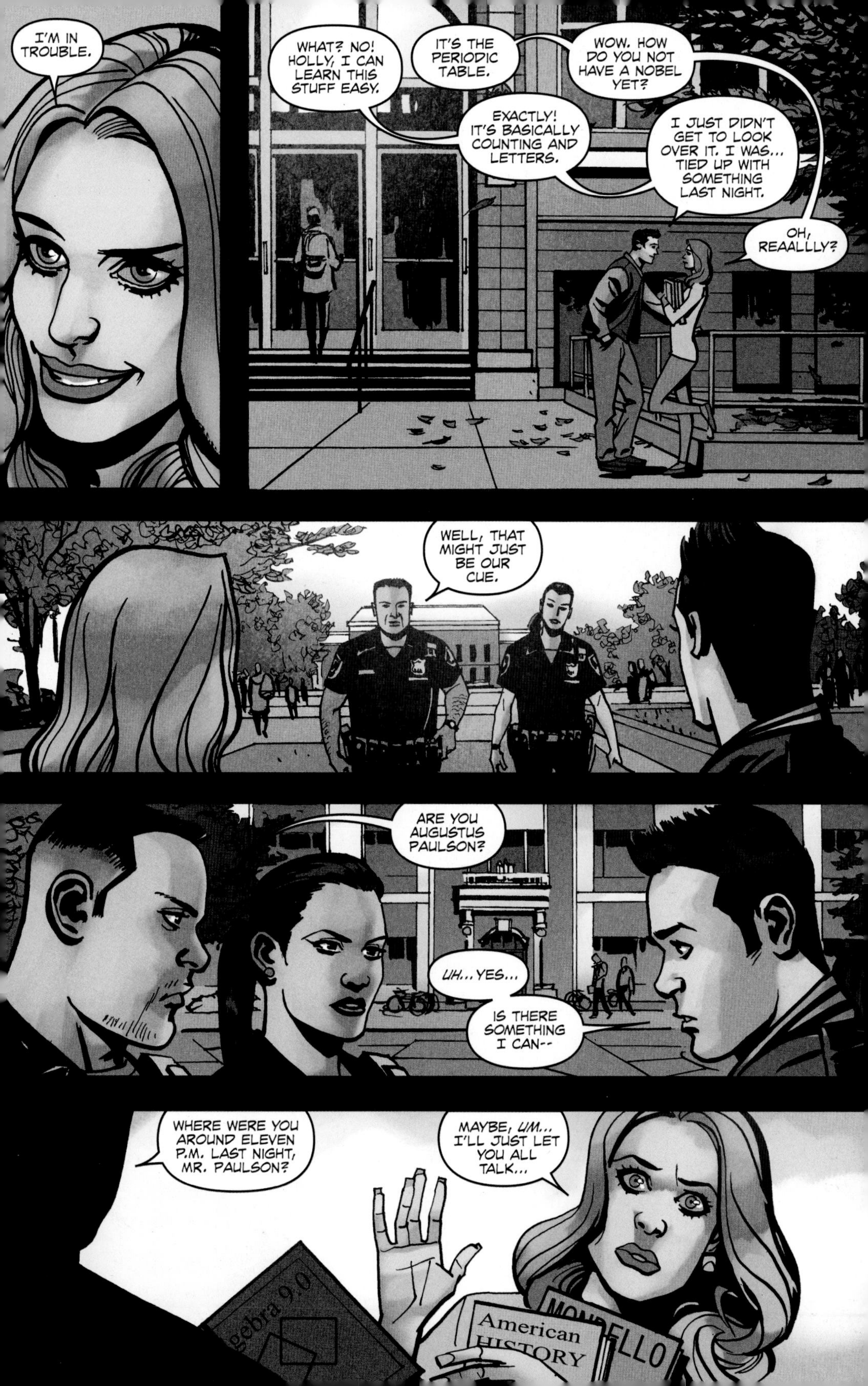
I'M IN TROUBLE.
WHAT? NO! HOLLY, I CAN LEARN THIS STUFF EASY.
IT'S THE PERIODIC TABLE.
WOW. HOW DO YOU NOT HAVE A NOBEL YET?
EXACTLY! IT'S BASICALLY COUNTING AND LETTERS.
I JUST DIDN'T GET TO LOOK OVER IT. I WAS... TIED UP WITH SOMETHING LAST NIGHT.
OH, REAALLLY?
WELL, THAT MIGHT JUST BE OUR CUE.
ARE YOU AUGUSTUS PAULSON?
UH... YES...
IS THERE SOMETHING I CAN--
WHERE WERE YOU AROUND ELEVEN P.M. LAST NIGHT, MR. PAULSON?
MAYBE, UM... I'LL JUST LET YOU ALL TALK...
gebra 9.0
American HISTORY
MONDELLO

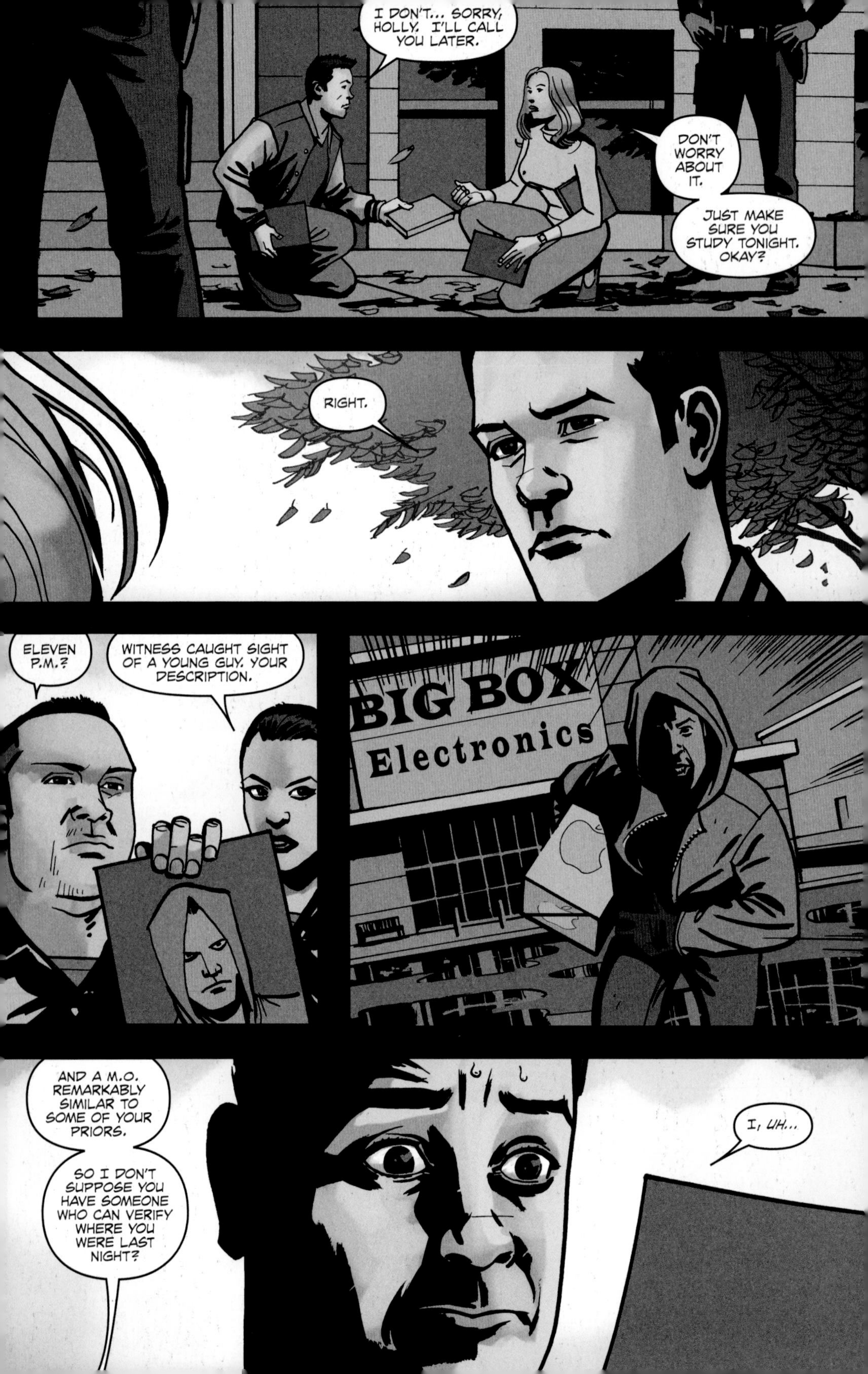
I DON'T... SORRY, HOLLY. I'LL CALL YOU LATER.
DON'T WORRY ABOUT IT.
JUST MAKE SURE YOU STUDY TONIGHT. OKAY?
RIGHT.
ELEVEN P.M.?
WITNESS CAUGHT SIGHT OF A YOUNG GUY. YOUR DESCRIPTION.
BIG BOX
Electronics
AND A M.O. REMARKABLY SIMILAR TO SOME OF YOUR PRIORS.
SO I DON'T SUPPOSE YOU HAVE SOMEONE WHO CAN VERIFY WHERE YOU WERE LAST NIGHT?
I, UH...

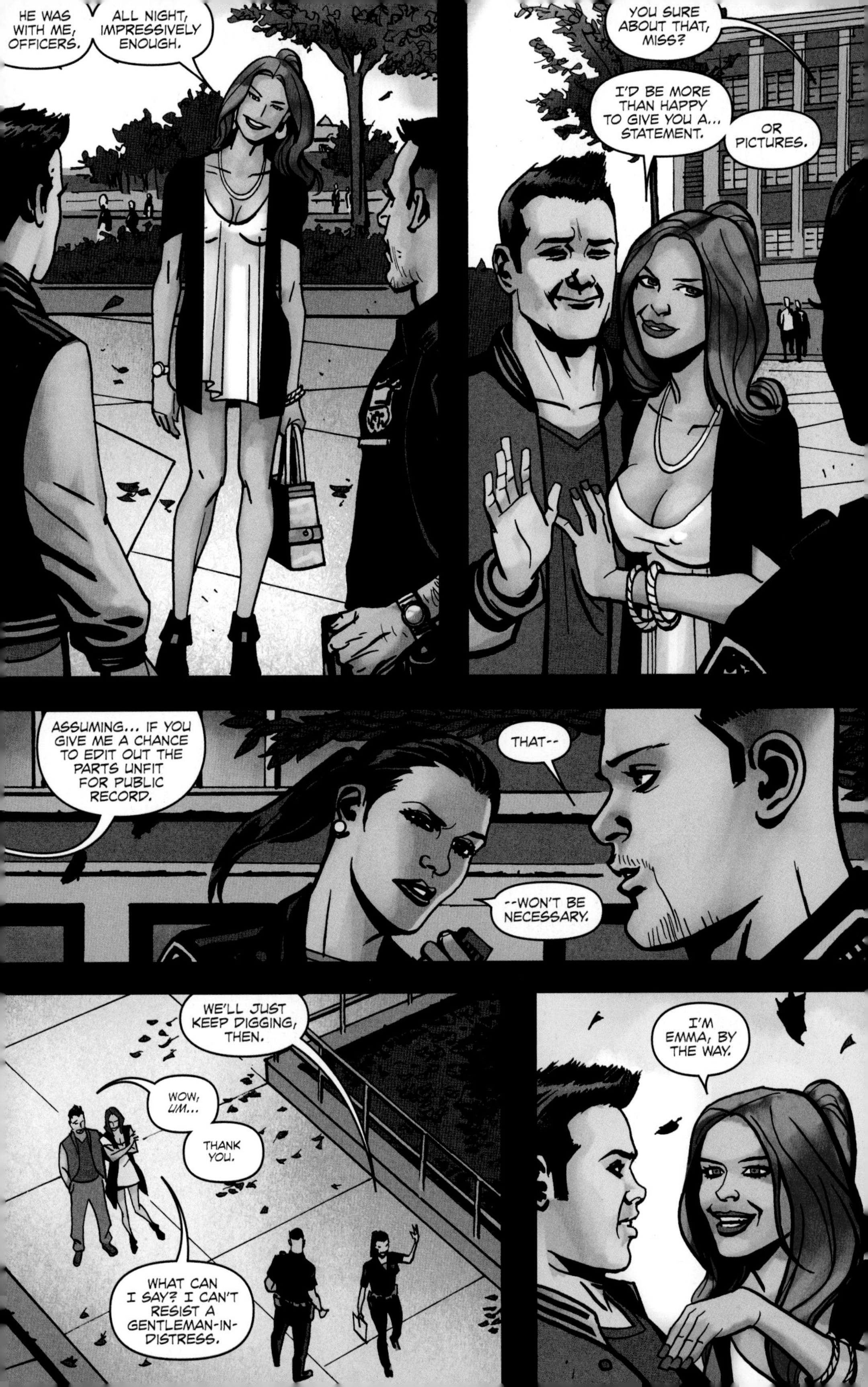

HE WAS WITH ME, OFFICERS.
ALL NIGHT, IMPRESSIVELY ENOUGH.
YOU SURE ABOUT THAT, MISS?
I'D BE MORE THAN HAPPY TO GIVE YOU A... STATEMENT.
OR PICTURES.
ASSUMING... IF YOU GIVE ME A CHANCE TO EDIT OUT THE PARTS UNFIT FOR PUBLIC RECORD.
THAT--
--WON'T BE NECESSARY.
WE'LL JUST KEEP DIGGING, THEN.
WOW, UM...
THANK YOU.
WHAT CAN I SAY? I CAN'T RESIST A GENTLEMAN-IN-DISTRESS.
I'M EMMA, BY THE WAY.

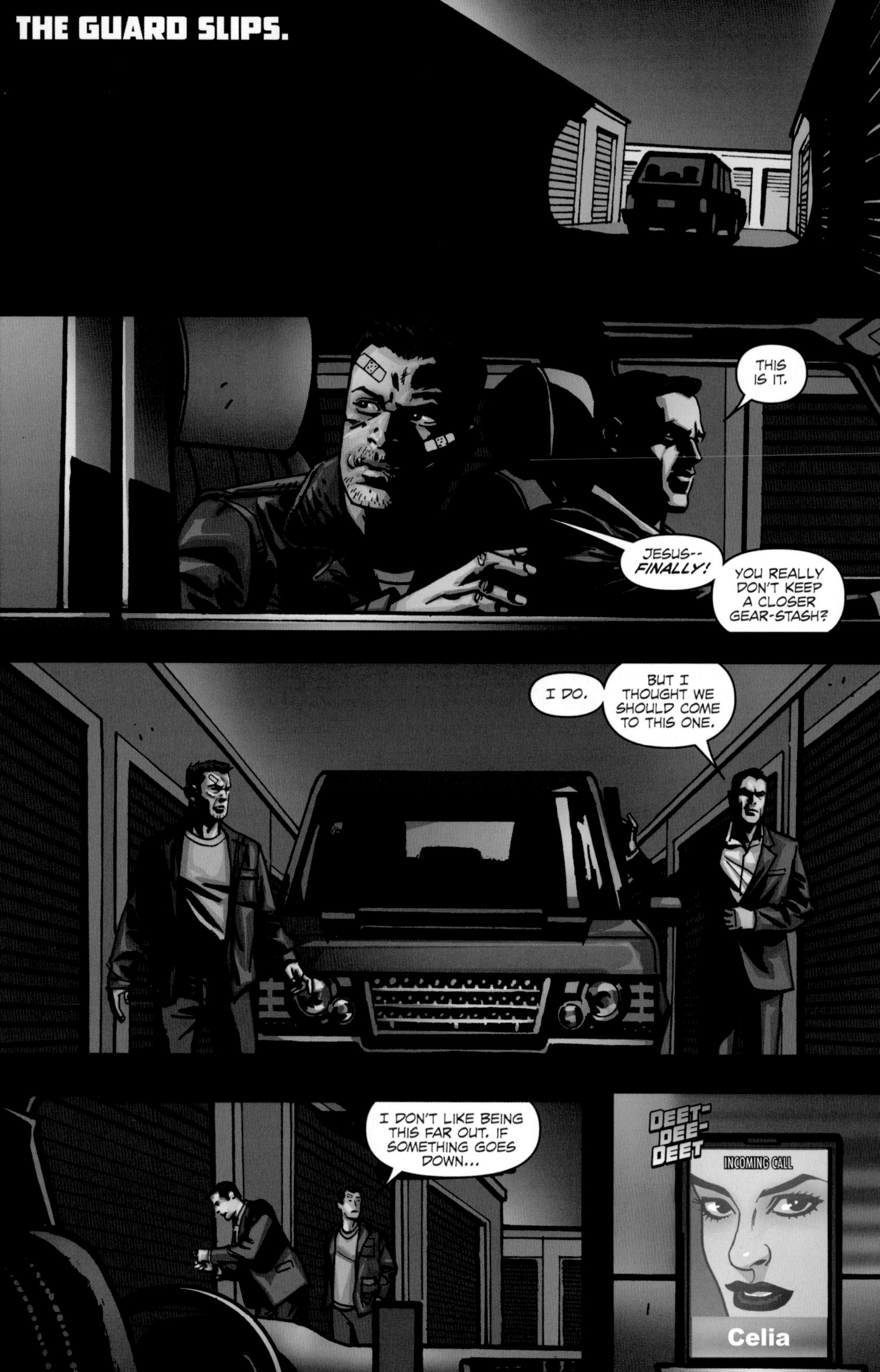
THE GUARD SLIPS.
THIS IS IT.
JESUS-- FINALLY!
YOU REALLY DON'T KEEP A CLOSER GEAR-STASH?
I DO.
BUT I THOUGHT WE SHOULD COME TO THIS ONE.
I DON'T LIKE BEING THIS FAR OUT. IF SOMETHING GOES DOWN...
DEET-DEE-DEET
INCOMING CALL
Celia

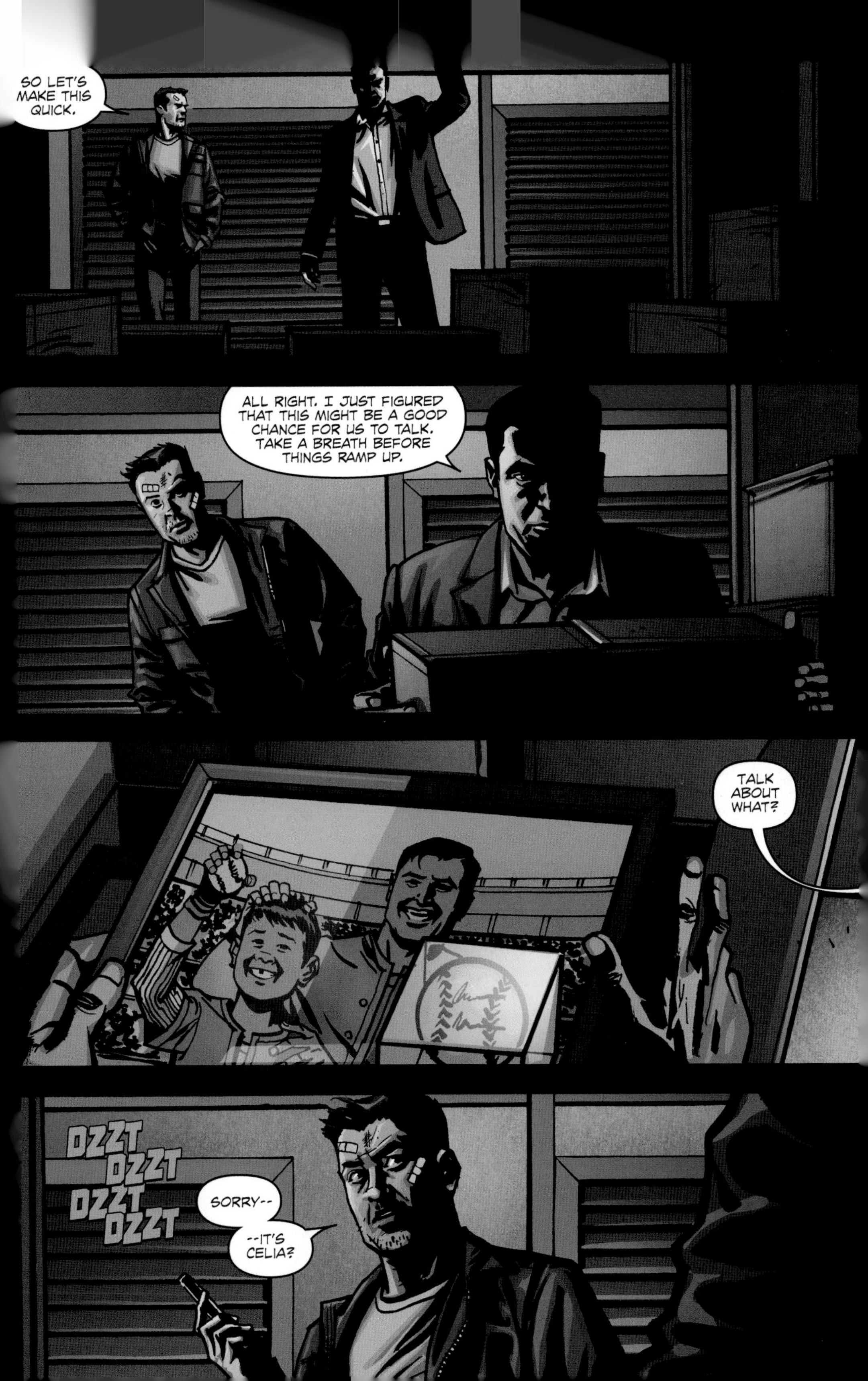
SO LET'S MAKE THIS QUICK.
ALL RIGHT. I JUST FIGURED THAT THIS MIGHT BE A GOOD CHANCE FOR US TO TALK. TAKE A BREATH BEFORE THINGS RAMP UP.
TALK ABOUT WHAT?
DZZT DZZT DZZT DZZT
SORRY--
--IT'S CELIA?

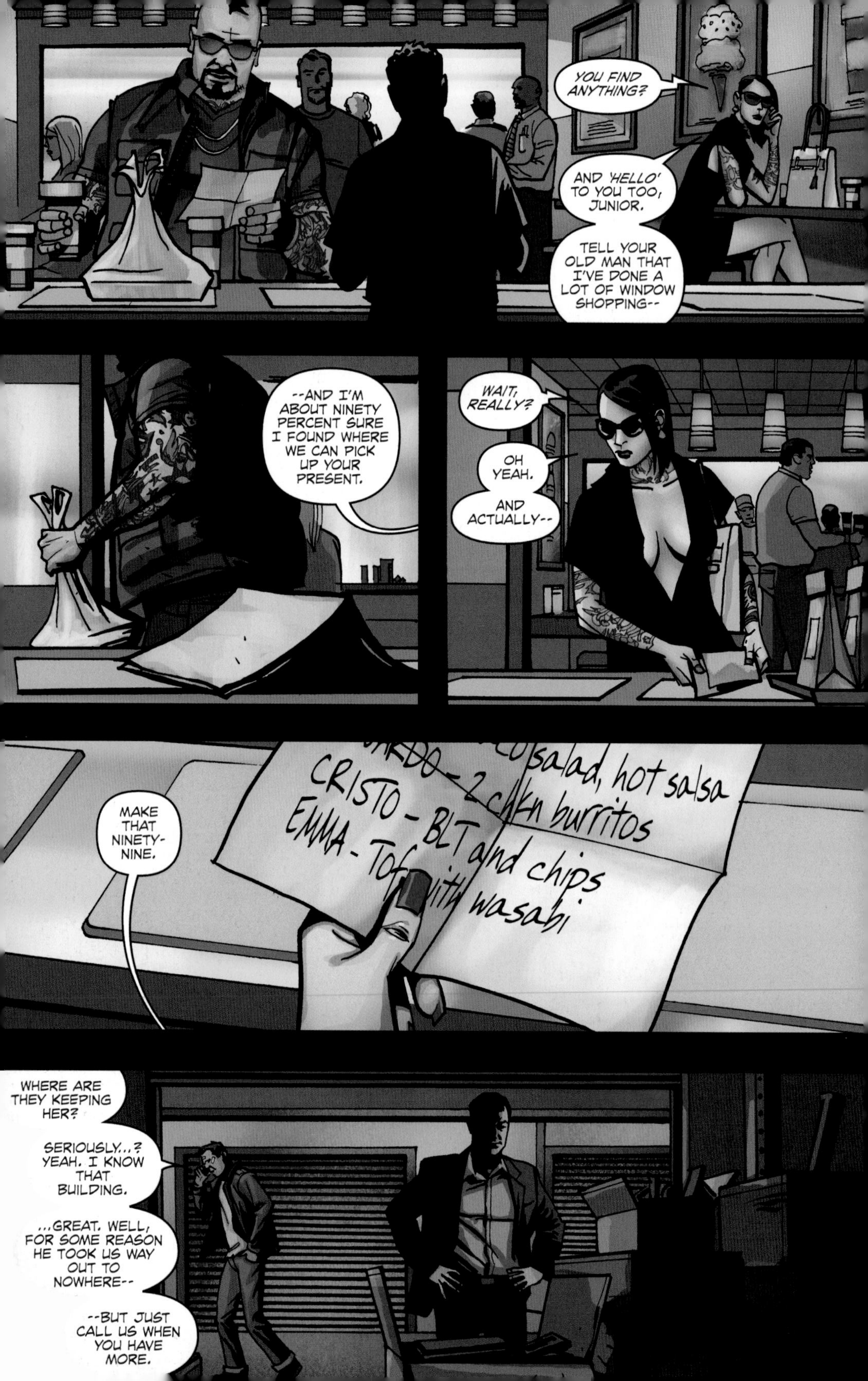
YOU FIND ANYTHING?
AND 'HELLO' TO YOU TOO, JUNIOR.
TELL YOUR OLD MAN THAT I'VE DONE A LOT OF WINDOW SHOPPING--
--AND I'M ABOUT NINETY PERCENT SURE I FOUND WHERE WE CAN PICK UP YOUR PRESENT.
WAIT, REALLY?
OH YEAH.
AND ACTUALLY--
salad, hot salsa
CRISTO - 2 chkn burritos
BLT and chips
EMMA - Tof with wasabi
MAKE THAT NINETY-NINE.
WHERE ARE THEY KEEPING HER?
SERIOUSLY...? YEAH. I KNOW THAT BUILDING.
...GREAT. WELL, FOR SOME REASON HE TOOK US WAY OUT TO NOWHERE--
--BUT JUST CALL US WHEN YOU HAVE MORE.

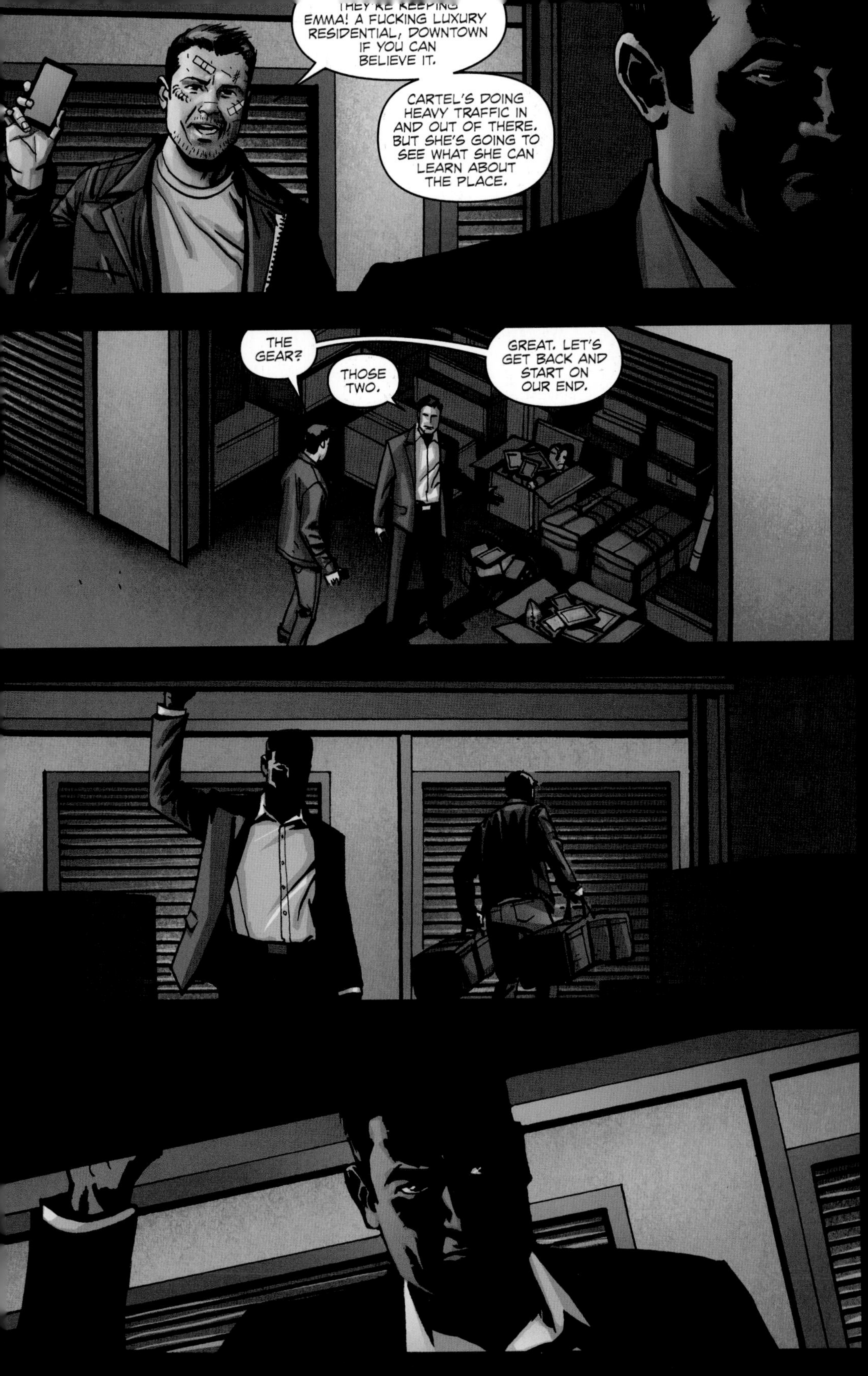
THEY'RE KEEPING EMMA! A FUCKING LUXURY RESIDENTIAL, DOWNTOWN IF YOU CAN BELIEVE IT.
CARTEL'S DOING HEAVY TRAFFIC IN AND OUT OF THERE. BUT SHE'S GOING TO SEE WHAT SHE CAN LEARN ABOUT THE PLACE.
THE GEAR?
THOSE TWO.
GREAT. LET'S GET BACK AND START ON OUR END.

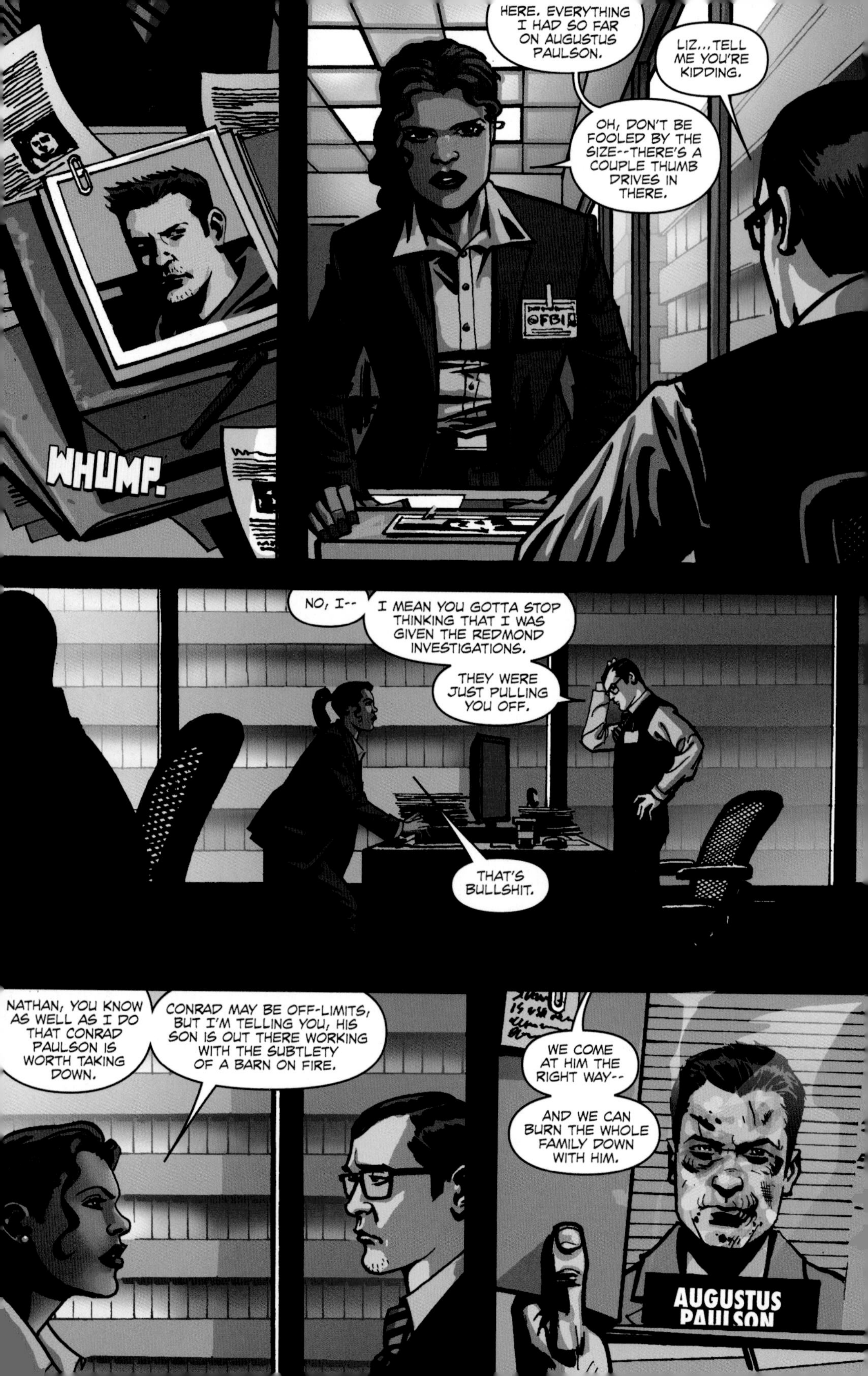
WHUMP.
HERE. EVERYTHING I HAD SO FAR ON AUGUSTUS PAULSON.
LIZ...TELL ME YOU'RE KIDDING.
OH, DON'T BE FOOLED BY THE SIZE--THERE'S A COUPLE THUMB DRIVES IN THERE.
NO, I--
I MEAN YOU GOTTA STOP THINKING THAT I WAS GIVEN THE REDMOND INVESTIGATIONS.
THEY WERE JUST PULLING YOU OFF.
THAT'S BULLSHIT.
NATHAN, YOU KNOW AS WELL AS I DO THAT CONRAD PAULSON IS WORTH TAKING DOWN.
CONRAD MAY BE OFF-LIMITS, BUT I'M TELLING YOU, HIS SON IS OUT THERE WORKING WITH THE SUBTLETY OF A BARN ON FIRE.
WE COME AT HIM THE RIGHT WAY--
AND WE CAN BURN THE WHOLE FAMILY DOWN WITH HIM.
AUGUSTUS PAULSON

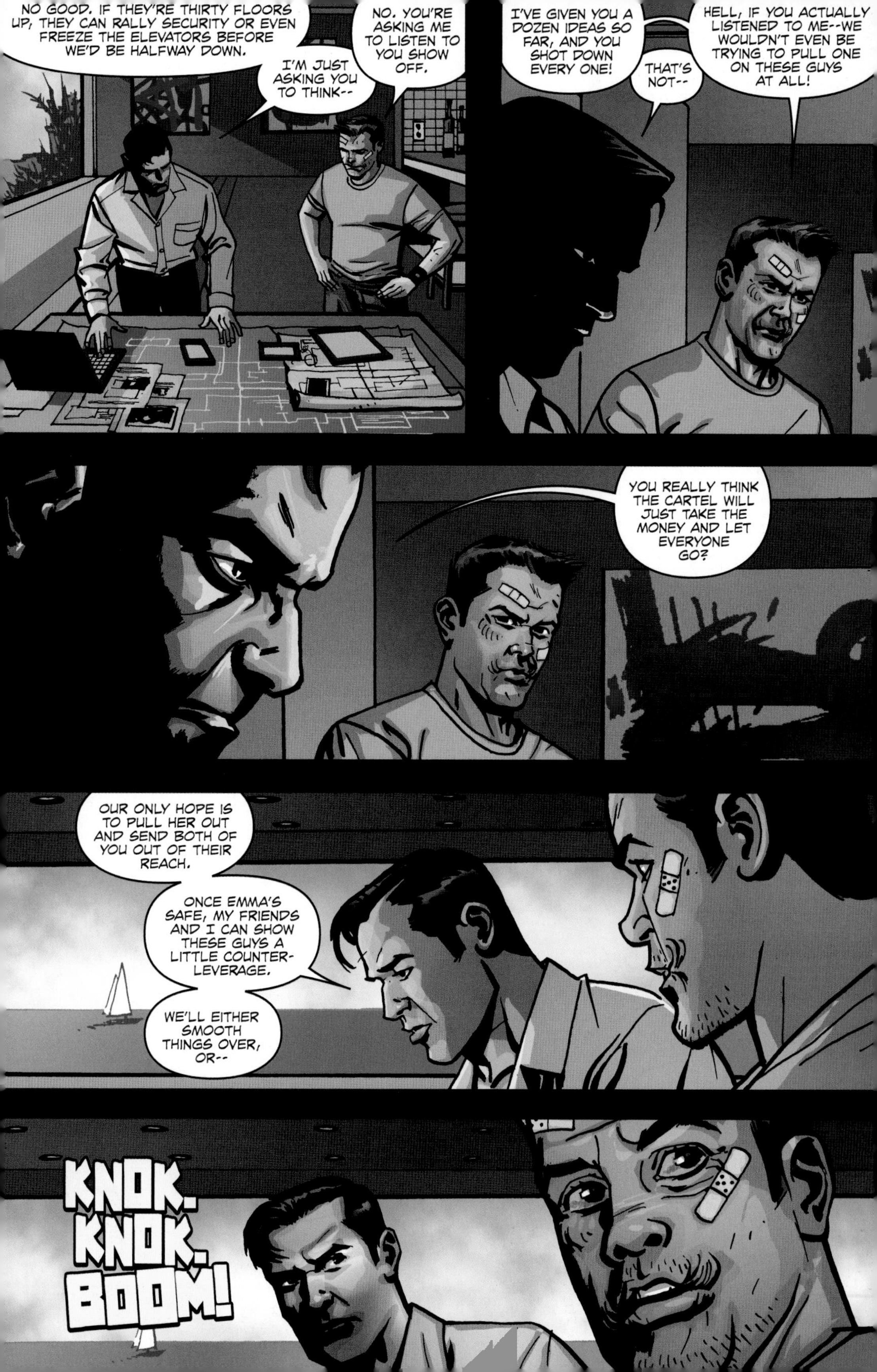

NO GOOD. IF THEY'RE THIRTY FLOORS UP, THEY CAN RALLY SECURITY OR EVEN FREEZE THE ELEVATORS BEFORE WE'D BE HALFWAY DOWN.
I'M JUST ASKING YOU TO THINK--
NO. YOU'RE ASKING ME TO LISTEN TO YOU SHOW OFF.
I'VE GIVEN YOU A DOZEN IDEAS SO FAR, AND YOU SHOT DOWN EVERY ONE!
THAT'S NOT--
HELL, IF YOU ACTUALLY LISTENED TO ME--WE WOULDN'T EVEN BE TRYING TO PULL ONE ON THESE GUYS AT ALL!
YOU REALLY THINK THE CARTEL WILL JUST TAKE THE MONEY AND LET EVERYONE GO?
OUR ONLY HOPE IS TO PULL HER OUT AND SEND BOTH OF YOU OUT OF THEIR REACH.
ONCE EMMA'S SAFE, MY FRIENDS AND I CAN SHOW THESE GUYS A LITTLE COUNTER-LEVERAGE.
WE'LL EITHER SMOOTH THINGS OVER, OR--
KNOK. KNOK. BOOM!

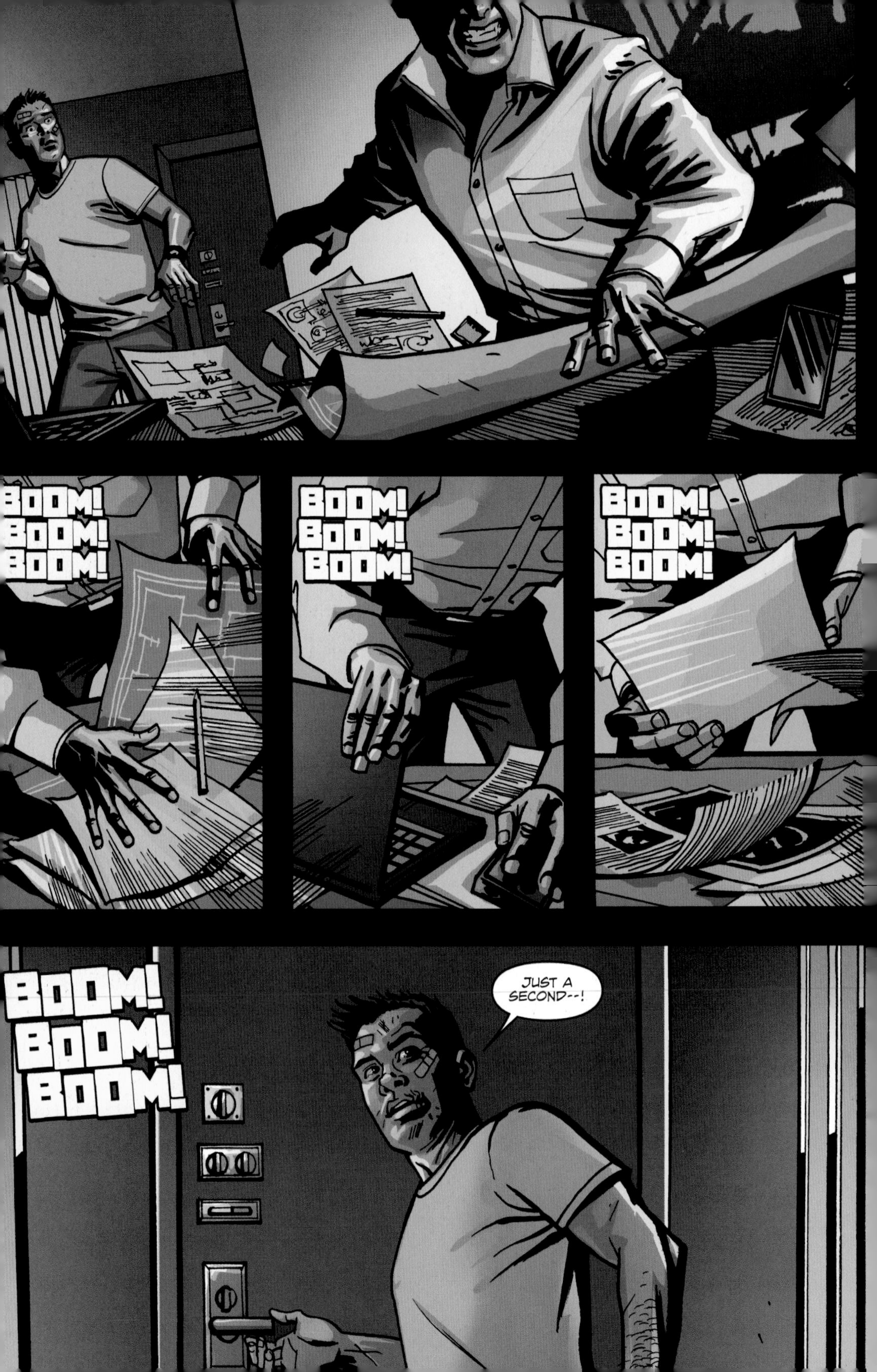
BOOM! BOOM! BOOM!
BOOM! BOOM! BOOM!
BOOM! BOOM! BOOM!
BOOM! BOOM! BOOM!
JUST A SECOND--!

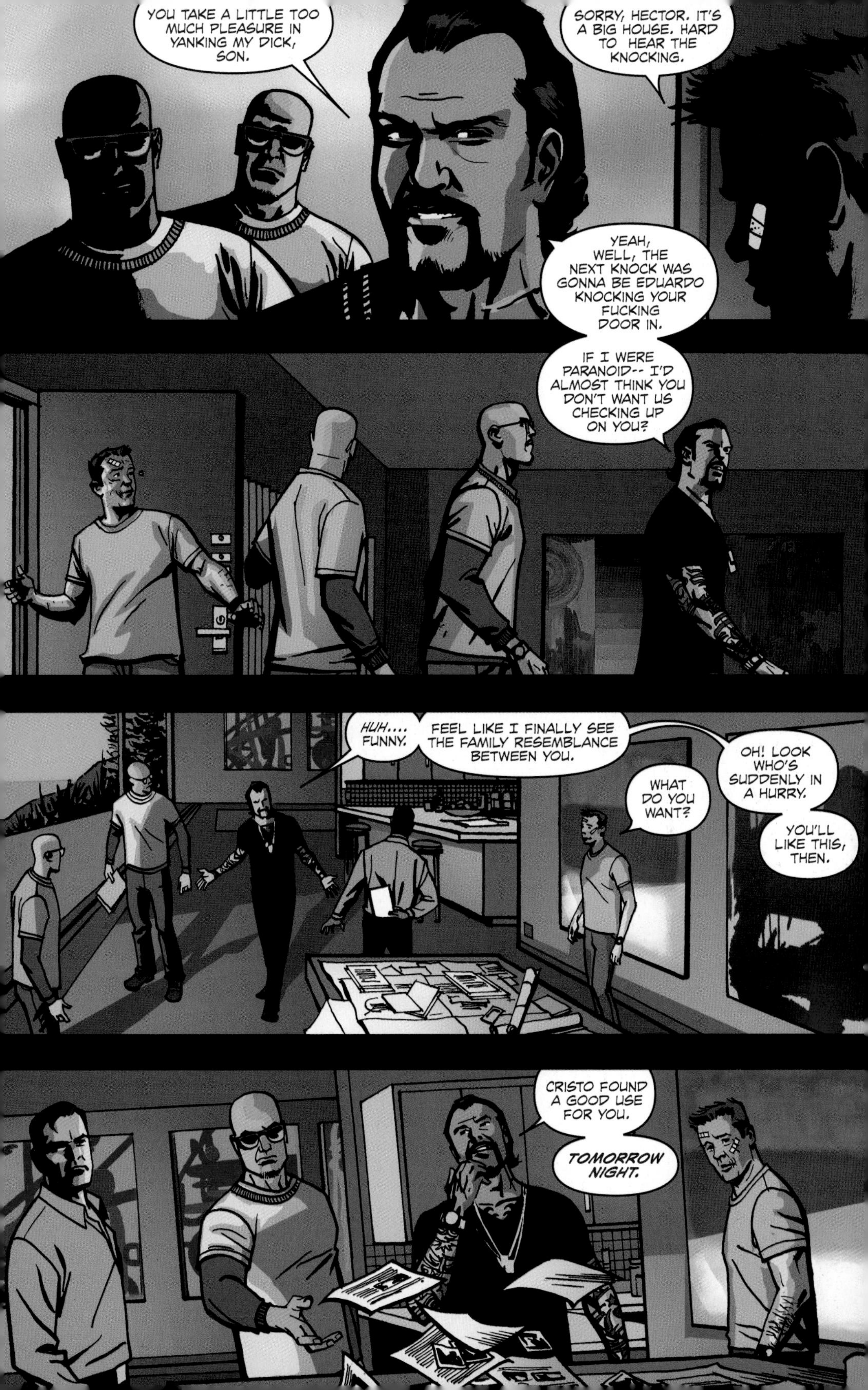
YOU TAKE A LITTLE TOO MUCH PLEASURE IN YANKING MY DICK, SON.
SORRY, HECTOR. IT'S A BIG HOUSE. HARD TO HEAR THE KNOCKING.
YEAH, WELL, THE NEXT KNOCK WAS GONNA BE EDUARDO KNOCKING YOUR FUCKING DOOR IN.
IF I WERE PARANOID-- I'D ALMOST THINK YOU DON'T WANT US CHECKING UP ON YOU?
HUH.... FUNNY.
FEEL LIKE I FINALLY SEE THE FAMILY RESEMBLANCE BETWEEN YOU.
OH! LOOK WHO'S SUDDENLY IN A HURRY.
WHAT DO YOU WANT?
YOU'LL LIKE THIS, THEN.
CRISTO FOUND A GOOD USE FOR YOU.
TOMORROW NIGHT.

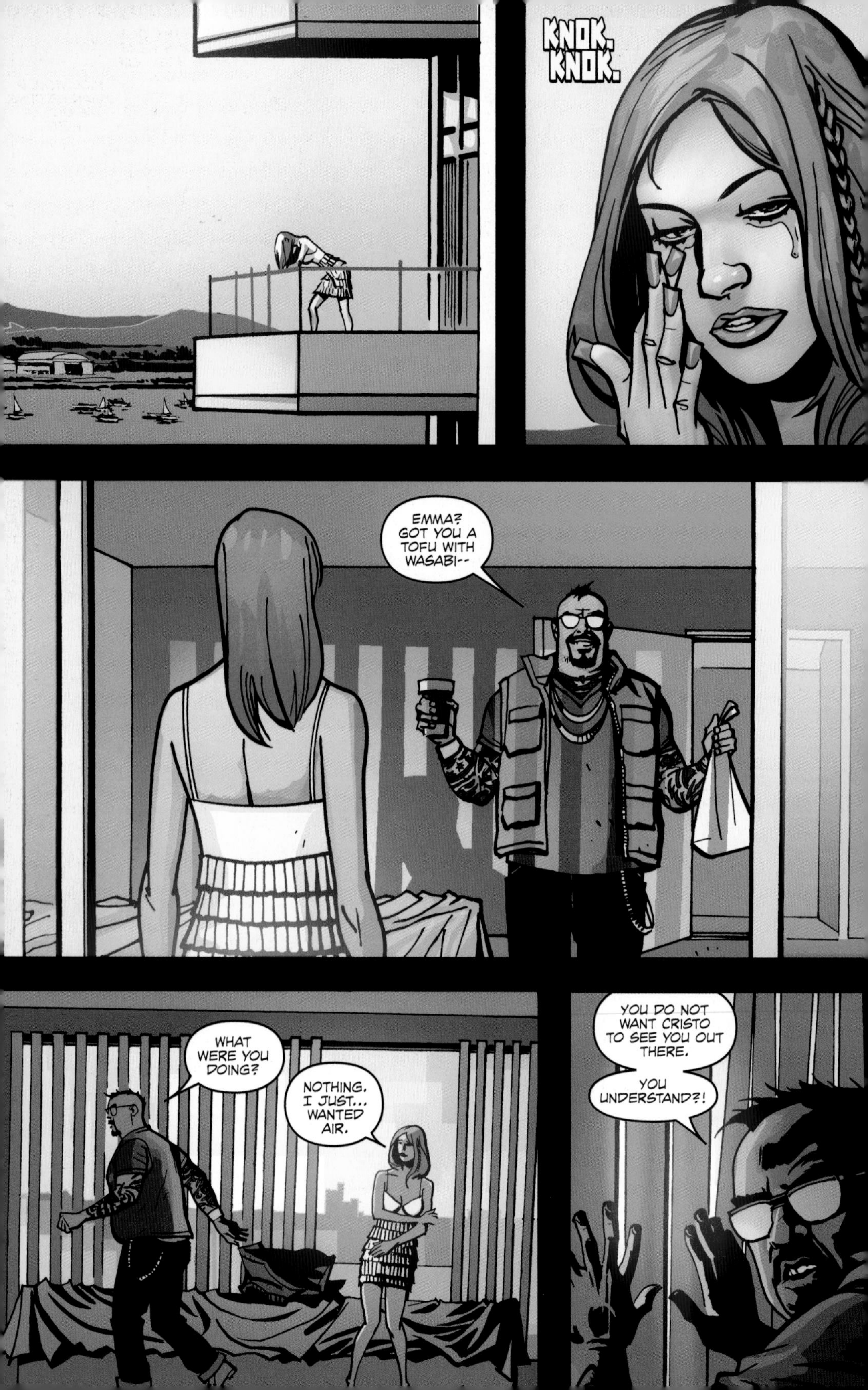
KNOK. KNOK.
EMMA? GOT YOU A TOFU WITH WASABI--
WHAT WERE YOU DOING?
NOTHING. I JUST... WANTED AIR.
YOU DO NOT WANT CRISTO TO SEE YOU OUT THERE.
YOU UNDERSTAND?!

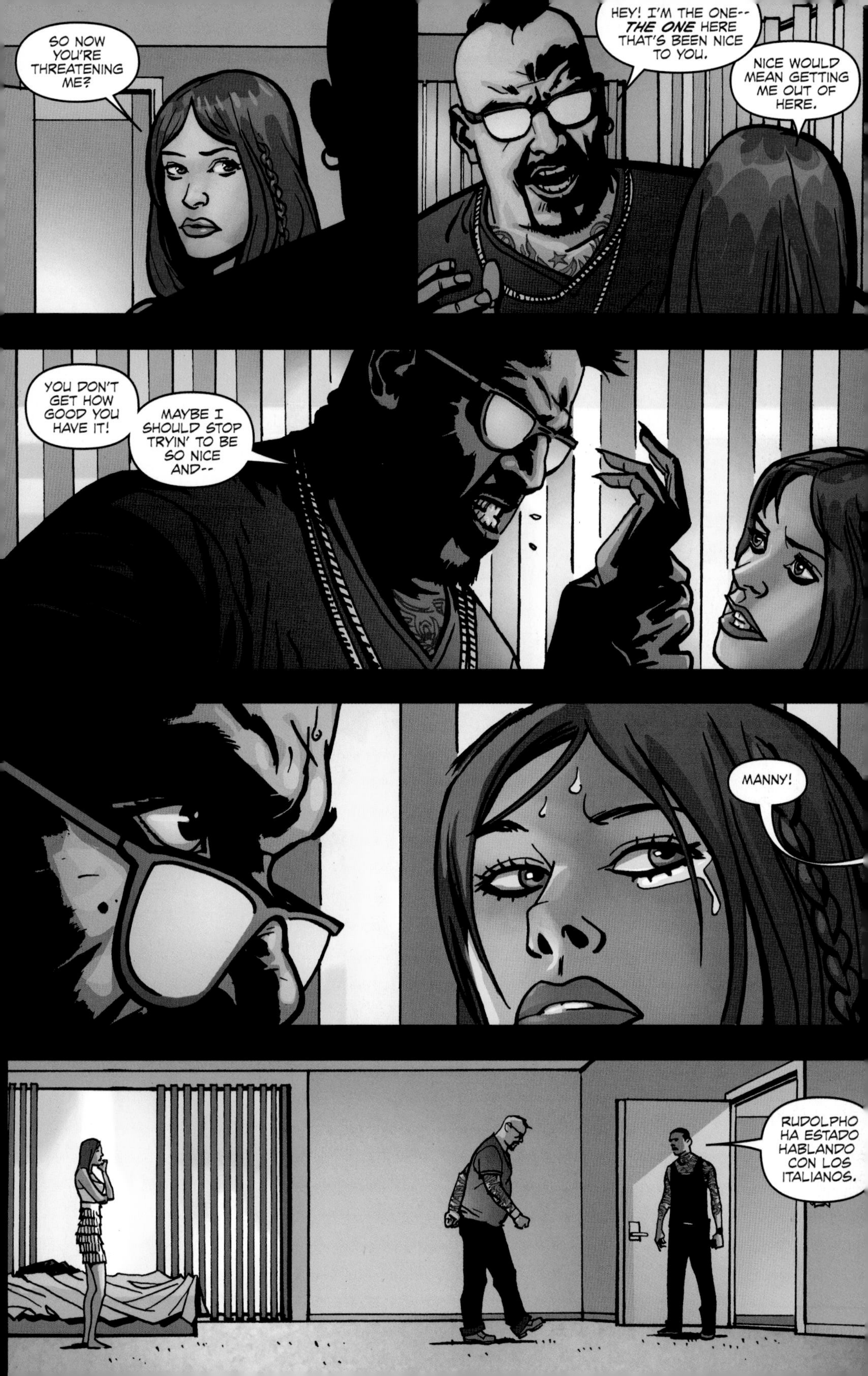
SO NOW YOU'RE THREATENING ME?
HEY! I'M THE ONE-- THE ONE HERE THAT'S BEEN NICE TO YOU.
NICE WOULD MEAN GETTING ME OUT OF HERE.
YOU DON'T GET HOW GOOD YOU HAVE IT!
MAYBE I SHOULD STOP TRYIN' TO BE SO NICE AND--
MANNY!
RUDOLPHO HA ESTADO HABLANDO CON LOS ITALIANOS.

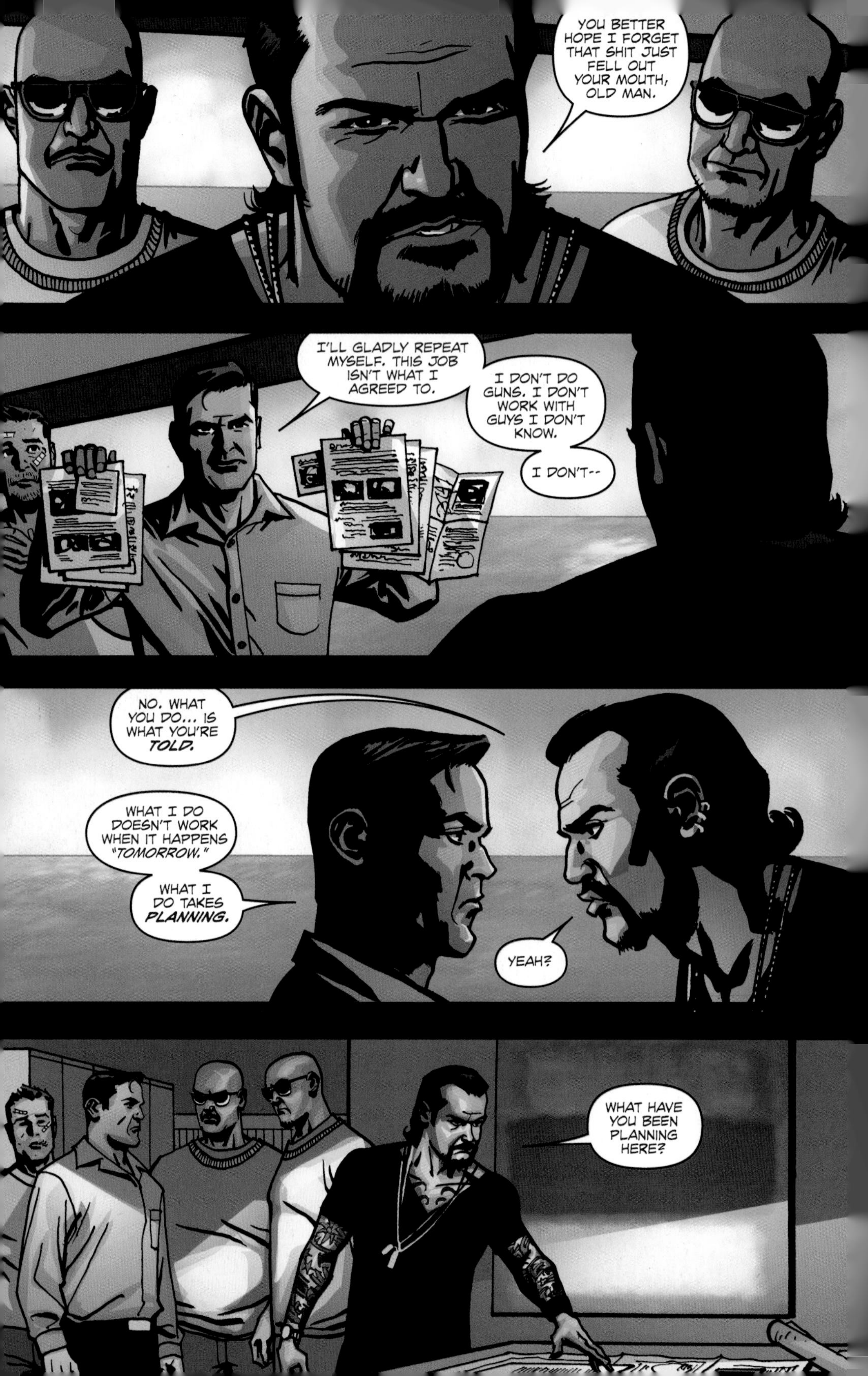
YOU BETTER HOPE I FORGET THAT SHIT JUST FELL OUT YOUR MOUTH, OLD MAN.
I'LL GLADLY REPEAT MYSELF. THIS JOB ISN'T WHAT I AGREED TO.
I DON'T DO GUNS. I DON'T WORK WITH GUYS I DON'T KNOW.
I DON'T--
NO. WHAT YOU DO... IS WHAT YOU'RE *TOLD.*
WHAT I DO DOESN'T WORK WHEN IT HAPPENS *"TOMORROW."*
WHAT I DO TAKES ***PLANNING.***
YEAH?
WHAT HAVE YOU BEEN PLANNING HERE?

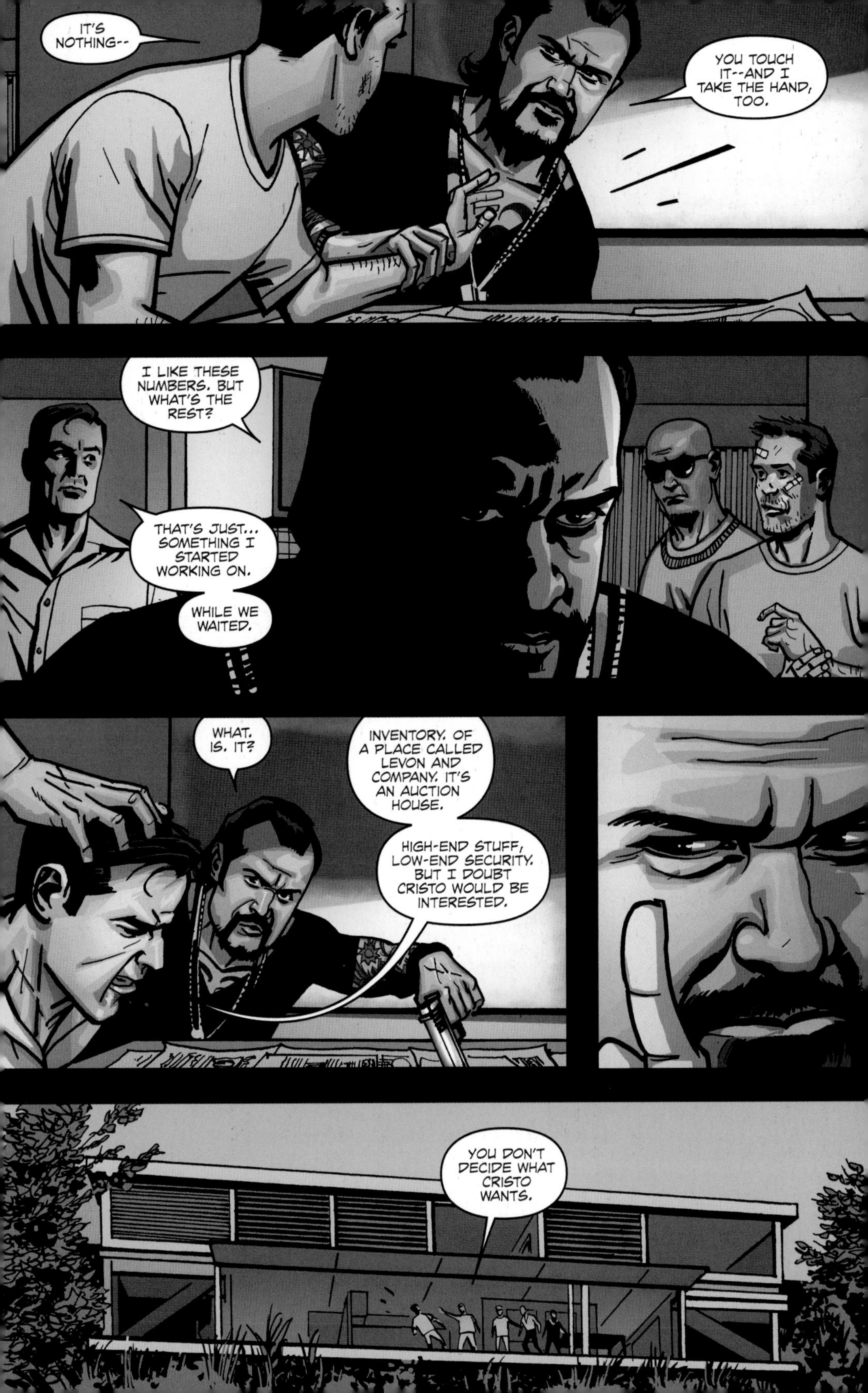
IT'S NOTHING--
YOU TOUCH IT--AND I TAKE THE HAND, TOO.
I LIKE THESE NUMBERS. BUT WHAT'S THE REST?
THAT'S JUST... SOMETHING I STARTED WORKING ON.
WHILE WE WAITED.
WHAT. IS. IT?
INVENTORY. OF A PLACE CALLED LEVON AND COMPANY. IT'S AN AUCTION HOUSE.
HIGH-END STUFF, LOW-END SECURITY. BUT I DOUBT CRISTO WOULD BE INTERESTED.
YOU DON'T DECIDE WHAT CRISTO WANTS.

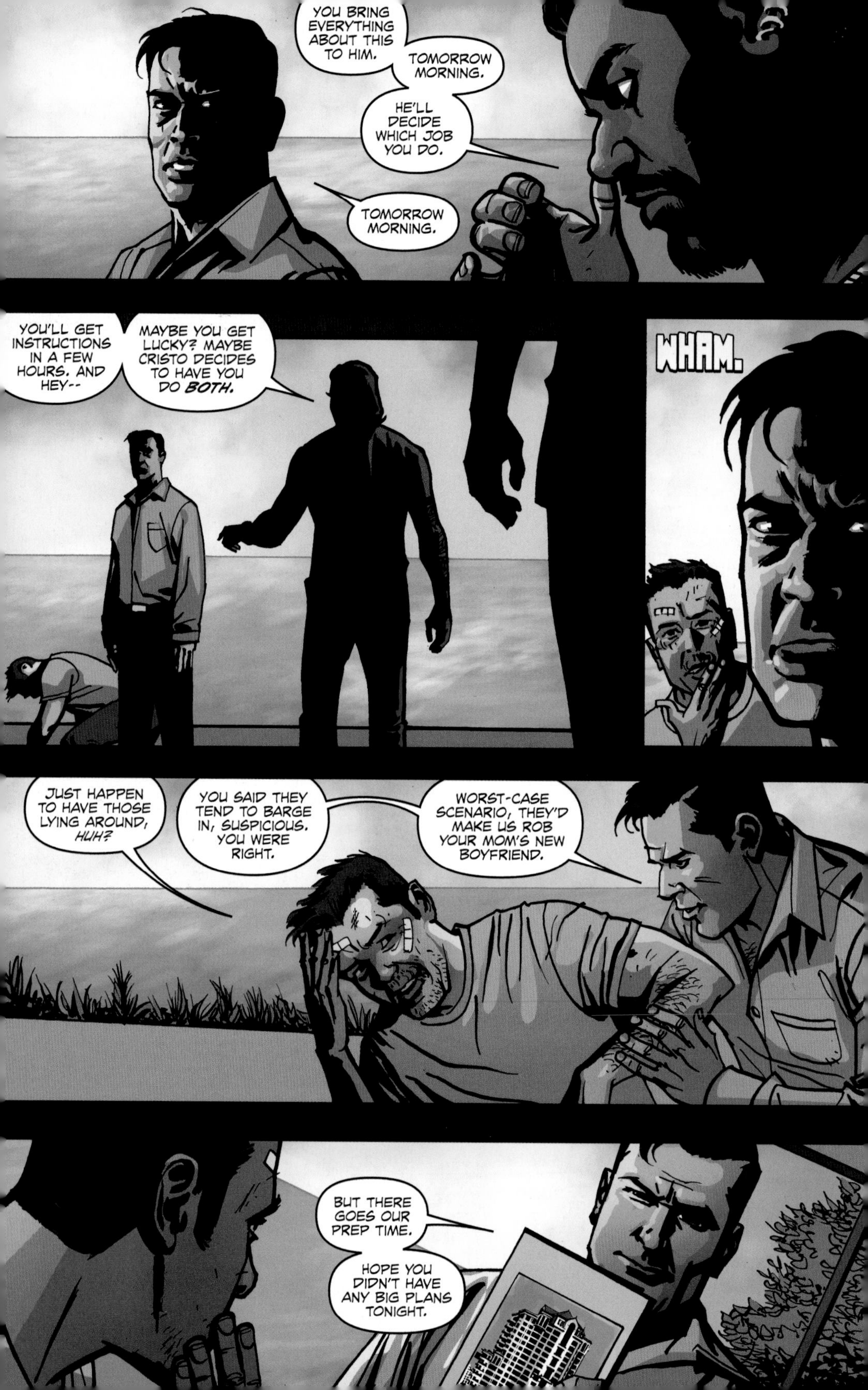
YOU BRING EVERYTHING ABOUT THIS TO HIM.
TOMORROW MORNING.
HE'LL DECIDE WHICH JOB YOU DO.
TOMORROW MORNING.
YOU'LL GET INSTRUCTIONS IN A FEW HOURS. AND HEY--
MAYBE YOU GET LUCKY? MAYBE CRISTO DECIDES TO HAVE YOU DO *BOTH.*
WHAM.
JUST HAPPEN TO HAVE THOSE LYING AROUND, *HUH?*
YOU SAID THEY TEND TO BARGE IN, SUSPICIOUS. YOU WERE RIGHT.
WORST-CASE SCENARIO, THEY'D MAKE US ROB YOUR MOM'S NEW BOYFRIEND.
BUT THERE GOES OUR PREP TIME.
HOPE YOU DIDN'T HAVE ANY BIG PLANS TONIGHT.

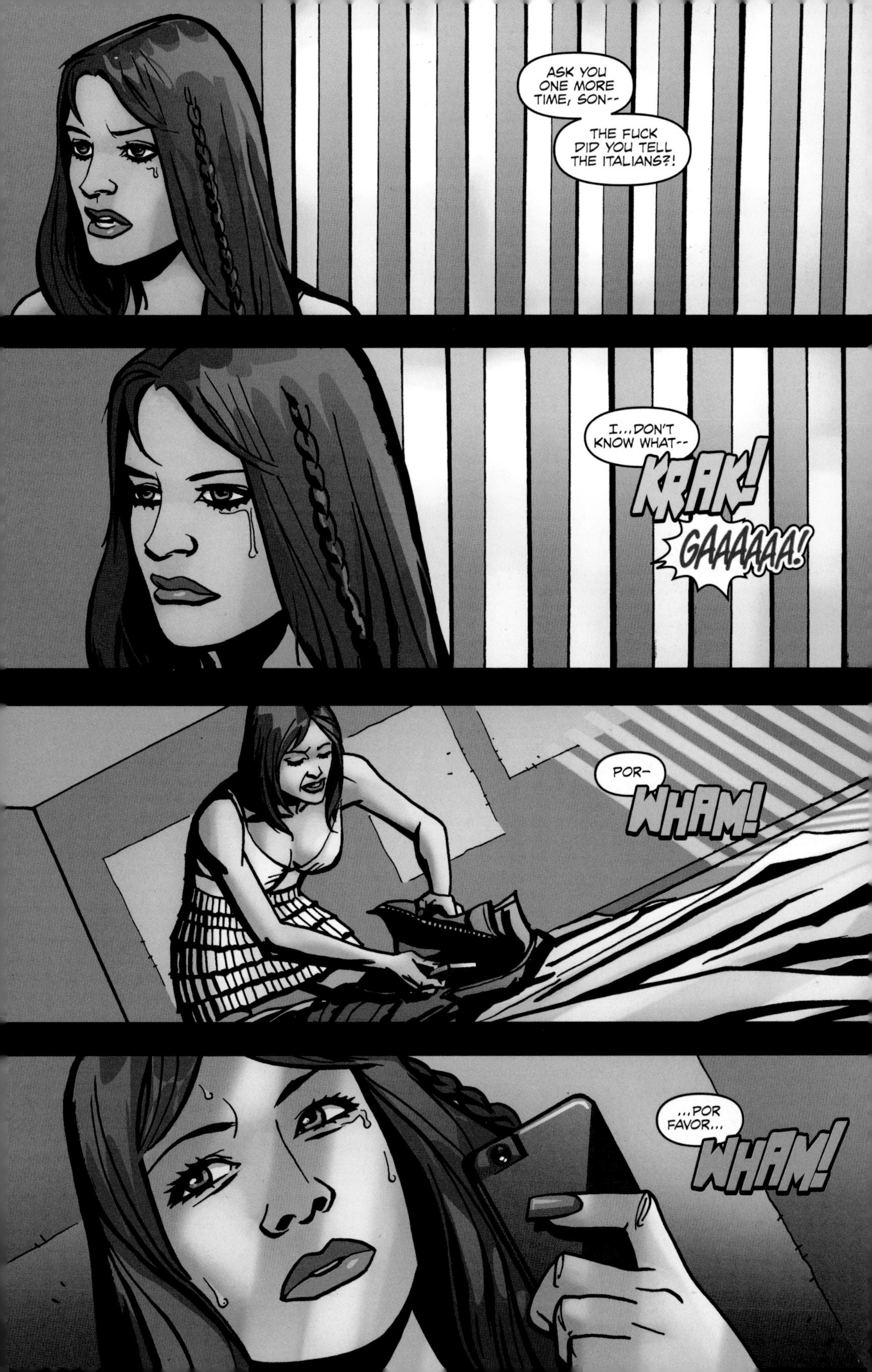
ASK YOU ONE MORE TIME, SON--
THE FUCK DID YOU TELL THE ITALIANS?!
I...DON'T KNOW WHAT--
KRAK!
GAAAAAA!
POR-
WHAM!
...POR FAVOR...
WHAM!

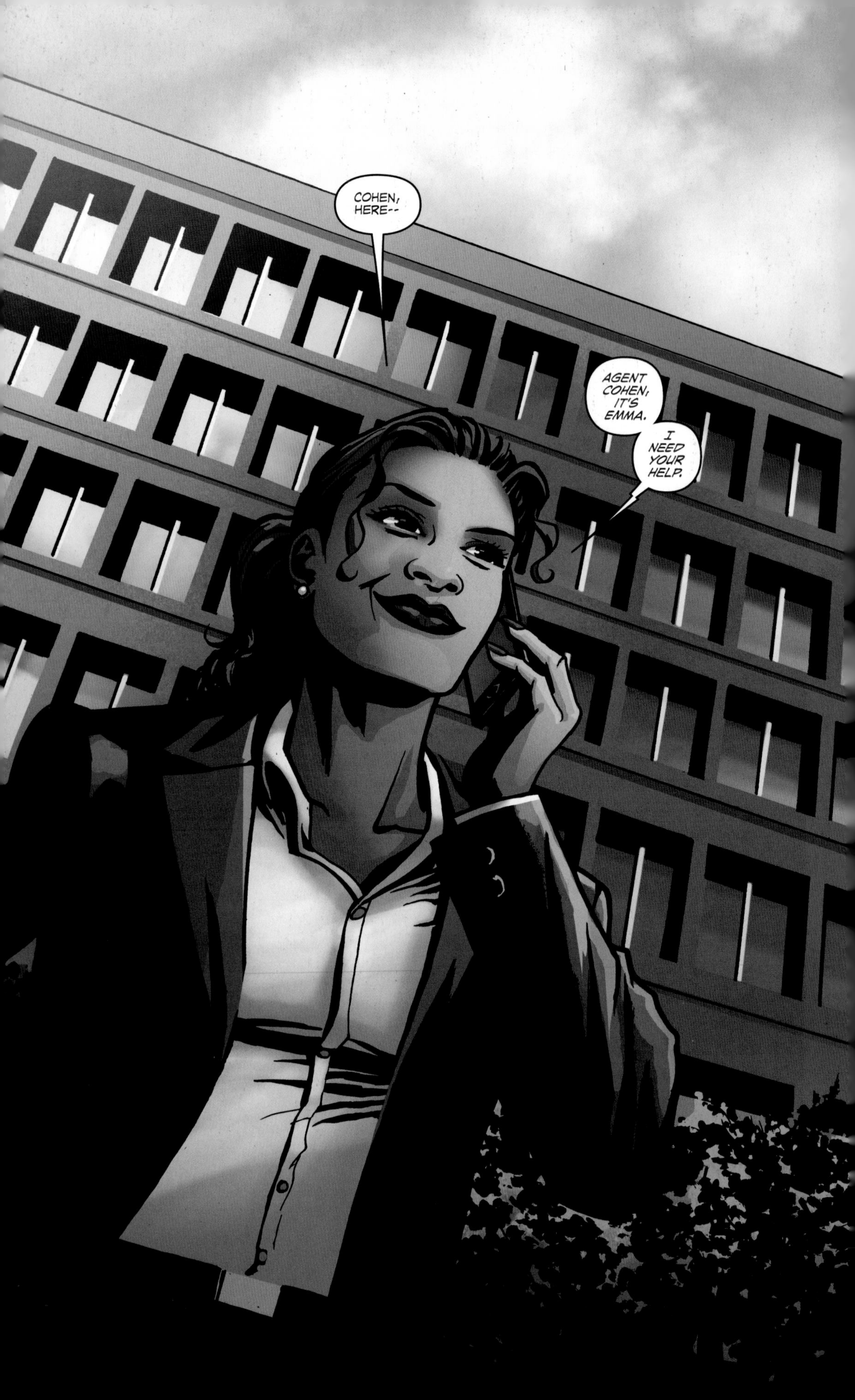
COHEN, HERE--
AGENT COHEN, IT'S EMMA.
I NEED YOUR HELP.

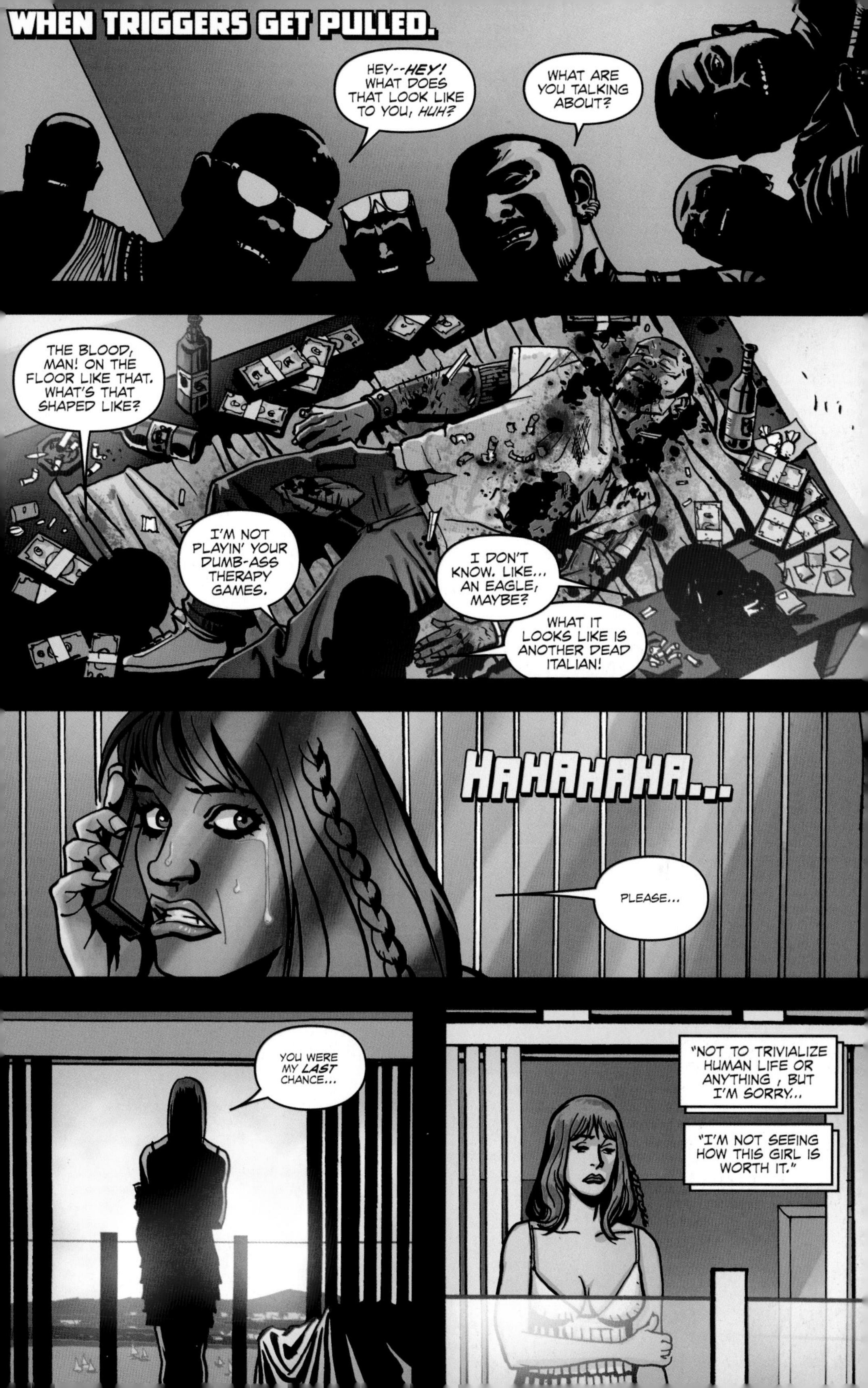
WHEN TRIGGERS GET PULLED.
HEY--HEY! WHAT DOES THAT LOOK LIKE TO YOU, HUH?
WHAT ARE YOU TALKING ABOUT?
THE BLOOD, MAN! ON THE FLOOR LIKE THAT. WHAT'S THAT SHAPED LIKE?
I'M NOT PLAYIN' YOUR DUMB-ASS THERAPY GAMES.
I DON'T KNOW. LIKE... AN EAGLE, MAYBE?
WHAT IT LOOKS LIKE IS ANOTHER DEAD ITALIAN!
HAHAHAHA...
PLEASE...
YOU WERE MY LAST CHANCE...
"NOT TO TRIVIALIZE HUMAN LIFE OR ANYTHING , BUT I'M SORRY...
"I'M NOT SEEING HOW THIS GIRL IS WORTH IT."

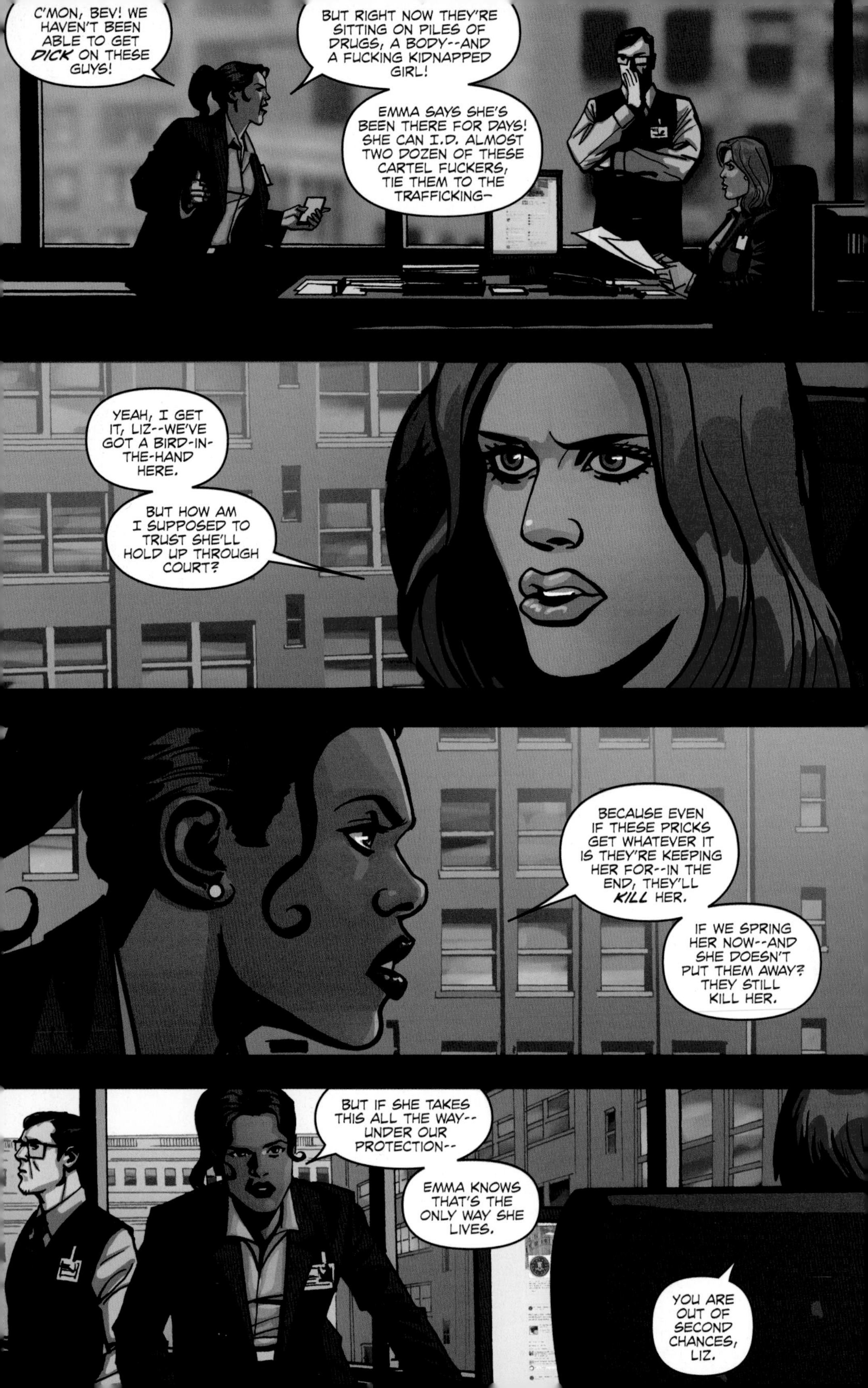
C'MON, BEV! WE HAVEN'T BEEN ABLE TO GET DICK ON THESE GUYS!
BUT RIGHT NOW THEY'RE SITTING ON PILES OF DRUGS, A BODY--AND A FUCKING KIDNAPPED GIRL!
EMMA SAYS SHE'S BEEN THERE FOR DAYS! SHE CAN I.D. ALMOST TWO DOZEN OF THESE CARTEL FUCKERS, TIE THEM TO THE TRAFFICKING–
YEAH, I GET IT, LIZ--WE'VE GOT A BIRD-IN-THE-HAND HERE.
BUT HOW AM I SUPPOSED TO TRUST SHE'LL HOLD UP THROUGH COURT?
BECAUSE EVEN IF THESE PRICKS GET WHATEVER IT IS THEY'RE KEEPING HER FOR--IN THE END, THEY'LL KILL HER.
IF WE SPRING HER NOW--AND SHE DOESN'T PUT THEM AWAY? THEY STILL KILL HER.
BUT IF SHE TAKES THIS ALL THE WAY--UNDER OUR PROTECTION--
EMMA KNOWS THAT'S THE ONLY WAY SHE LIVES.
YOU ARE OUT OF SECOND CHANCES, LIZ.

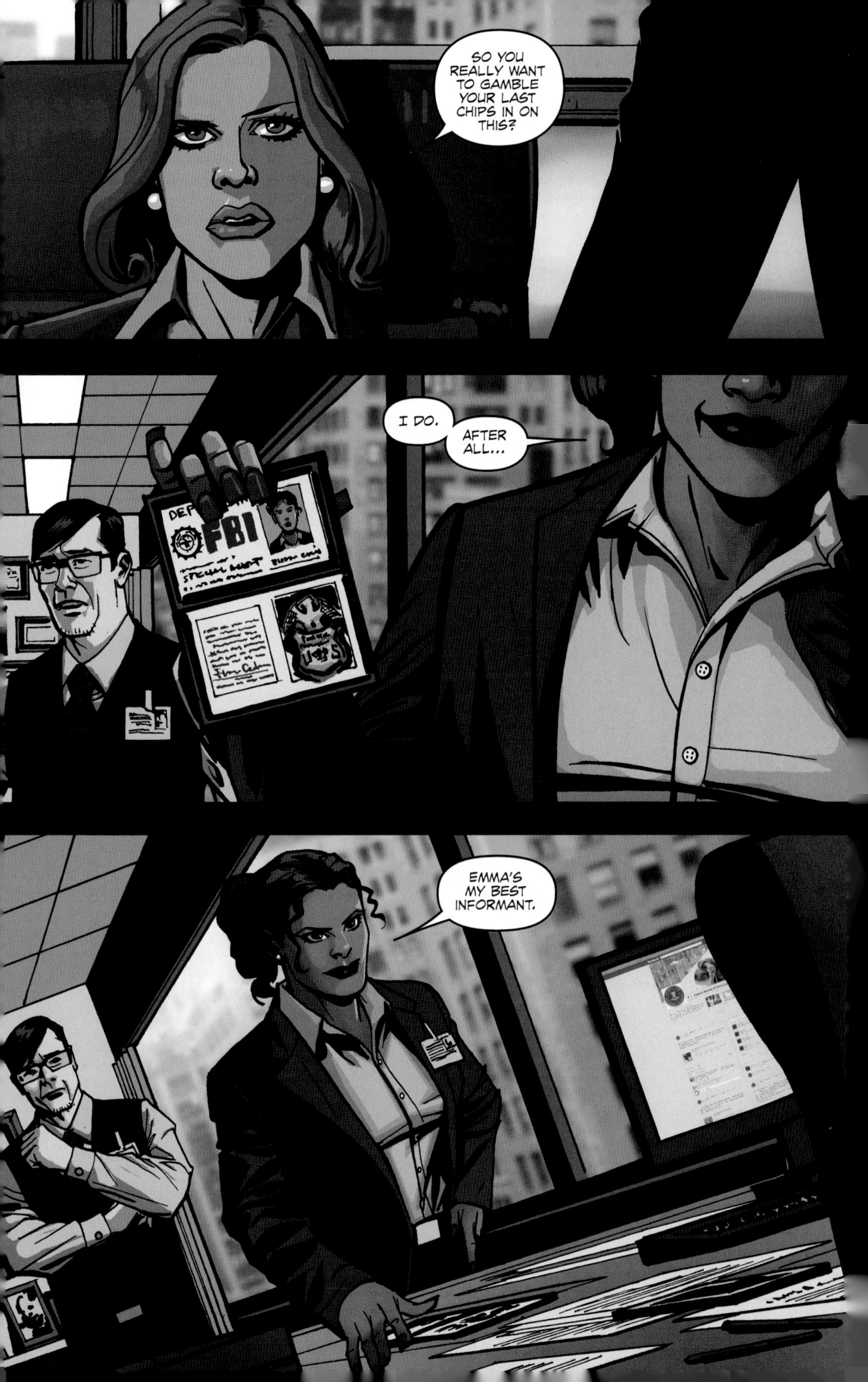
SO YOU REALLY WANT TO GAMBLE YOUR LAST CHIPS IN ON THIS?
I DO.
AFTER ALL...
FBI
EMMA'S MY BEST INFORMANT.

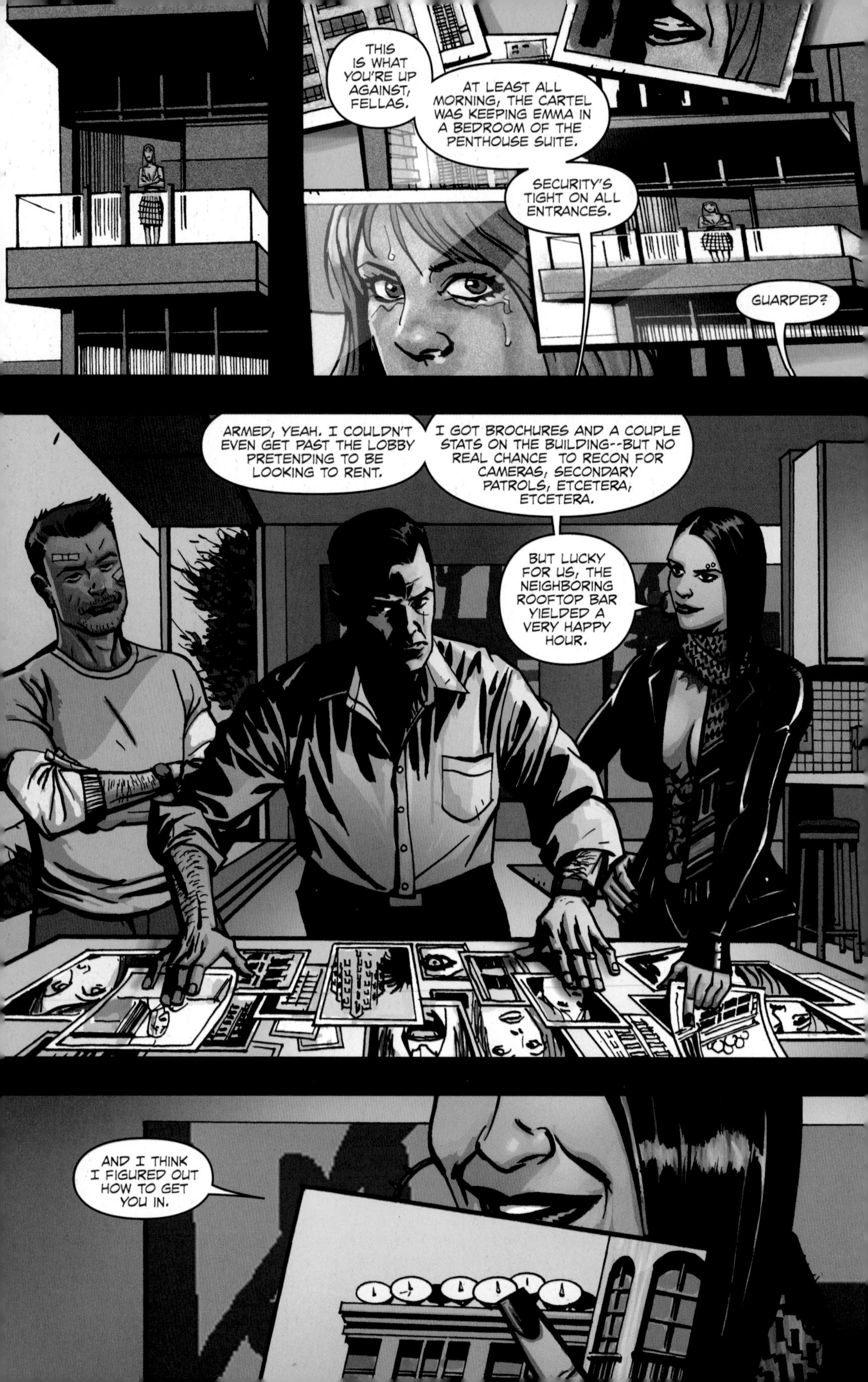
THIS IS WHAT YOU'RE UP AGAINST, FELLAS.
AT LEAST ALL MORNING, THE CARTEL WAS KEEPING EMMA IN A BEDROOM OF THE PENTHOUSE SUITE.
SECURITY'S TIGHT ON ALL ENTRANCES.
GUARDED?
ARMED, YEAH. I COULDN'T EVEN GET PAST THE LOBBY PRETENDING TO BE LOOKING TO RENT.
I GOT BROCHURES AND A COUPLE STATS ON THE BUILDING--BUT NO REAL CHANCE TO RECON FOR CAMERAS, SECONDARY PATROLS, ETCETERA, ETCETERA.
BUT LUCKY FOR US, THE NEIGHBORING ROOFTOP BAR YIELDED A VERY HAPPY HOUR.
AND I THINK I FIGURED OUT HOW TO GET YOU IN.

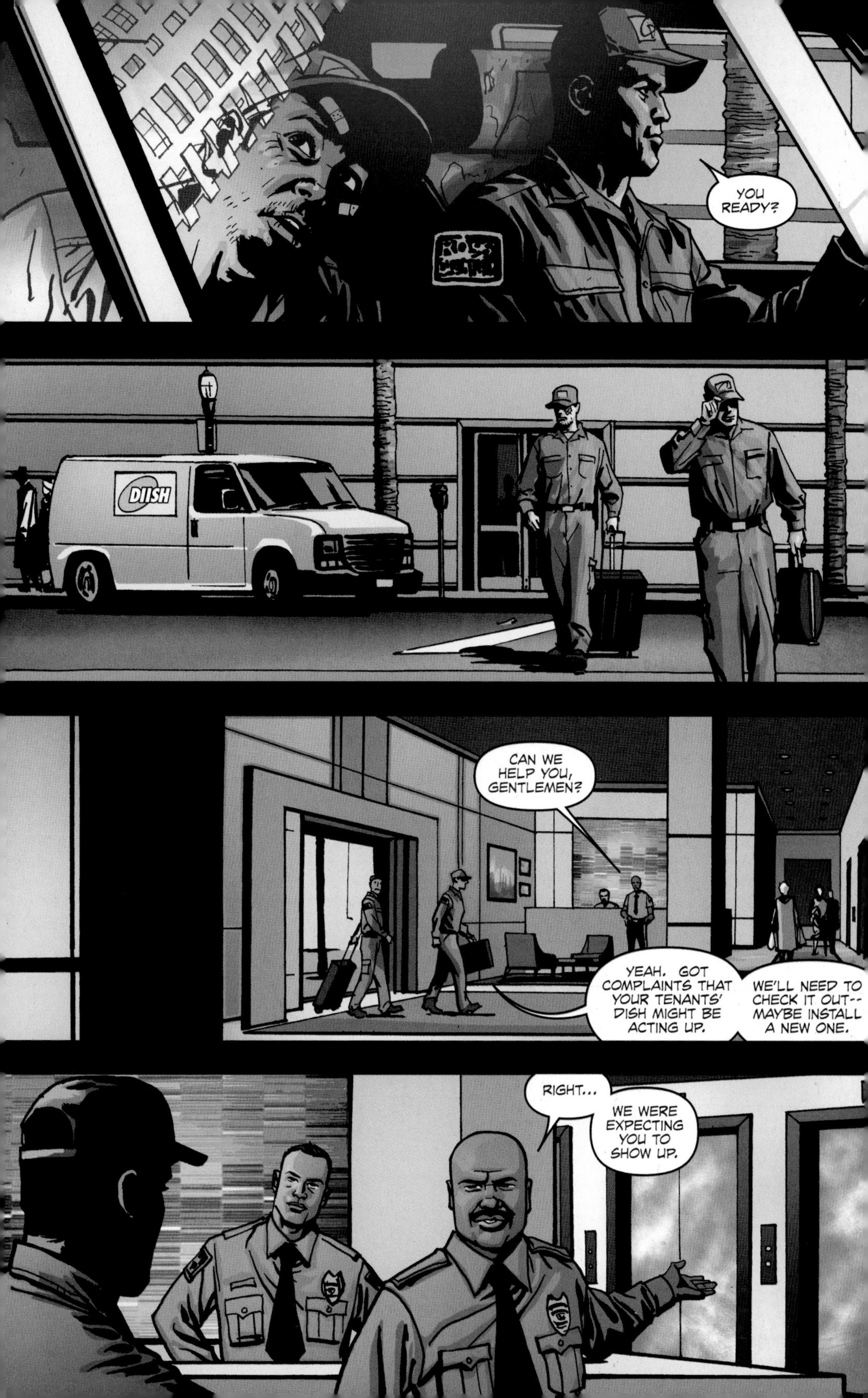
YOU READY?
DIISH
CAN WE HELP YOU, GENTLEMEN?
YEAH. GOT COMPLAINTS THAT YOUR TENANTS' DISH MIGHT BE ACTING UP.
WE'LL NEED TO CHECK IT OUT-- MAYBE INSTALL A NEW ONE.
RIGHT...
WE WERE EXPECTING YOU TO SHOW UP.

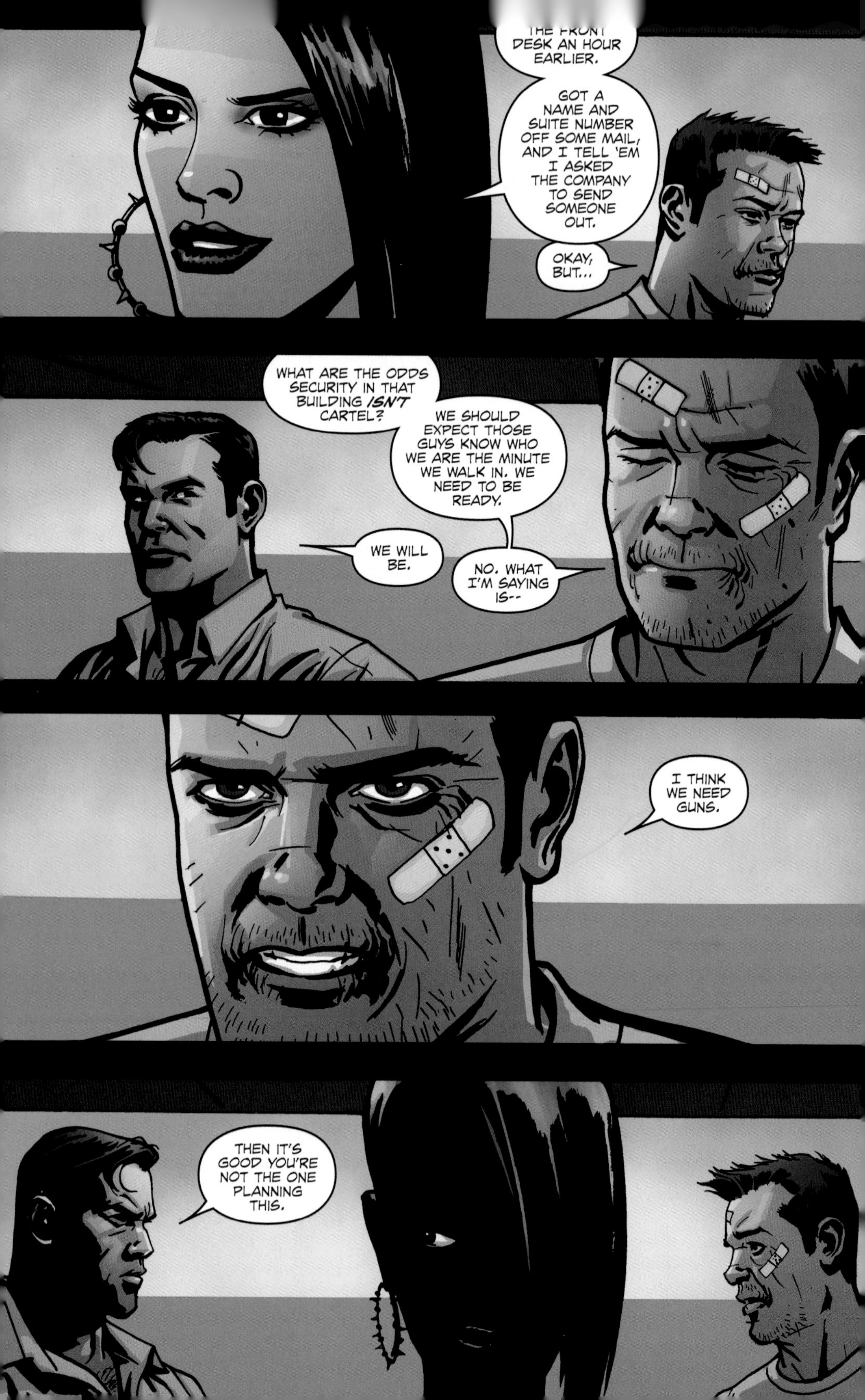
THE FRONT DESK AN HOUR EARLIER.
GOT A NAME AND SUITE NUMBER OFF SOME MAIL, AND I TELL 'EM I ASKED THE COMPANY TO SEND SOMEONE OUT.
OKAY, BUT...
WHAT ARE THE ODDS SECURITY IN THAT BUILDING *ISN'T* CARTEL?
WE SHOULD EXPECT THOSE GUYS KNOW WHO WE ARE THE MINUTE WE WALK IN. WE NEED TO BE READY.
WE WILL BE.
NO. WHAT I'M SAYING IS--
I THINK WE NEED GUNS.
THEN IT'S GOOD YOU'RE NOT THE ONE PLANNING THIS.

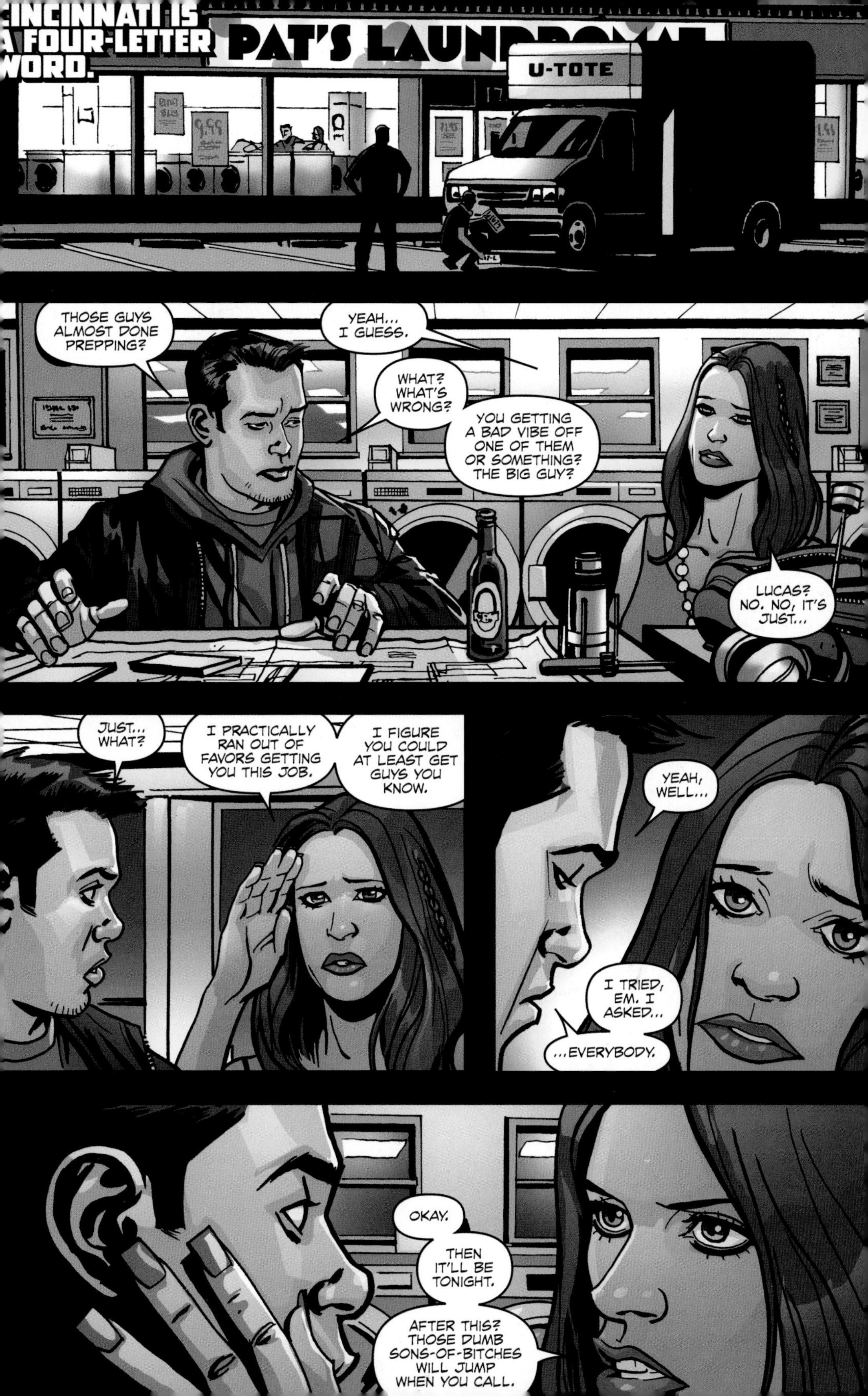
CINCINNATI IS A FOUR-LETTER WORD.
PAT'S LAUNDROMAT
U-TOTE
THOSE GUYS ALMOST DONE PREPPING?
YEAH... I GUESS.
WHAT? WHAT'S WRONG?
YOU GETTING A BAD VIBE OFF ONE OF THEM OR SOMETHING? THE BIG GUY?
LUCAS? NO. NO, IT'S JUST...
JUST... WHAT?
I PRACTICALLY RAN OUT OF FAVORS GETTING YOU THIS JOB.
I FIGURE YOU COULD AT LEAST GET GUYS YOU KNOW.
YEAH, WELL...
I TRIED, EM. I ASKED...
...EVERYBODY.
OKAY.
THEN IT'LL BE TONIGHT.
AFTER THIS? THOSE DUMB SONS-OF-BITCHES WILL JUMP WHEN YOU CALL.

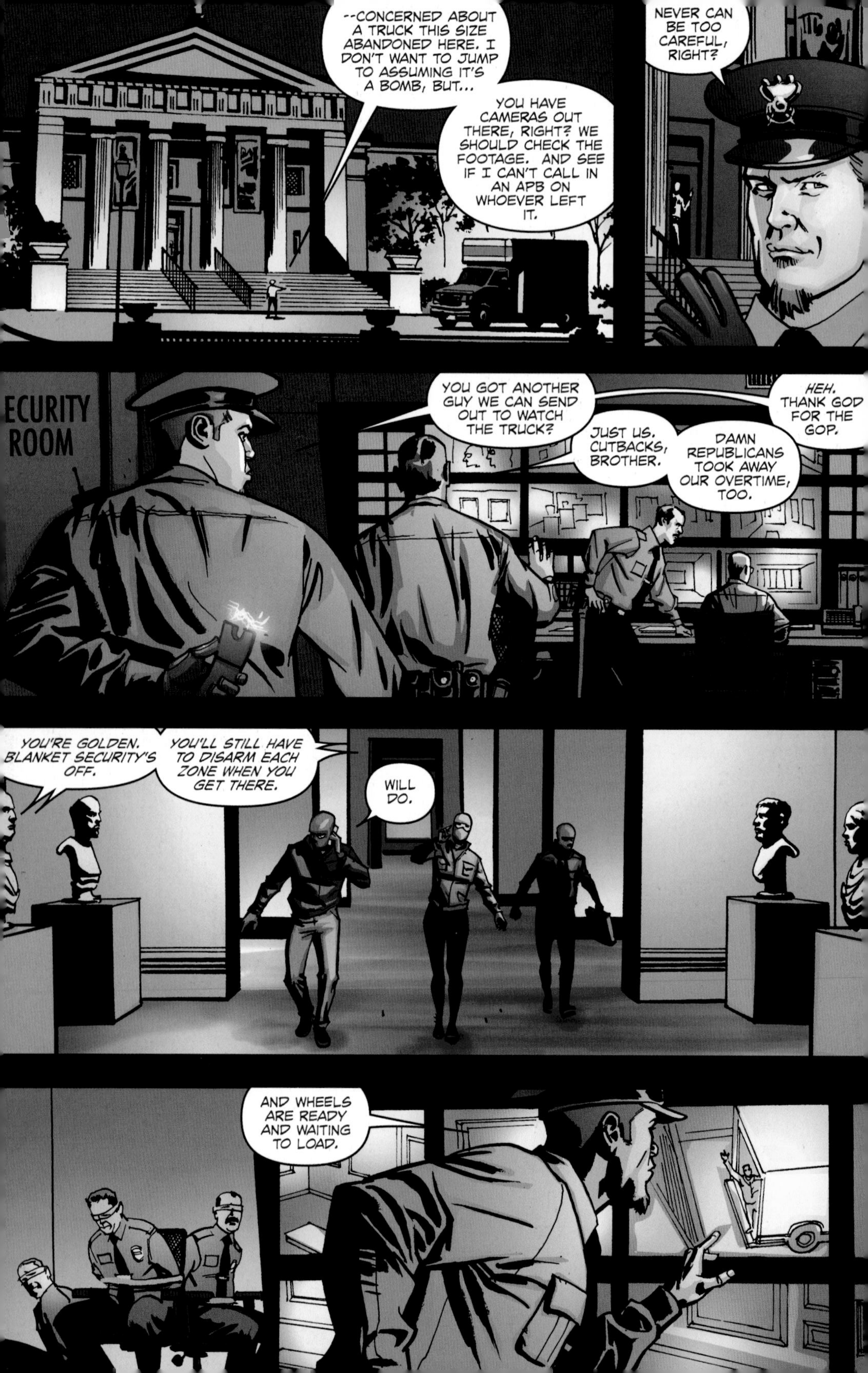
--CONCERNED ABOUT A TRUCK THIS SIZE ABANDONED HERE. I DON'T WANT TO JUMP TO ASSUMING IT'S A BOMB, BUT...
YOU HAVE CAMERAS OUT THERE, RIGHT? WE SHOULD CHECK THE FOOTAGE. AND SEE IF I CAN'T CALL IN AN APB ON WHOEVER LEFT IT.
NEVER CAN BE TOO CAREFUL, RIGHT?
ECURITY ROOM
YOU GOT ANOTHER GUY WE CAN SEND OUT TO WATCH THE TRUCK?
JUST US. CUTBACKS, BROTHER.
DAMN REPUBLICANS TOOK AWAY OUR OVERTIME, TOO.
HEH. THANK GOD FOR THE GOP.
YOU'RE GOLDEN. BLANKET SECURITY'S OFF.
YOU'LL STILL HAVE TO DISARM EACH ZONE WHEN YOU GET THERE.
WILL DO.
AND WHEELS ARE READY AND WAITING TO LOAD.

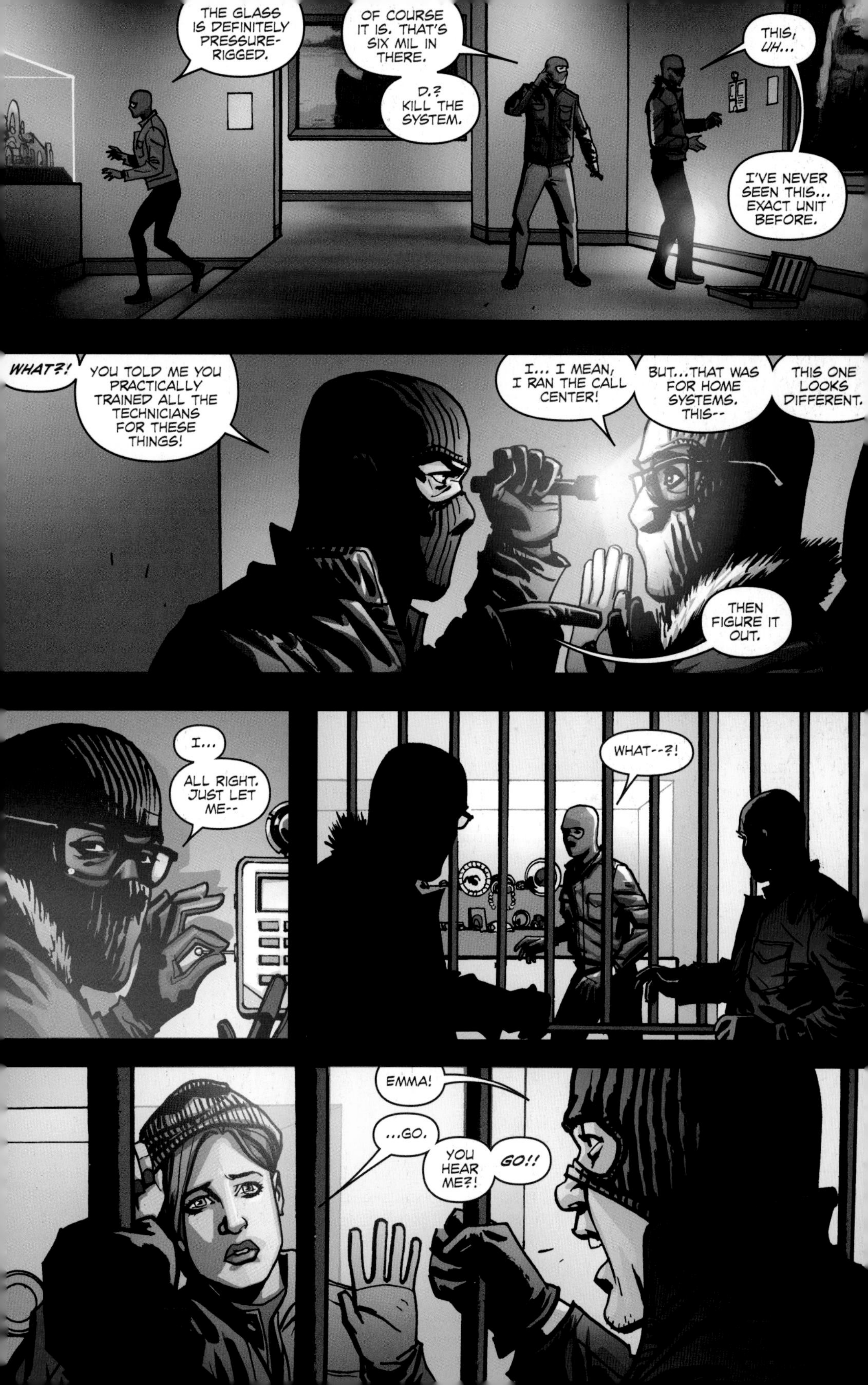
THE GLASS IS DEFINITELY PRESSURE-RIGGED.
OF COURSE IT IS. THAT'S SIX MIL IN THERE.
D.? KILL THE SYSTEM.
THIS, UH...
I'VE NEVER SEEN THIS... EXACT UNIT BEFORE.
WHAT?!
YOU TOLD ME YOU PRACTICALLY TRAINED ALL THE TECHNICIANS FOR THESE THINGS!
I... I MEAN, I RAN THE CALL CENTER!
BUT...THAT WAS FOR HOME SYSTEMS. THIS--
THIS ONE LOOKS DIFFERENT.
THEN FIGURE IT OUT.
I...
ALL RIGHT. JUST LET ME--
WHAT--?!
EMMA!
...GO.
YOU HEAR ME?!
GO!!

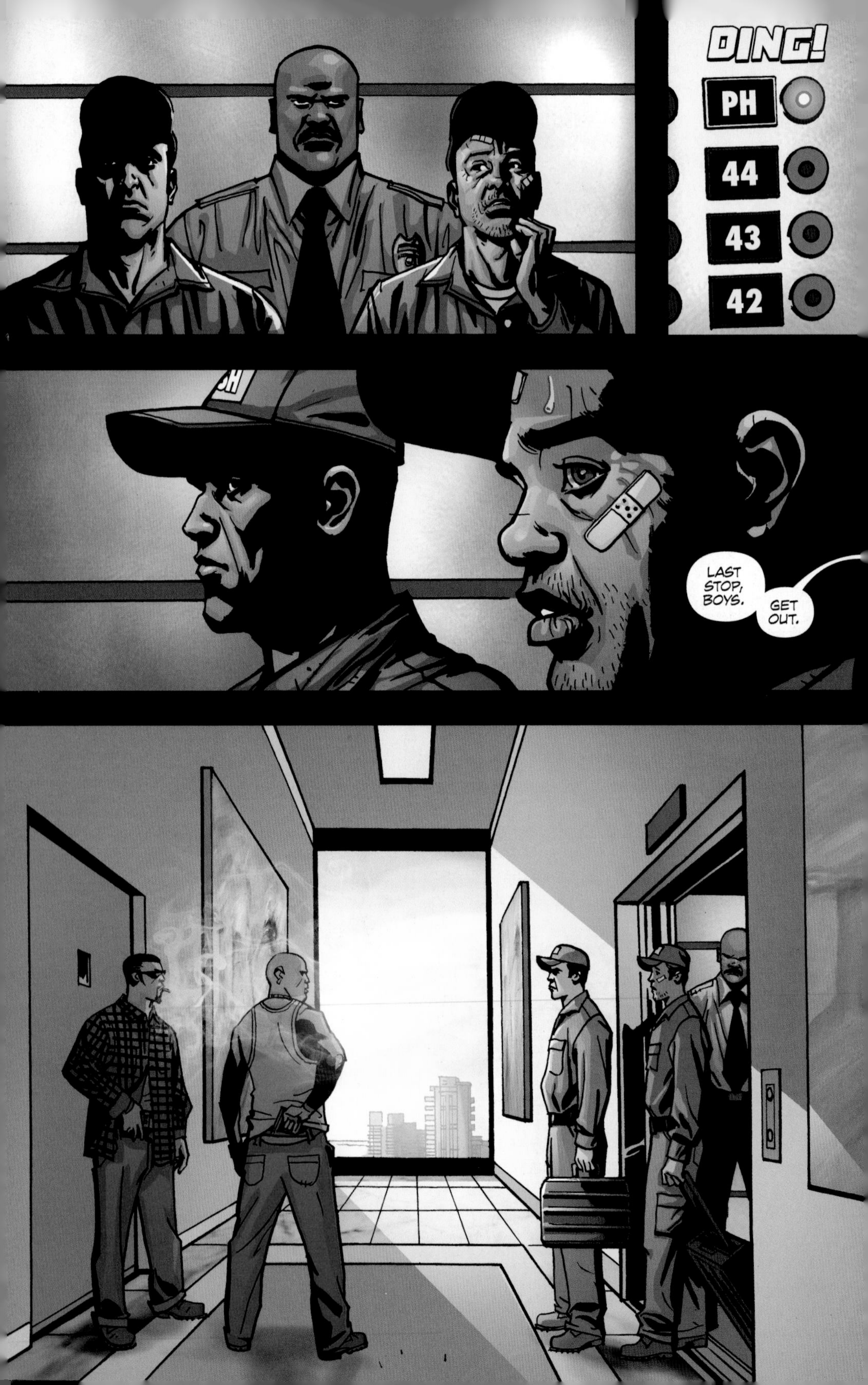
DING!
PH
44
43
42
LAST STOP, BOYS.
GET OUT.

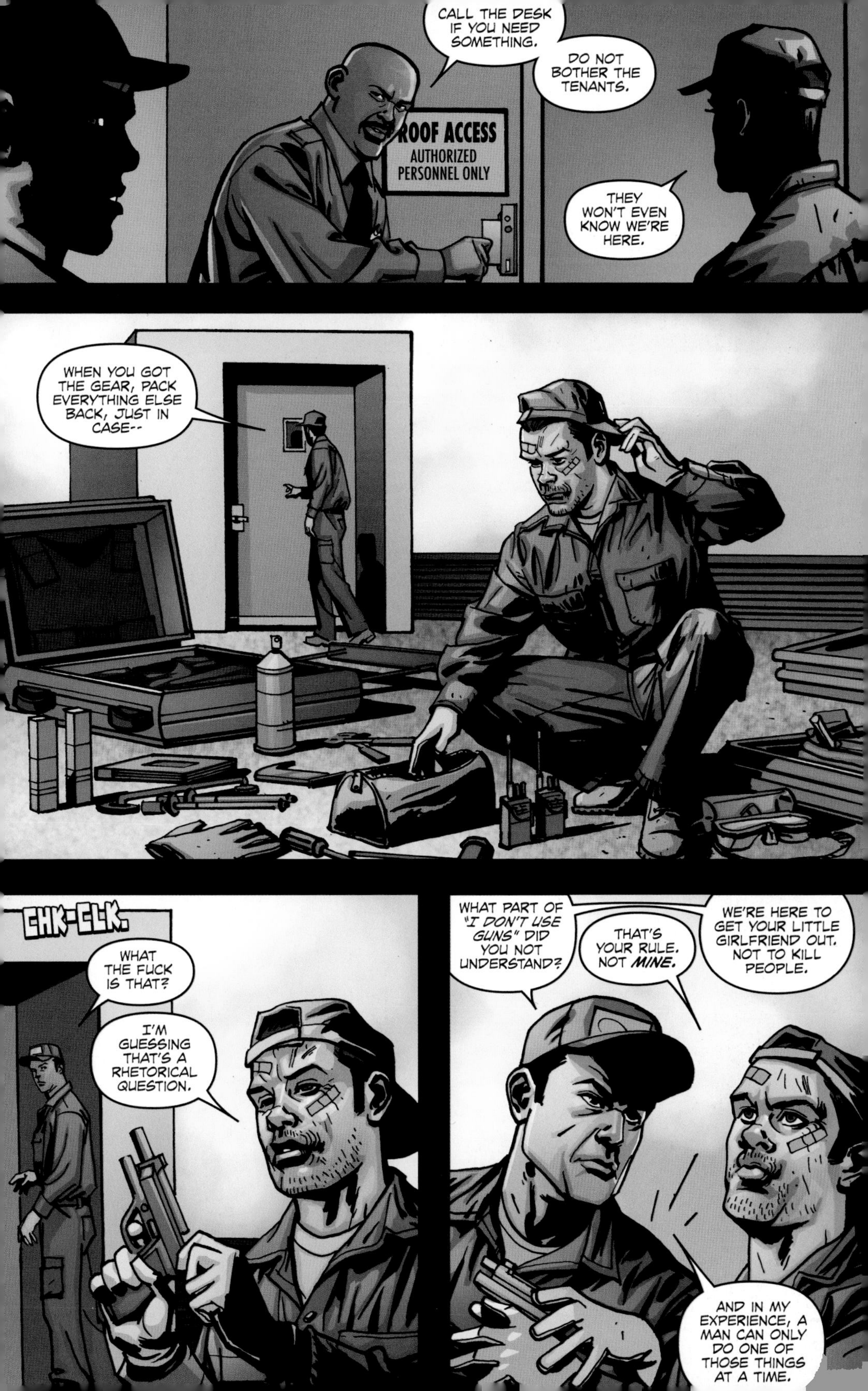
CALL THE DESK IF YOU NEED SOMETHING.
DO NOT BOTHER THE TENANTS.
ROOF ACCESS
AUTHORIZED PERSONNEL ONLY
THEY WON'T EVEN KNOW WE'RE HERE.
WHEN YOU GOT THE GEAR, PACK EVERYTHING ELSE BACK, JUST IN CASE--
CHK-CLK.
WHAT THE FUCK IS THAT?
I'M GUESSING THAT'S A RHETORICAL QUESTION.
WHAT PART OF *"I DON'T USE GUNS"* DID YOU NOT UNDERSTAND?
THAT'S YOUR RULE. NOT *MINE.*
WE'RE HERE TO GET YOUR LITTLE GIRLFRIEND OUT. NOT TO KILL PEOPLE.
AND IN MY EXPERIENCE, A MAN CAN ONLY DO ONE OF THOSE THINGS AT A TIME.

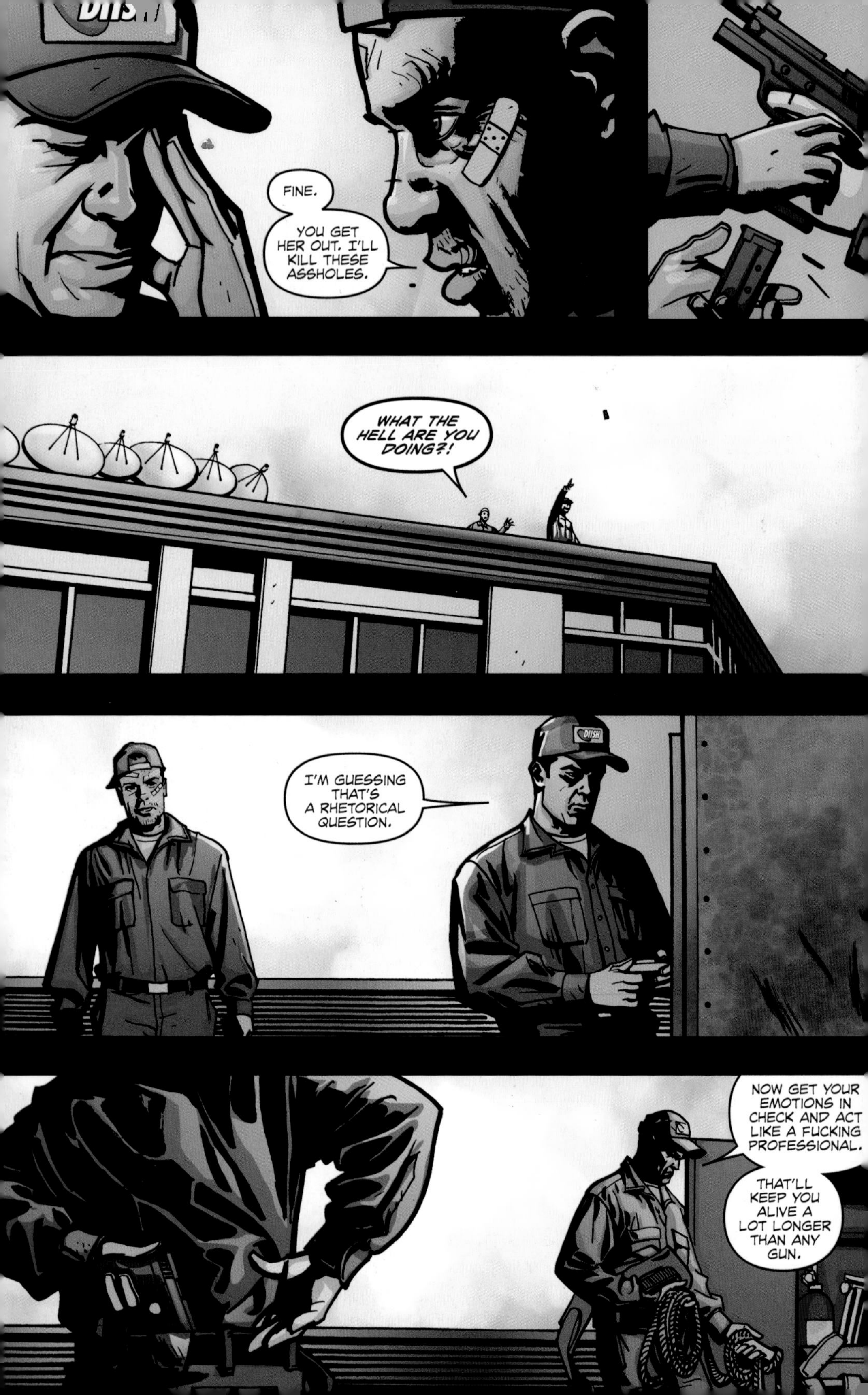
DIISH
FINE.
YOU GET HER OUT. I'LL KILL THESE ASSHOLES.
WHAT THE HELL ARE YOU DOING?!
DIISH
I'M GUESSING THAT'S A RHETORICAL QUESTION.
NOW GET YOUR EMOTIONS IN CHECK AND ACT LIKE A FUCKING PROFESSIONAL.
THAT'LL KEEP YOU ALIVE A LOT LONGER THAN ANY GUN.

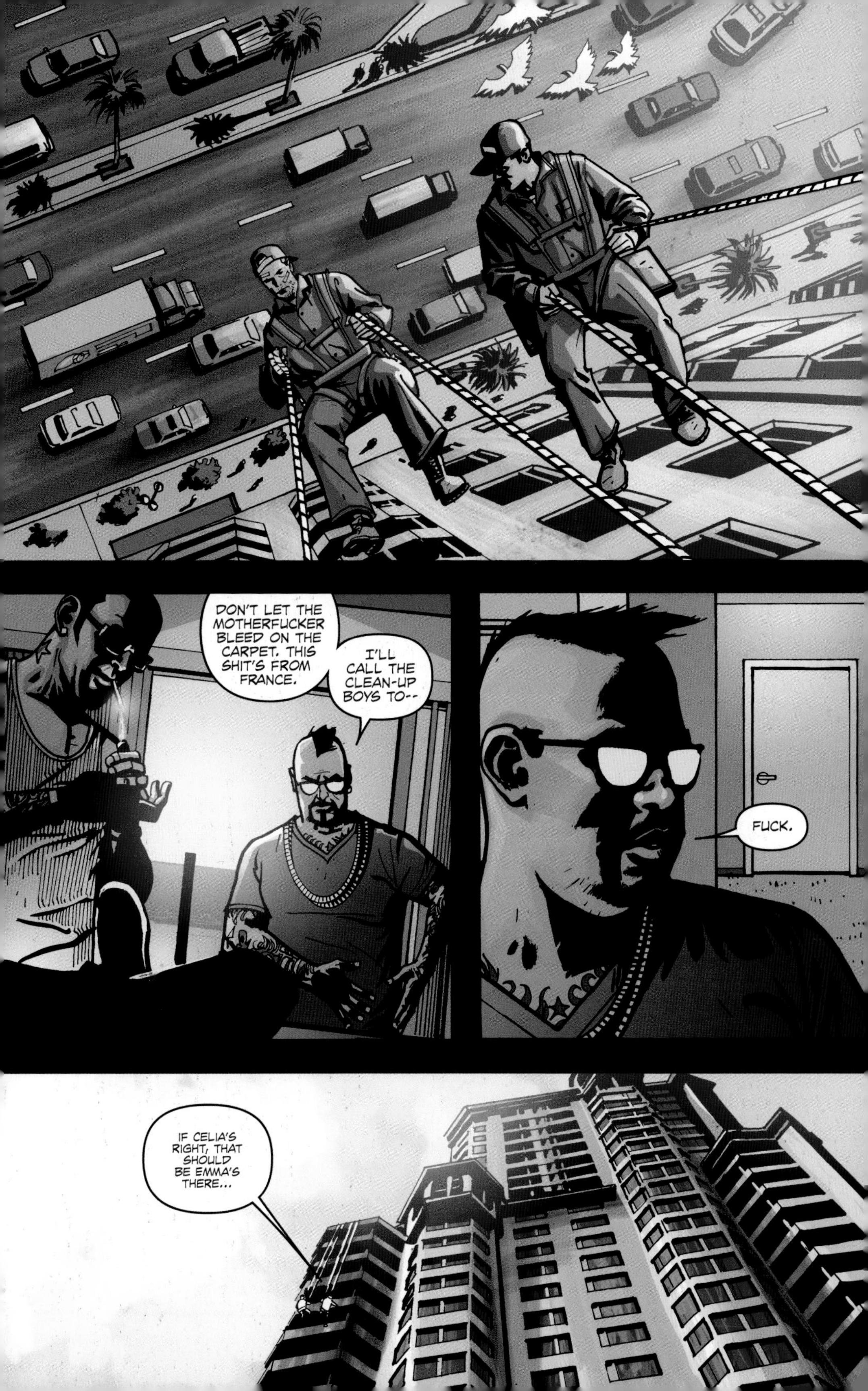
DON'T LET THE MOTHERFUCKER BLEED ON THE CARPET. THIS SHIT'S FROM FRANCE.
I'LL CALL THE CLEAN-UP BOYS TO--
FUCK.
IF CELIA'S RIGHT, THAT SHOULD BE EMMA'S THERE...

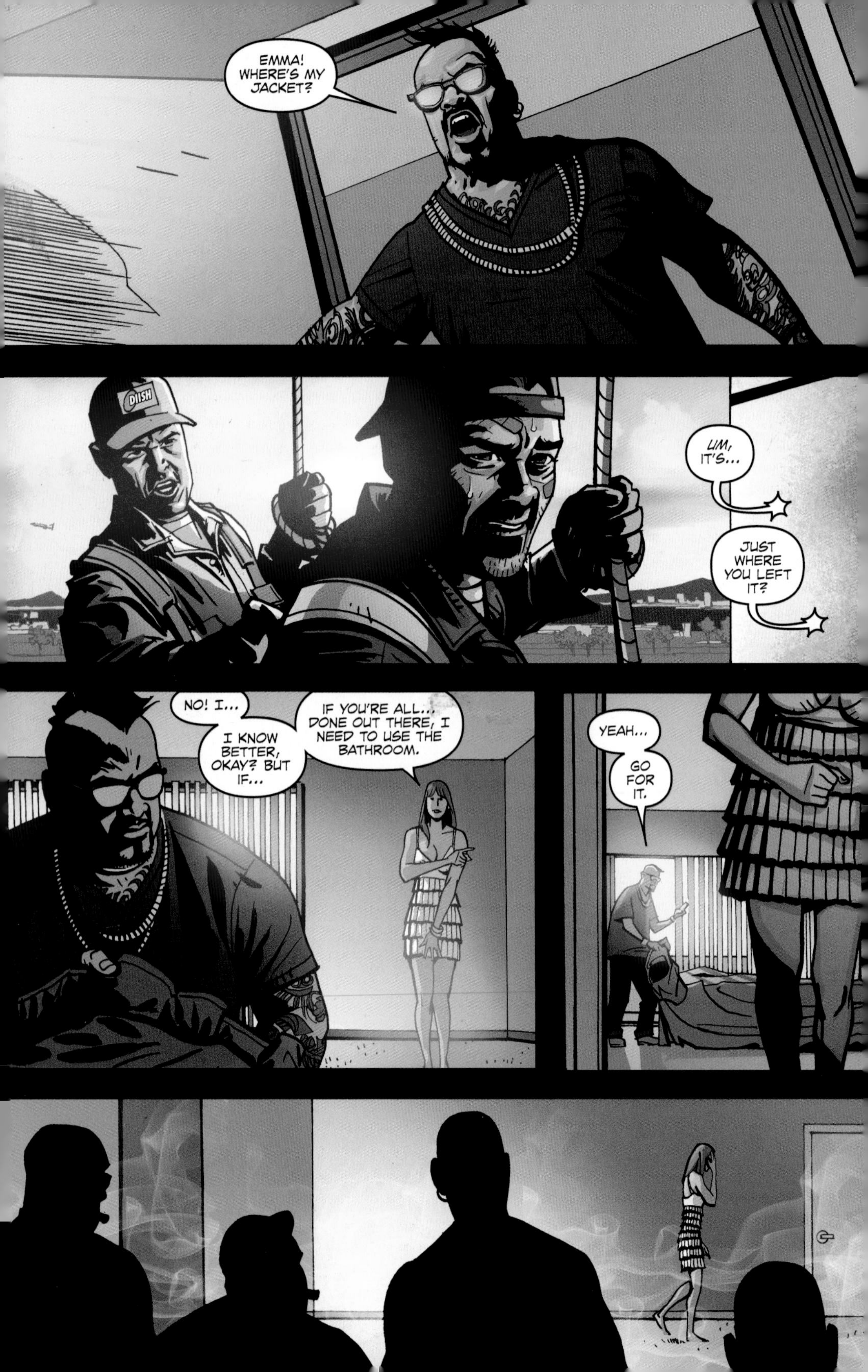
EMMA! WHERE'S MY JACKET?
UM, IT'S...
JUST WHERE YOU LEFT IT?
NO! I...
I KNOW BETTER, OKAY? BUT IF...
IF YOU'RE ALL... DONE OUT THERE, I NEED TO USE THE BATHROOM.
YEAH...
GO FOR IT.

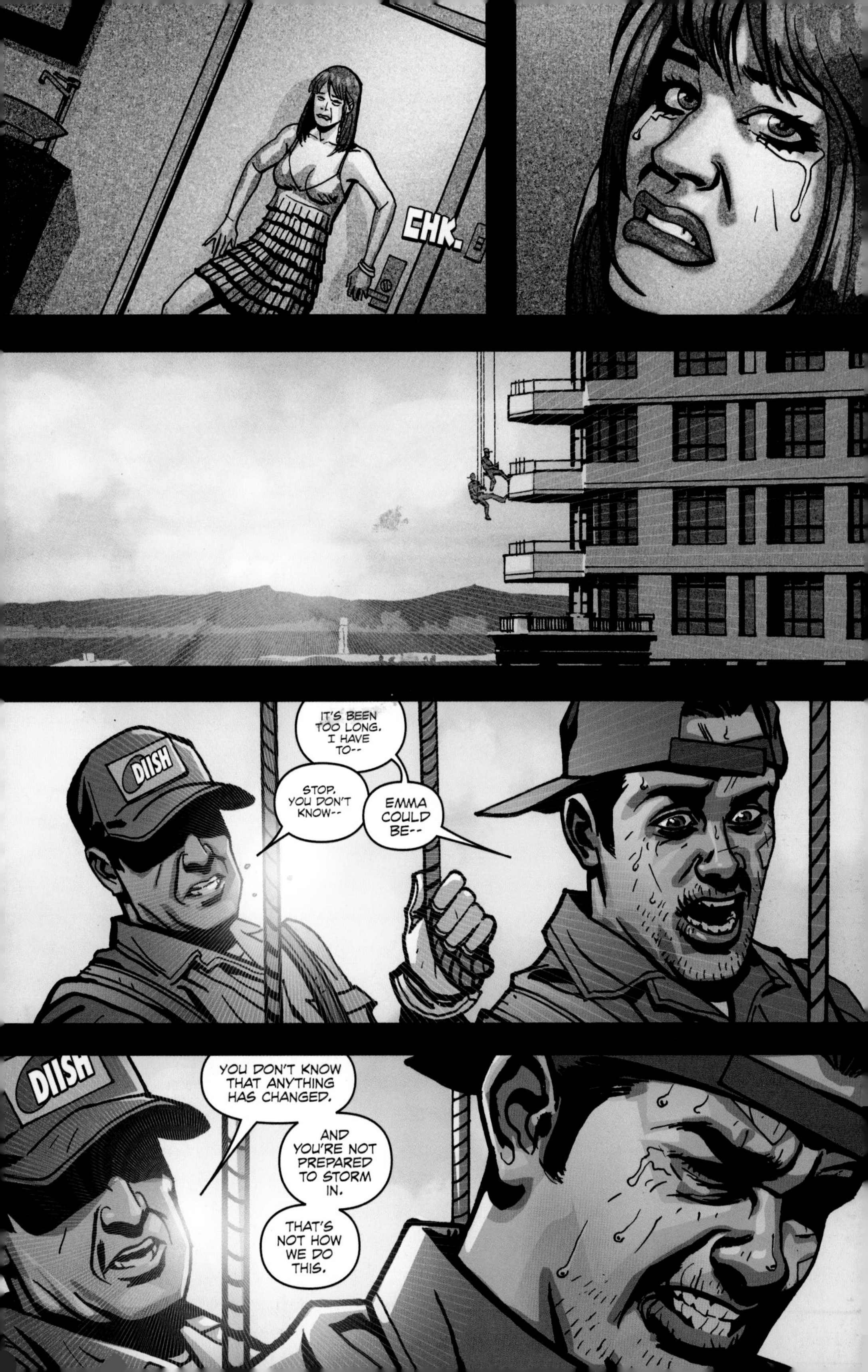
CHK.
IT'S BEEN TOO LONG. I HAVE TO--
STOP. YOU DON'T KNOW--
EMMA COULD BE--
DIISH
YOU DON'T KNOW THAT ANYTHING HAS CHANGED.
AND YOU'RE NOT PREPARED TO STORM IN.
THAT'S NOT HOW WE DO THIS.

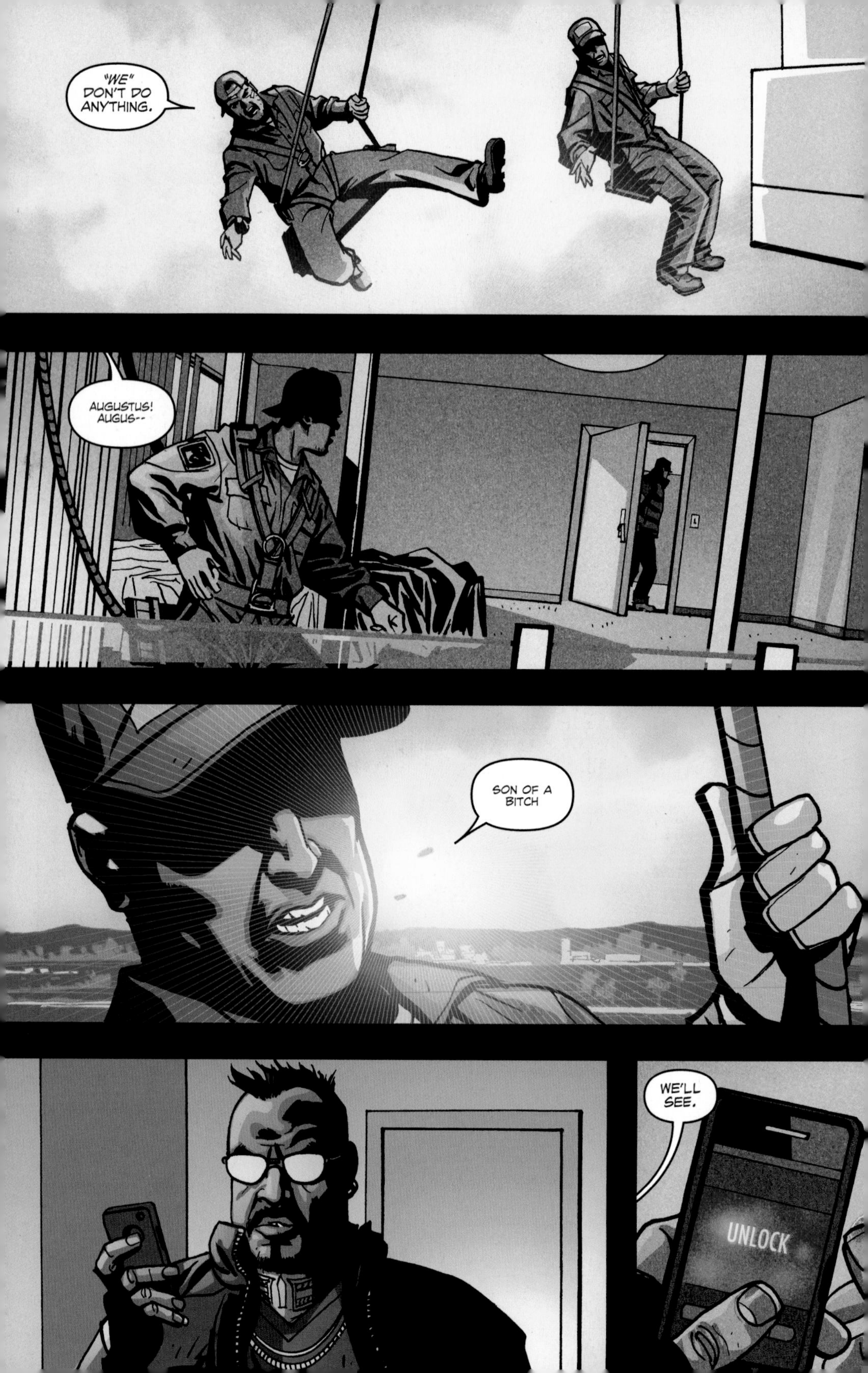
"WE" DON'T DO ANYTHING.
AUGUSTUS! AUGUS--
SON OF A BITCH
WE'LL SEE.
UNLOCK

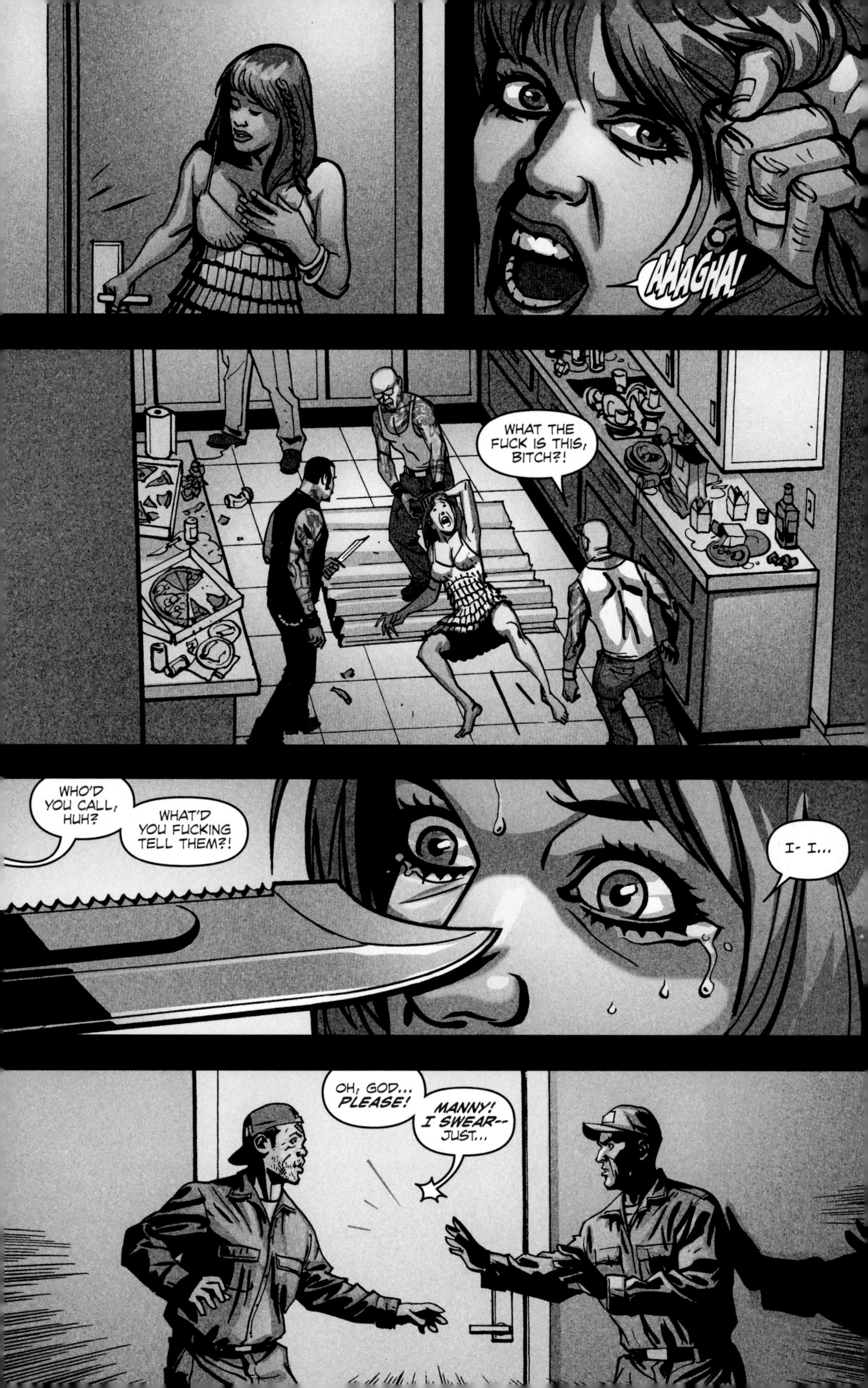
AAAGHA!
WHAT THE FUCK IS THIS, BITCH?!
WHO'D YOU CALL, HUH?
WHAT'D YOU FUCKING TELL THEM?!
I- I...
OH, GOD... PLEASE!
MANNY! I SWEAR-- JUST...

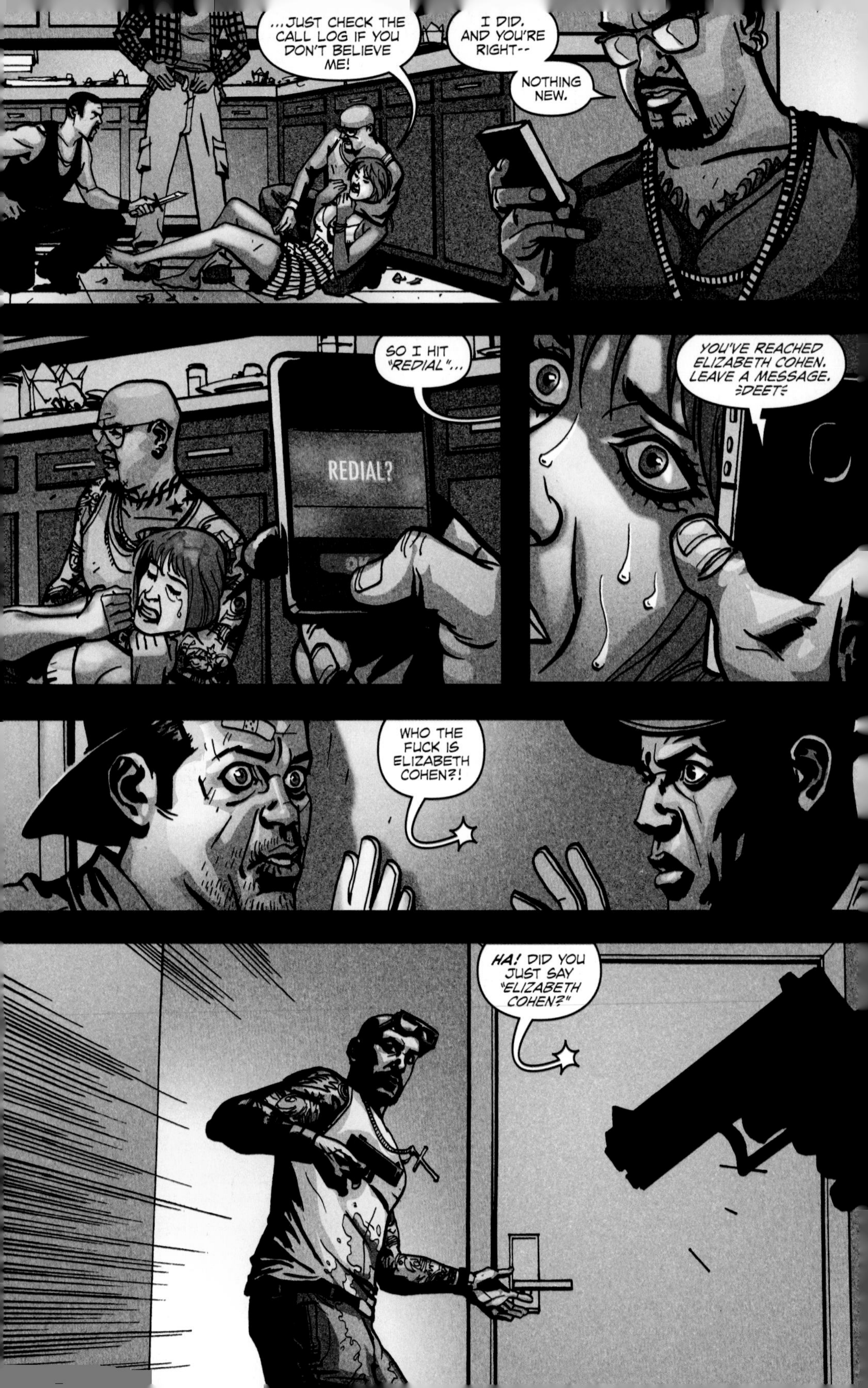
...JUST CHECK THE CALL LOG IF YOU DON'T BELIEVE ME!
I DID, AND YOU'RE RIGHT--
NOTHING NEW.
SO I HIT "REDIAL"...
REDIAL?
YOU'VE REACHED ELIZABETH COHEN. LEAVE A MESSAGE. ≷DEET≶
WHO THE FUCK IS ELIZABETH COHEN?!
HA! DID YOU JUST SAY "ELIZABETH COHEN?"

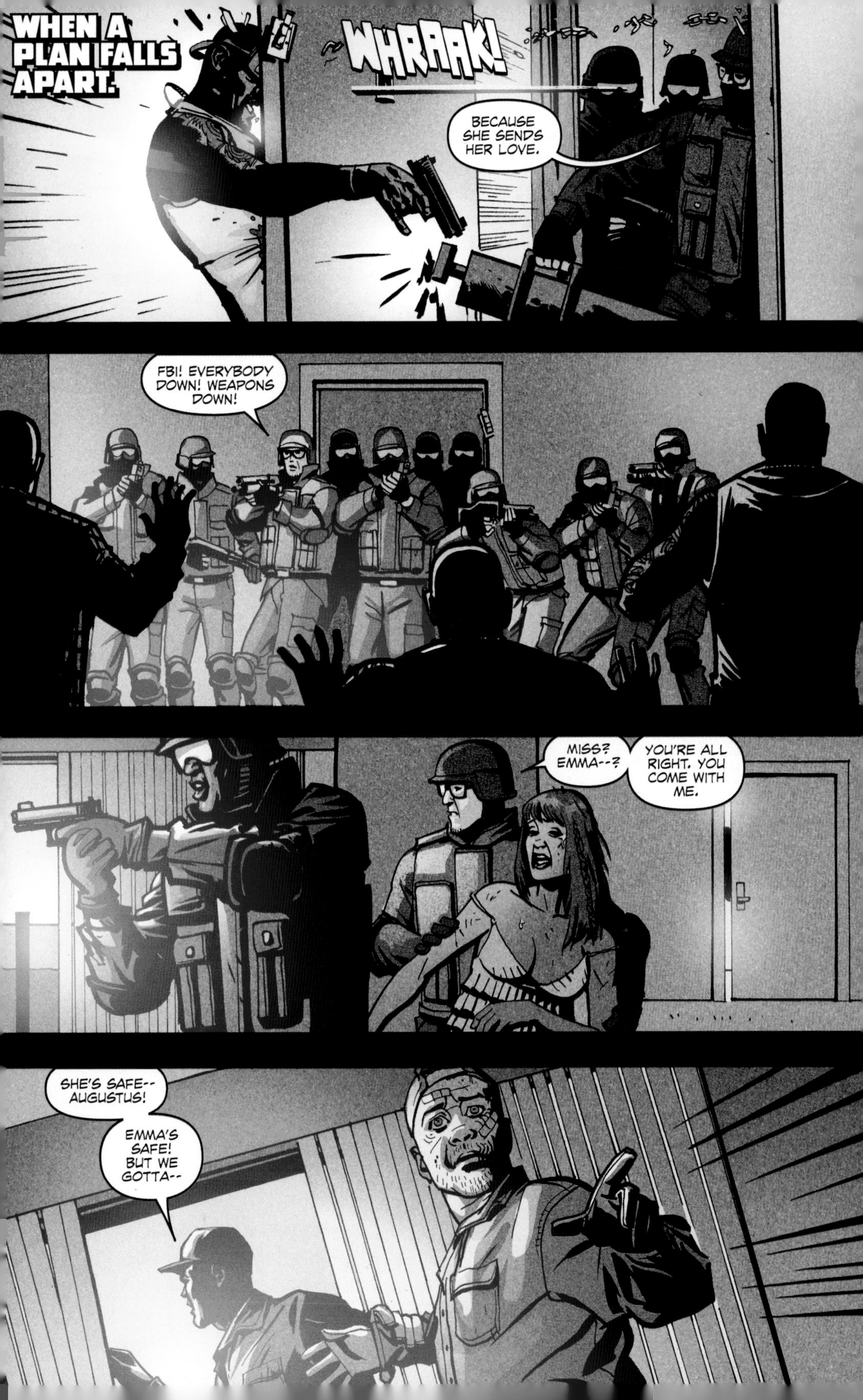
WHEN A PLAN FALLS APART.
WHRAAK!
BECAUSE SHE SENDS HER LOVE.
FBI! EVERYBODY DOWN! WEAPONS DOWN!
MISS? EMMA--?
YOU'RE ALL RIGHT. YOU COME WITH ME.
SHE'S SAFE-- AUGUSTUS!
EMMA'S SAFE! BUT WE GOTTA--

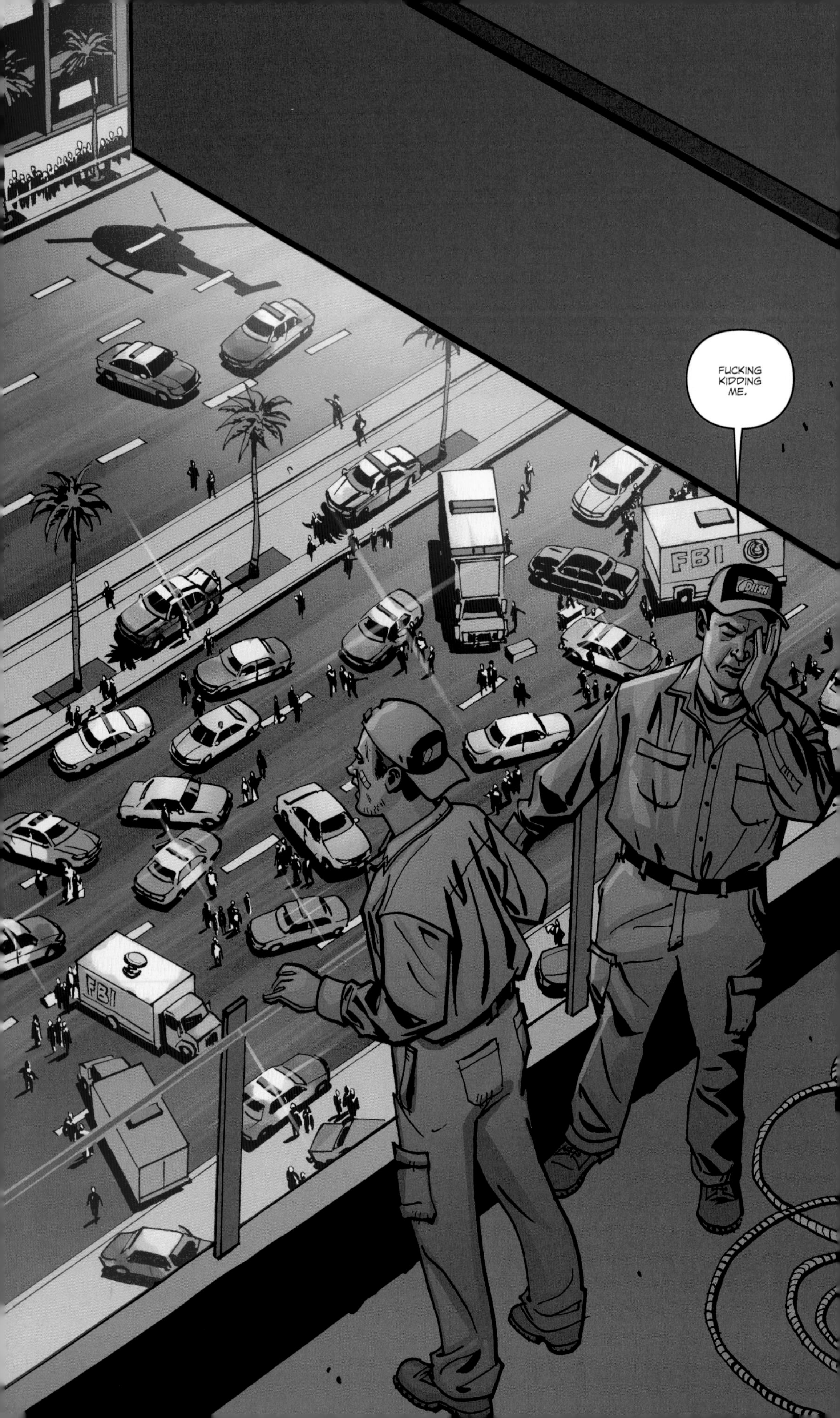
FUCKING
KIDDING
ME.
FBI
DISH
FBI

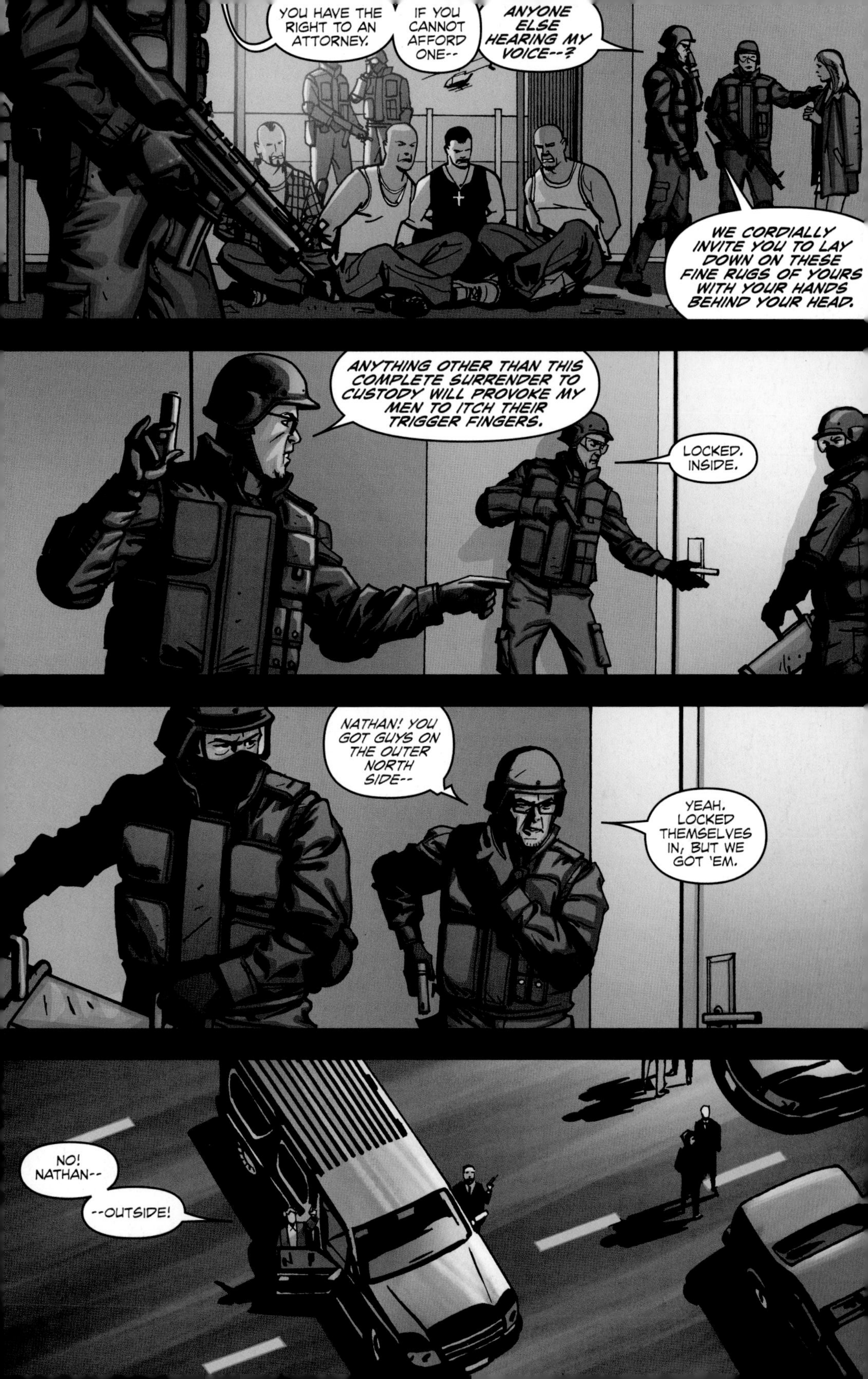
YOU HAVE THE RIGHT TO AN ATTORNEY.
IF YOU CANNOT AFFORD ONE--
ANYONE ELSE HEARING MY VOICE--?
WE CORDIALLY INVITE YOU TO LAY DOWN ON THESE FINE RUGS OF YOURS WITH YOUR HANDS BEHIND YOUR HEAD.
ANYTHING OTHER THAN THIS COMPLETE SURRENDER TO CUSTODY WILL PROVOKE MY MEN TO ITCH THEIR TRIGGER FINGERS.
LOCKED. INSIDE.
NATHAN! YOU GOT GUYS ON THE OUTER NORTH SIDE--
YEAH. LOCKED THEMSELVES IN, BUT WE GOT 'EM.
NO! NATHAN--
--OUTSIDE!

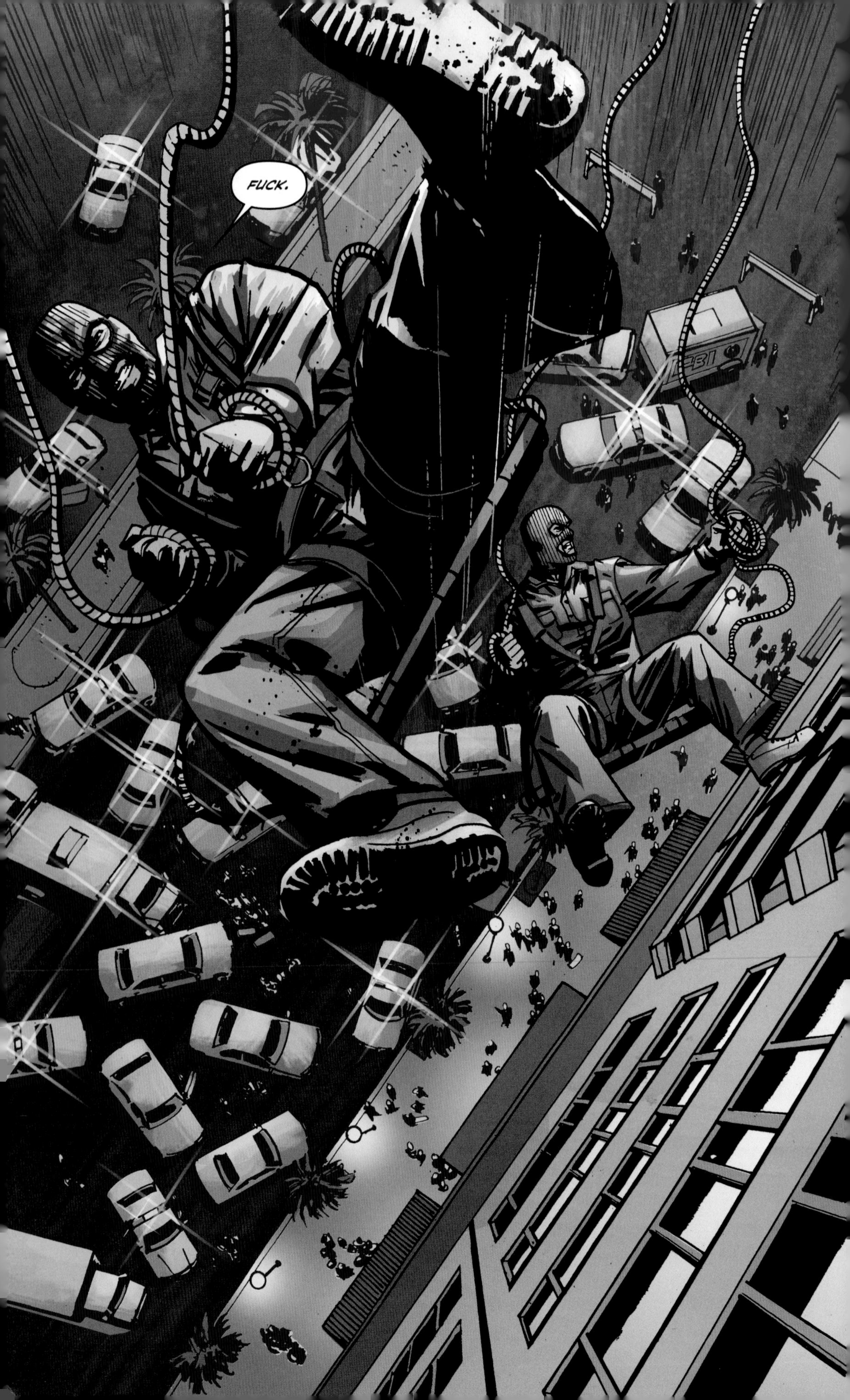
FUCK.
FBI

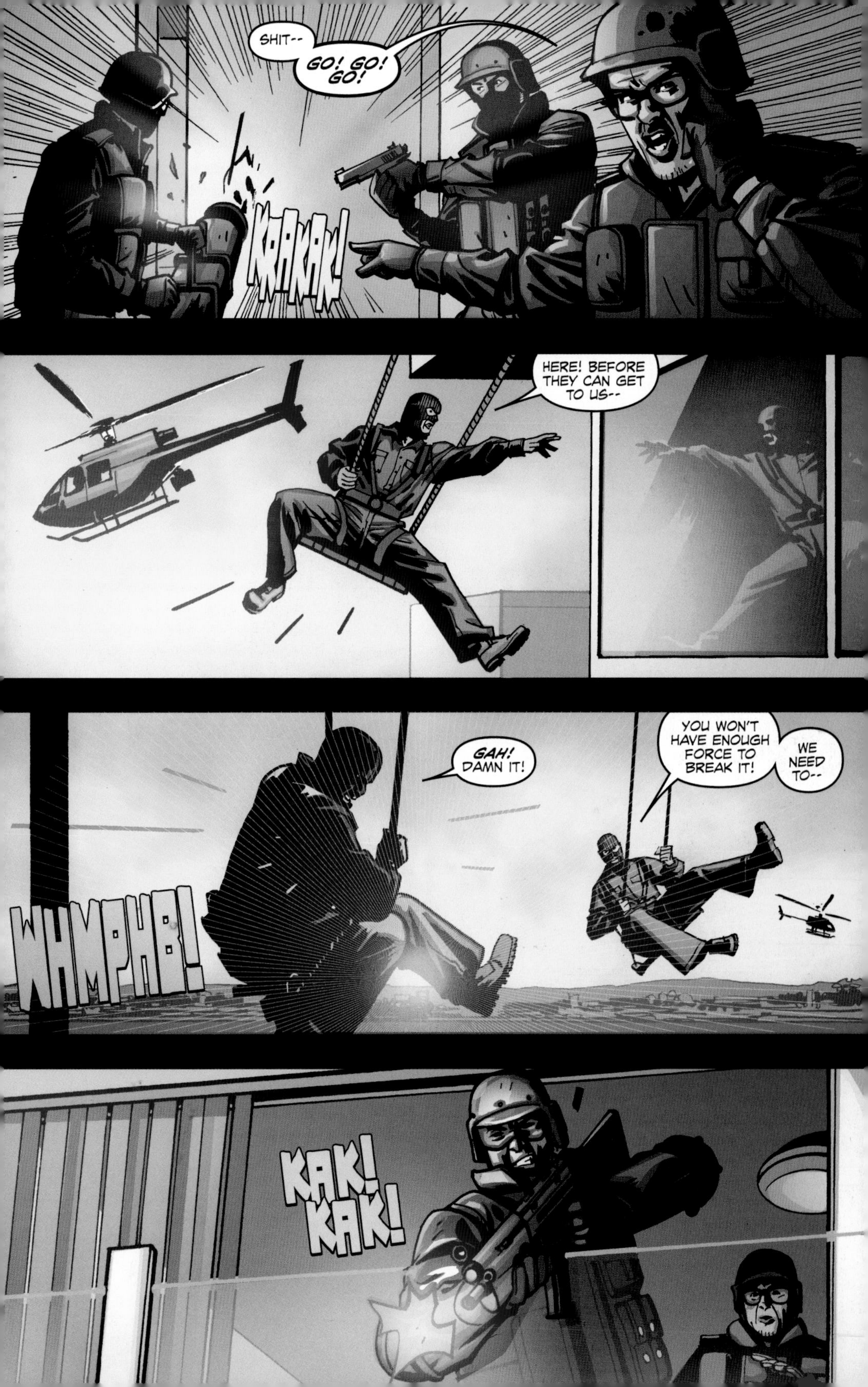
SHIT--
GO! GO! GO!
KRAKAK!
HERE! BEFORE THEY CAN GET TO US--
GAH! DAMN IT!
YOU WON'T HAVE ENOUGH FORCE TO BREAK IT!
WE NEED TO--
WHMPHB!
KAK! KAK!

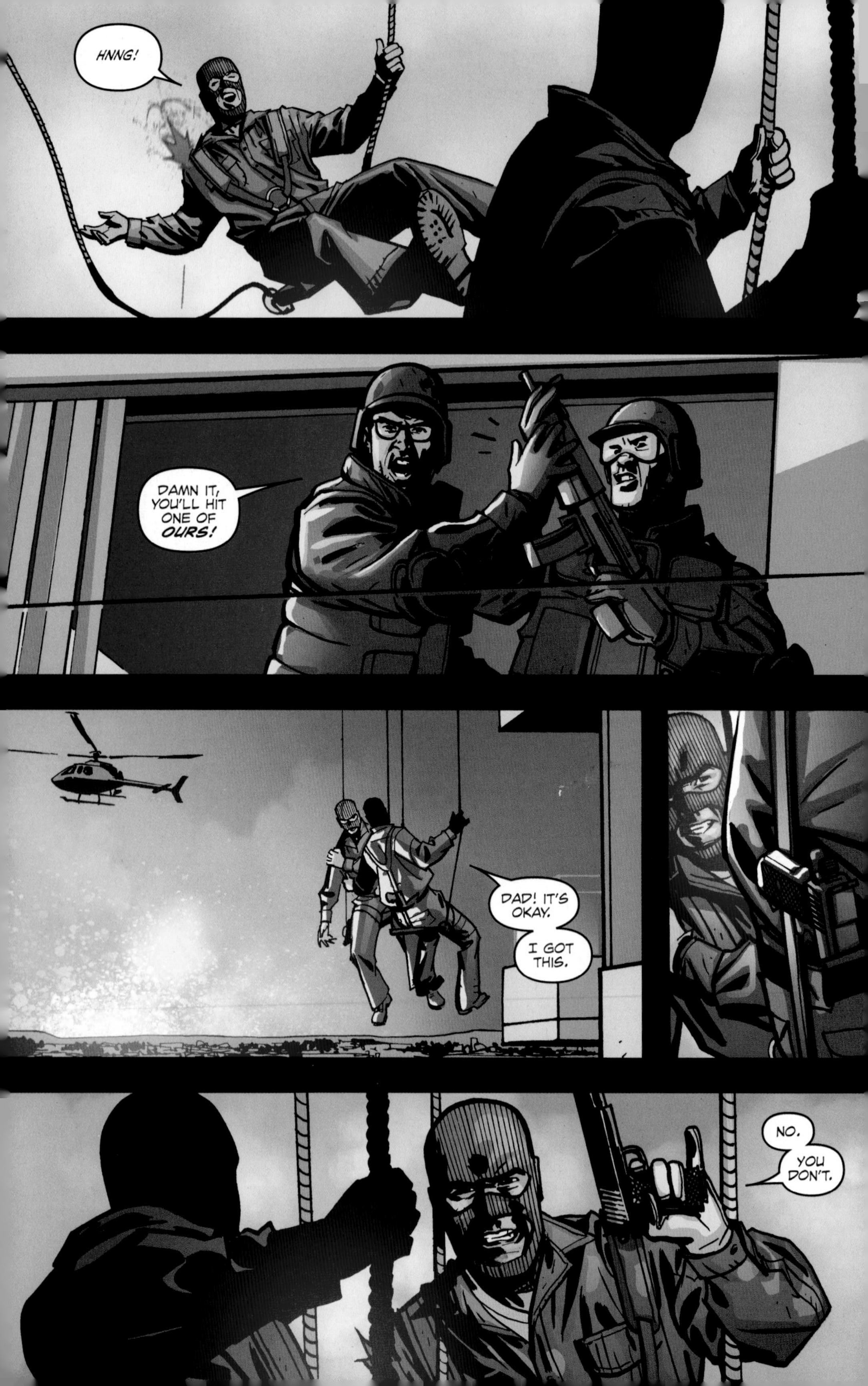
HNNG!
DAMN IT, YOU'LL HIT ONE OF OURS!
DAD! IT'S OKAY.
I GOT THIS.
NO.
YOU DON'T.

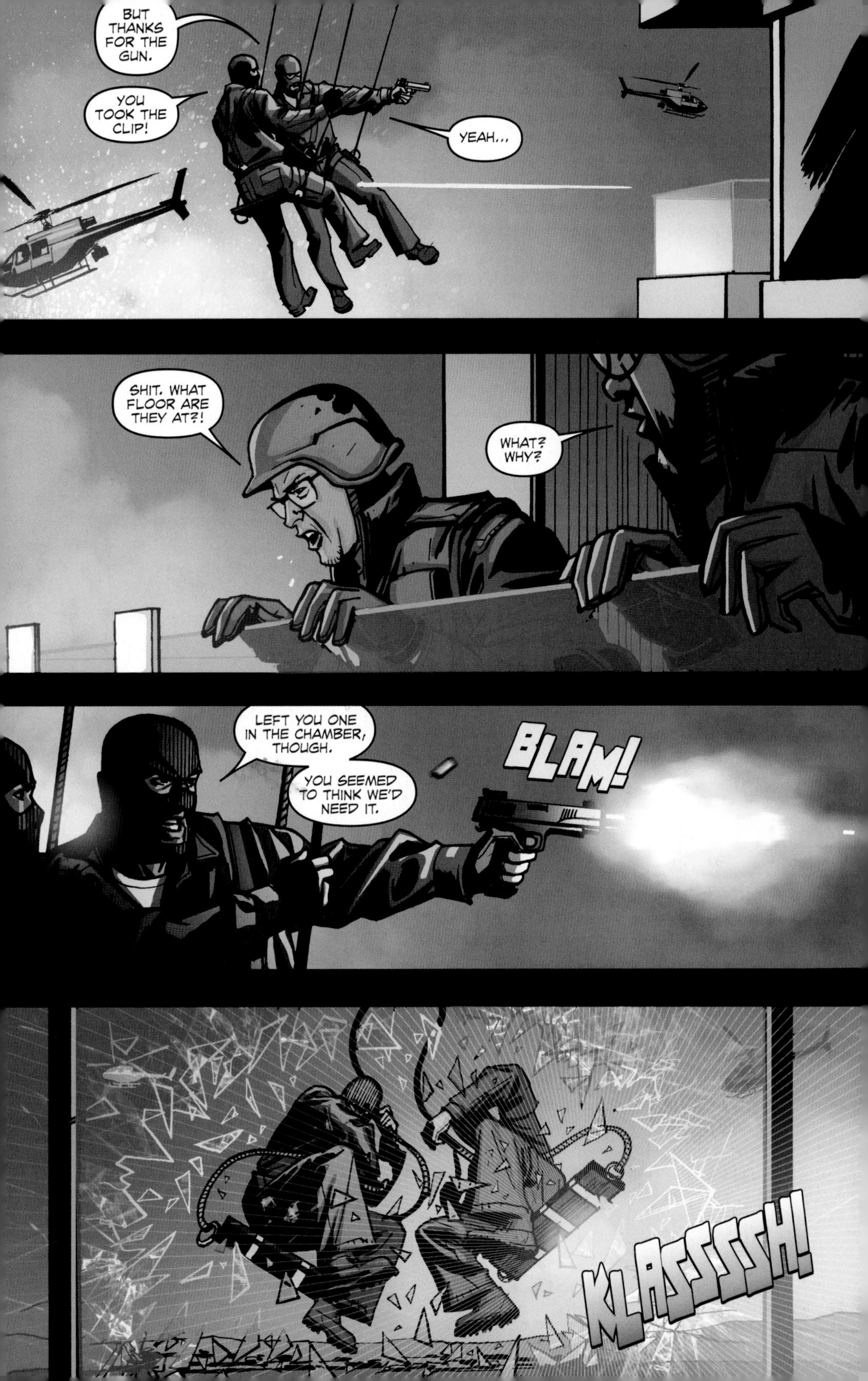
BUT THANKS FOR THE GUN.
YOU TOOK THE CLIP!
YEAH...
SHIT. WHAT FLOOR ARE THEY AT?!
WHAT? WHY?
LEFT YOU ONE IN THE CHAMBER, THOUGH.
YOU SEEMED TO THINK WE'D NEED IT.
BLAM!
KLASSSSH!

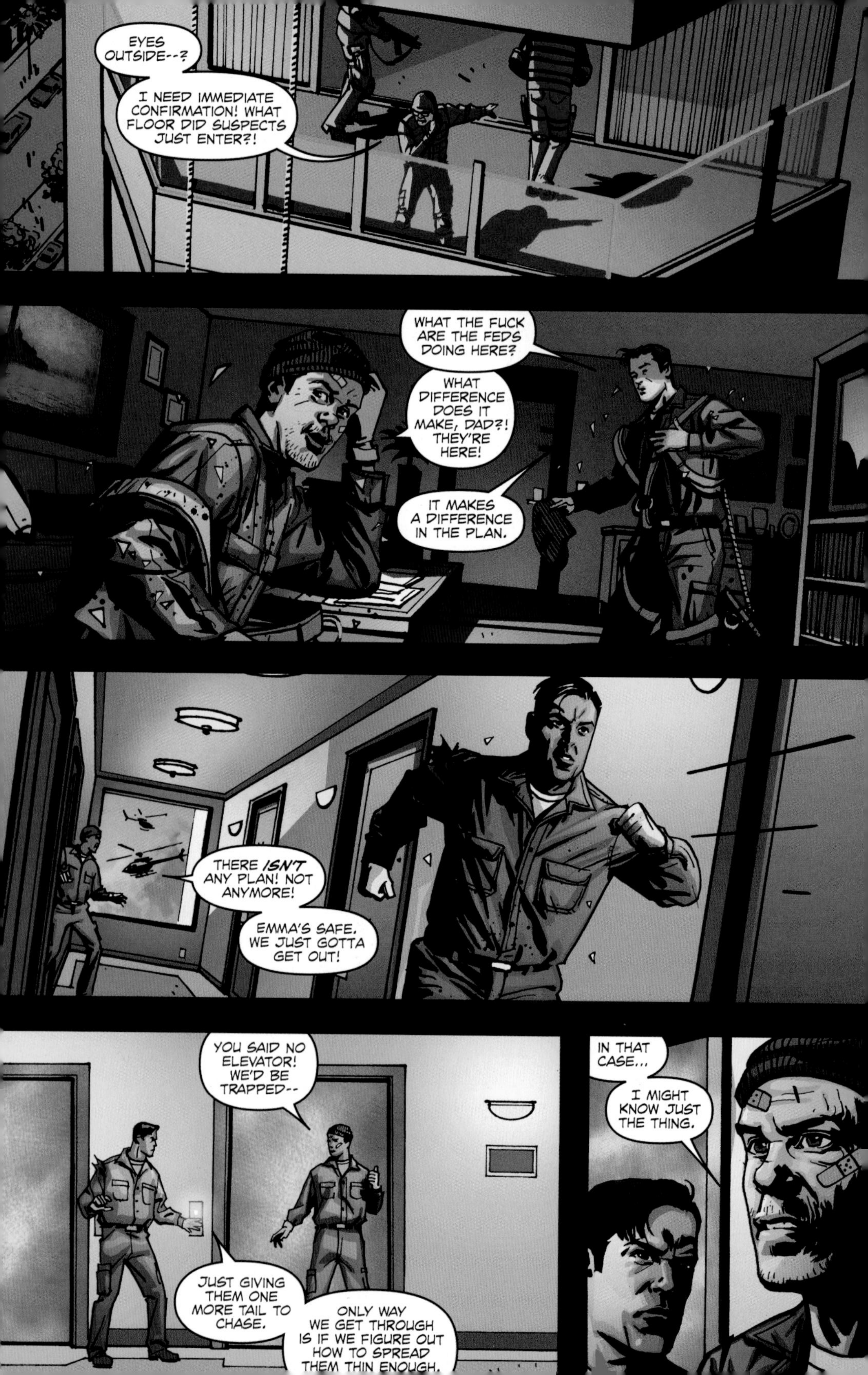
EYES OUTSIDE--?
I NEED IMMEDIATE CONFIRMATION! WHAT FLOOR DID SUSPECTS JUST ENTER?!
WHAT THE FUCK ARE THE FEDS DOING HERE?
WHAT DIFFERENCE DOES IT MAKE, DAD?! THEY'RE HERE!
IT MAKES A DIFFERENCE IN THE PLAN.
THERE *ISN'T* ANY PLAN! NOT ANYMORE!
EMMA'S SAFE. WE JUST GOTTA GET OUT!
YOU SAID NO ELEVATOR! WE'D BE TRAPPED--
JUST GIVING THEM ONE MORE TAIL TO CHASE.
ONLY WAY WE GET THROUGH IS IF WE FIGURE OUT HOW TO SPREAD THEM THIN ENOUGH.
IN THAT CASE...
I MIGHT KNOW JUST THE THING.

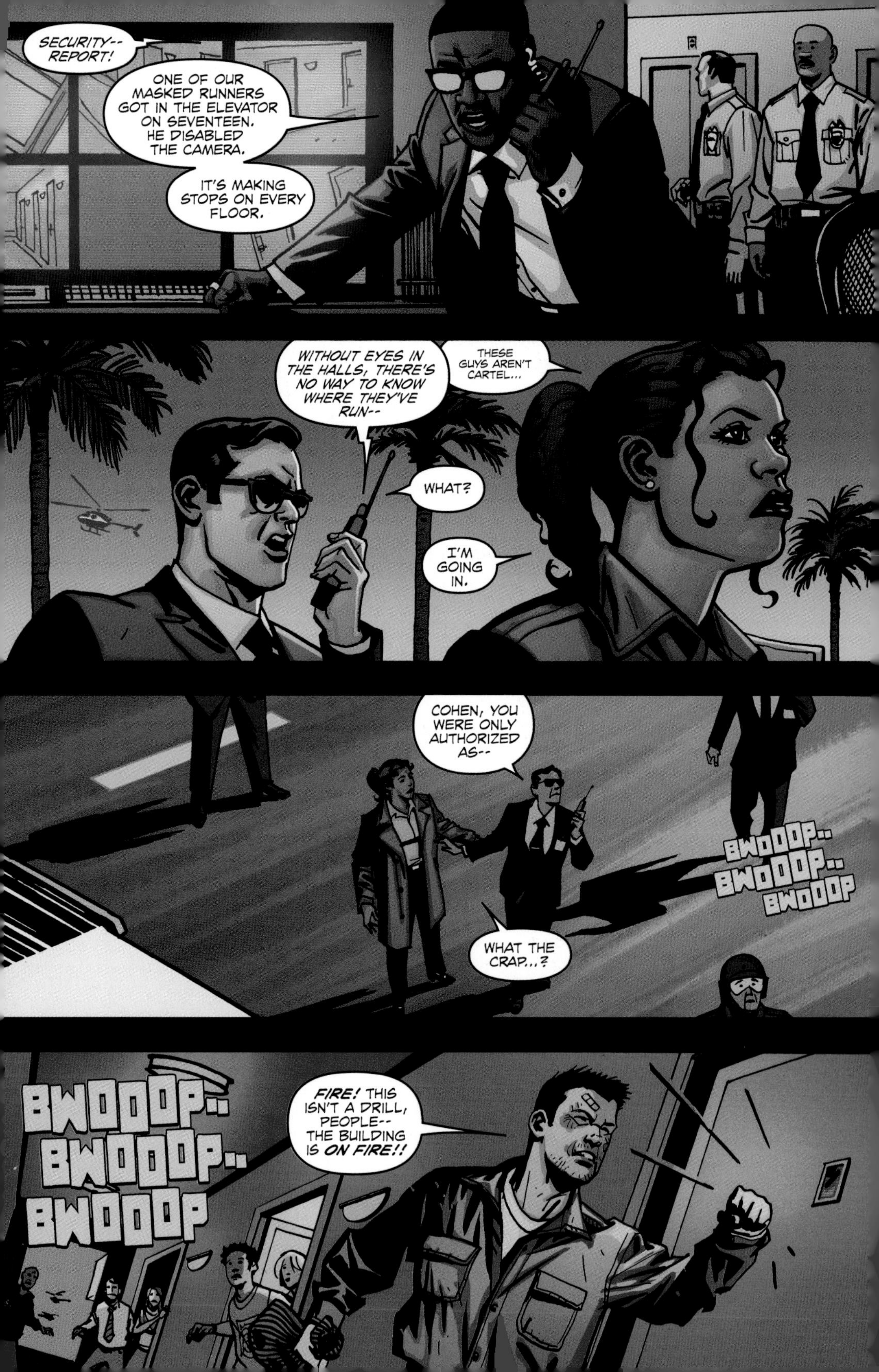
SECURITY-- REPORT!
ONE OF OUR MASKED RUNNERS GOT IN THE ELEVATOR ON SEVENTEEN. HE DISABLED THE CAMERA.
IT'S MAKING STOPS ON EVERY FLOOR.
WITHOUT EYES IN THE HALLS, THERE'S NO WAY TO KNOW WHERE THEY'VE RUN--
THESE GUYS AREN'T CARTEL...
WHAT?
I'M GOING IN.
COHEN, YOU WERE ONLY AUTHORIZED AS--
BWOOOP.. BWOOOP.. BWOOOP
WHAT THE CRAP...?
BWOOOP.. BWOOOP.. BWOOOP
FIRE! THIS ISN'T A DRILL, PEOPLE-- THE BUILDING IS ON FIRE!!

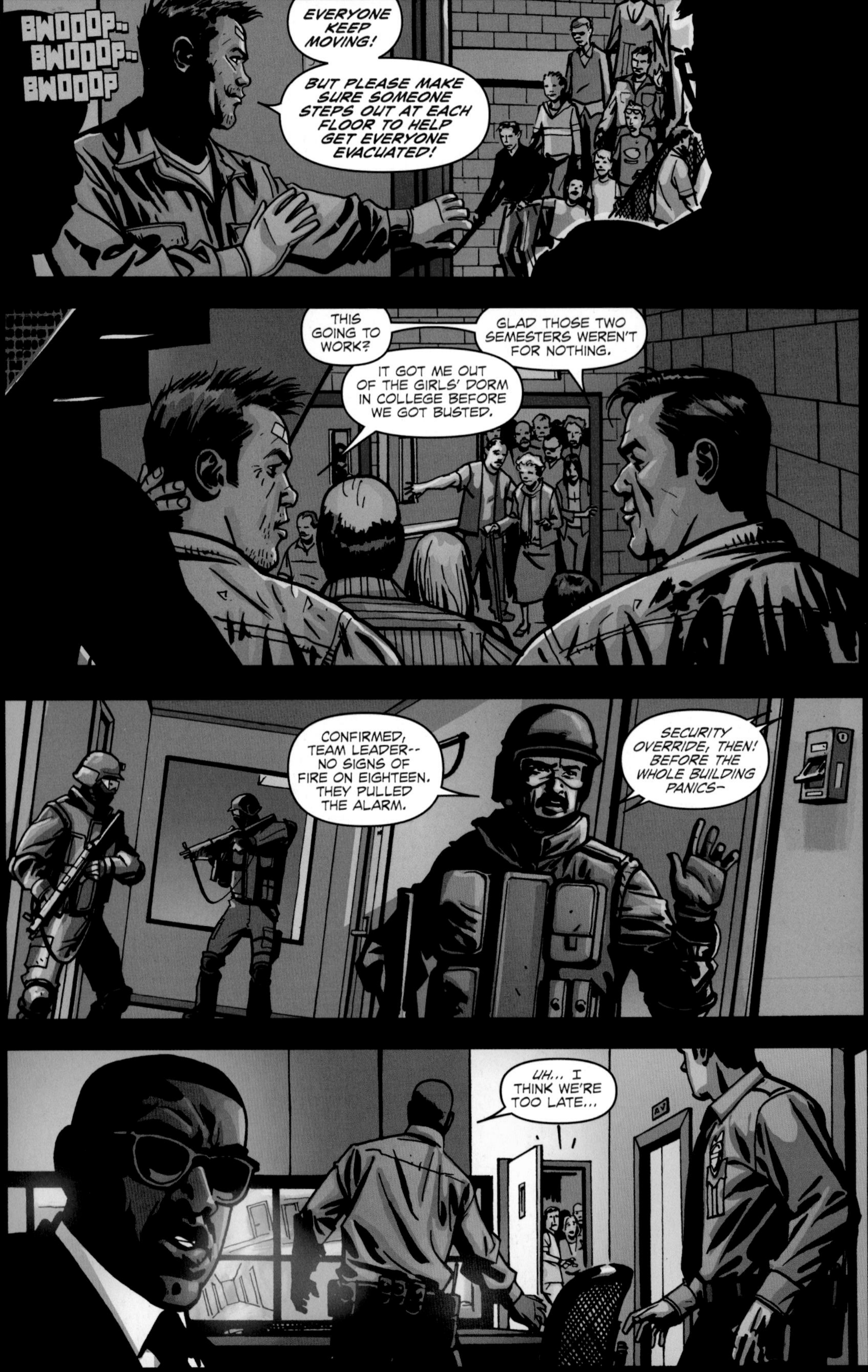
BWOOOP.. BWOOOP.. BWOOOP
EVERYONE KEEP MOVING!
BUT PLEASE MAKE SURE SOMEONE STEPS OUT AT EACH FLOOR TO HELP GET EVERYONE EVACUATED!
THIS GOING TO WORK?
IT GOT ME OUT OF THE GIRLS' DORM IN COLLEGE BEFORE WE GOT BUSTED.
GLAD THOSE TWO SEMESTERS WEREN'T FOR NOTHING.
CONFIRMED, TEAM LEADER-- NO SIGNS OF FIRE ON EIGHTEEN. THEY PULLED THE ALARM.
SECURITY OVERRIDE, THEN! BEFORE THE WHOLE BUILDING PANICS-
UH... I THINK WE'RE TOO LATE...

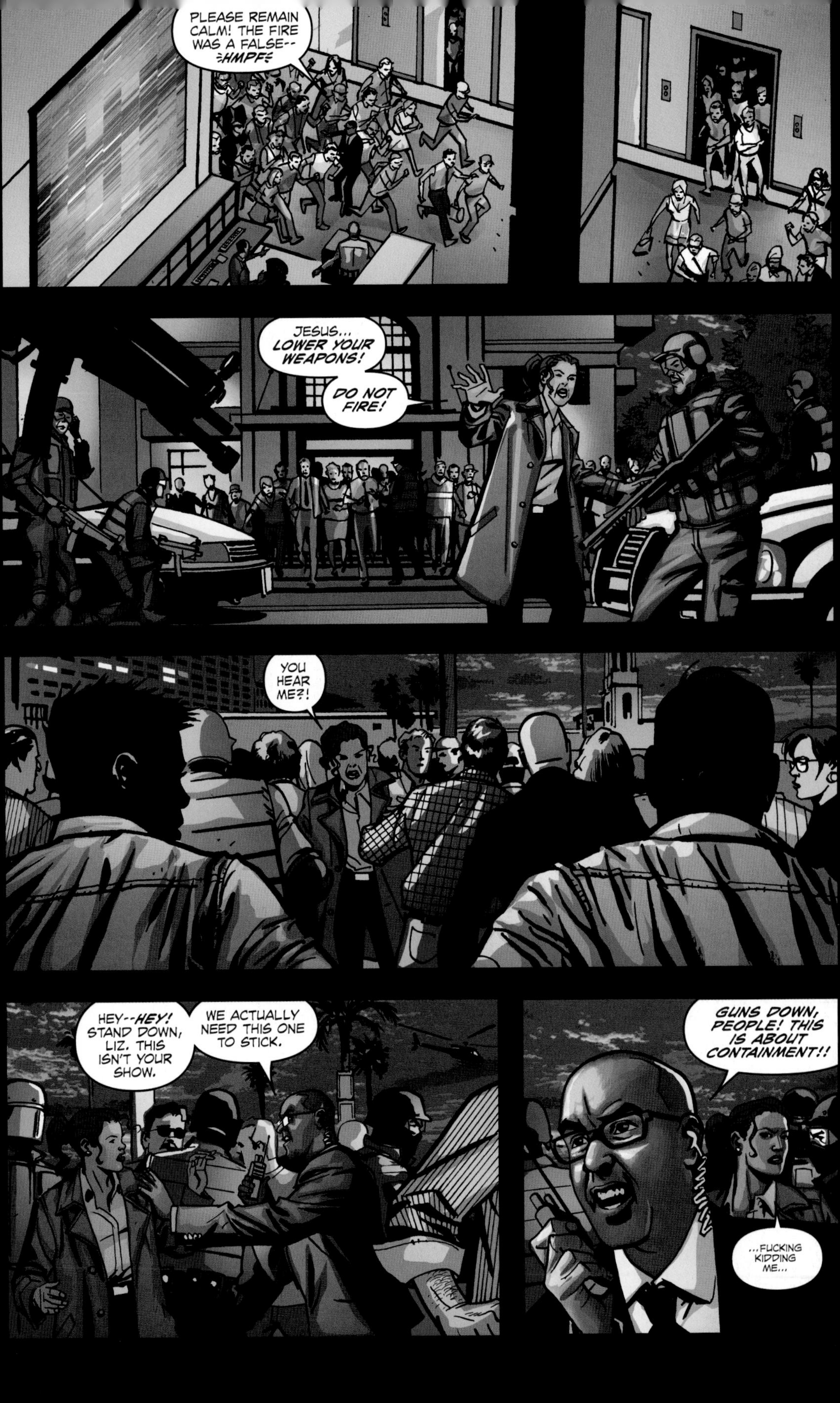
PLEASE REMAIN CALM! THE FIRE WAS A FALSE-- HMPF
JESUS... LOWER YOUR WEAPONS!
DO NOT FIRE!
YOU HEAR ME?!
HEY--HEY! STAND DOWN, LIZ. THIS ISN'T YOUR SHOW.
WE ACTUALLY NEED THIS ONE TO STICK.
GUNS DOWN, PEOPLE! THIS IS ABOUT CONTAINMENT!!
...FUCKING KIDDING ME...

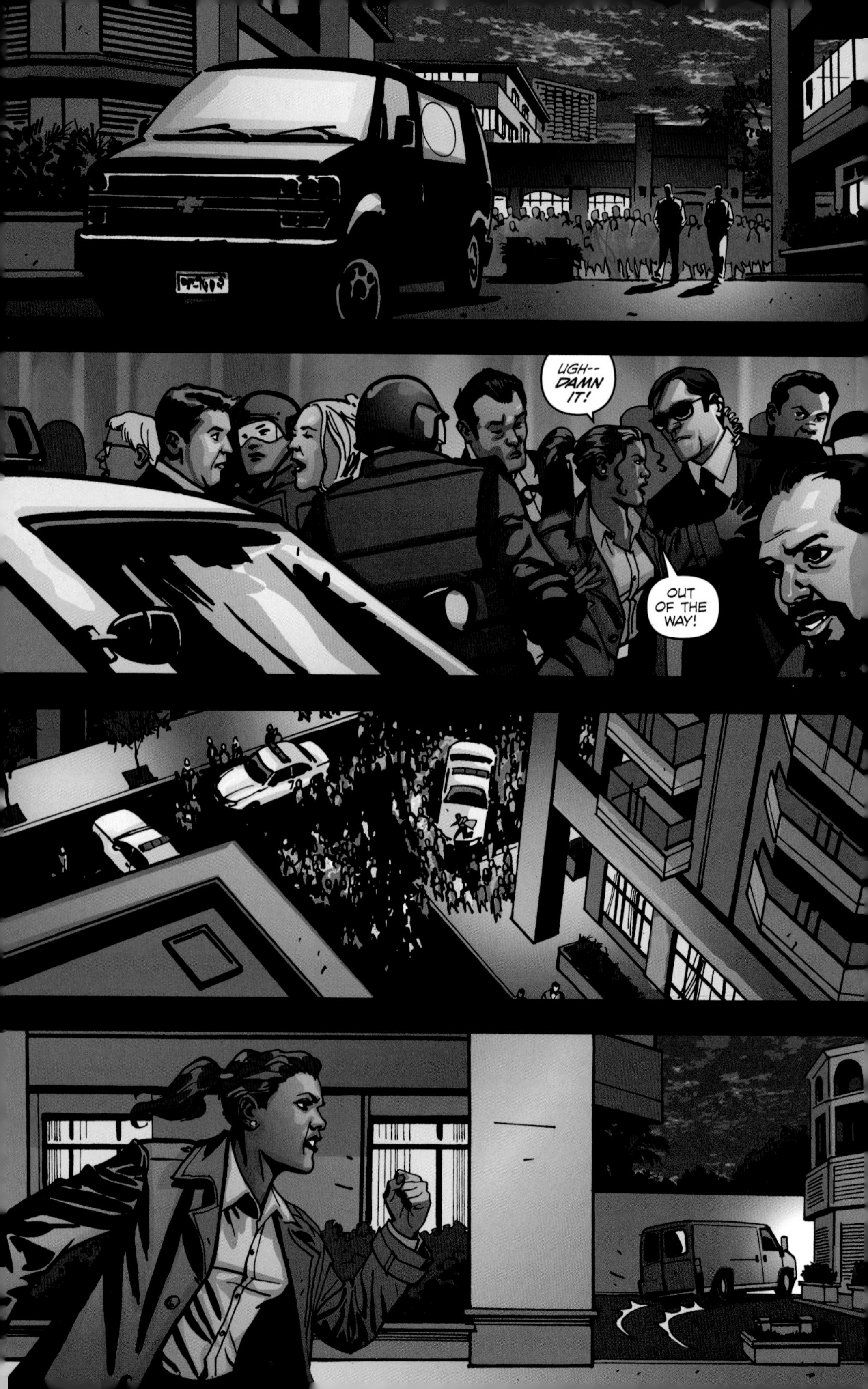
UGH--
DAMN IT!
OUT OF THE WAY!

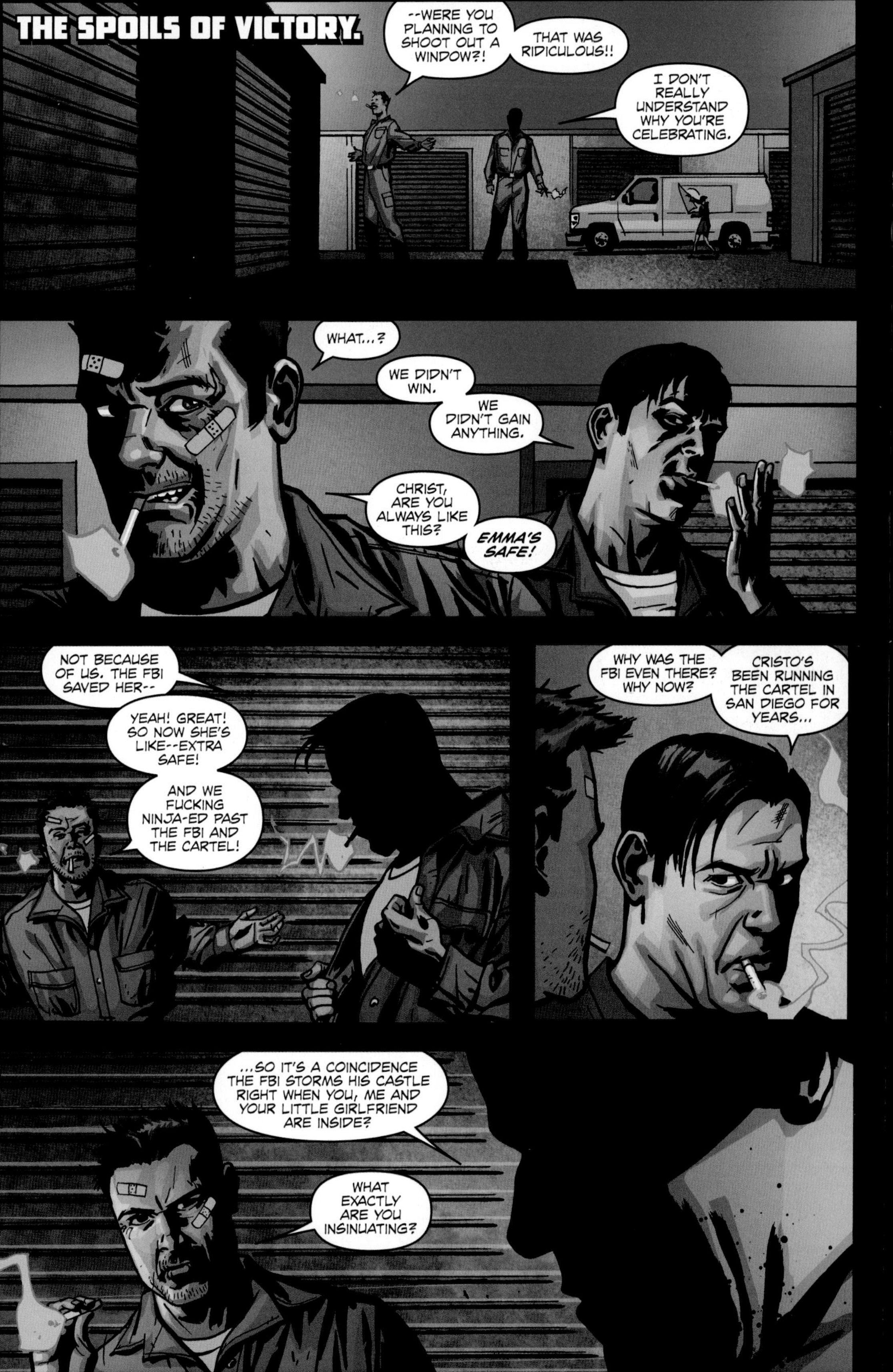
THE SPOILS OF VICTORY.
--WERE YOU PLANNING TO SHOOT OUT A WINDOW?!
THAT WAS RIDICULOUS!!
I DON'T REALLY UNDERSTAND WHY YOU'RE CELEBRATING.
WHAT...?
WE DIDN'T WIN.
WE DIDN'T GAIN ANYTHING.
CHRIST, ARE YOU ALWAYS LIKE THIS?
EMMA'S SAFE!
NOT BECAUSE OF US. THE FBI SAVED HER--
YEAH! GREAT! SO NOW SHE'S LIKE--EXTRA SAFE!
AND WE FUCKING NINJA-ED PAST THE FBI AND THE CARTEL!
WHY WAS THE FBI EVEN THERE? WHY NOW?
CRISTO'S BEEN RUNNING THE CARTEL IN SAN DIEGO FOR YEARS...
...SO IT'S A COINCIDENCE THE FBI STORMS HIS CASTLE RIGHT WHEN YOU, ME AND YOUR LITTLE GIRLFRIEND ARE INSIDE?
WHAT EXACTLY ARE YOU INSINUATING?

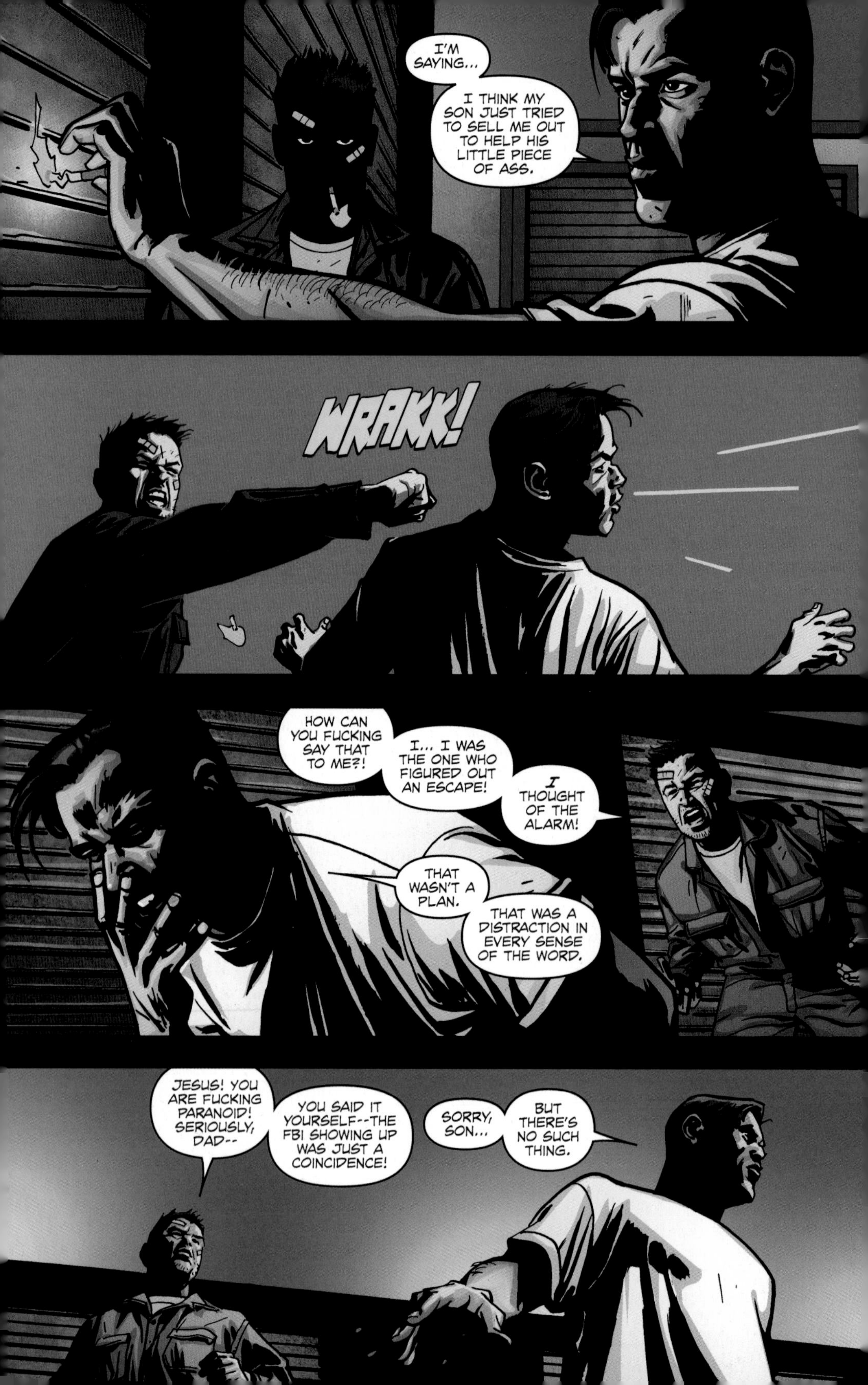

I'M SAYING...
I THINK MY SON JUST TRIED TO SELL ME OUT TO HELP HIS LITTLE PIECE OF ASS.
WRAKK!
HOW CAN YOU FUCKING SAY THAT TO ME?!
I... I WAS THE ONE WHO FIGURED OUT AN ESCAPE!
I THOUGHT OF THE ALARM!
THAT WASN'T A PLAN.
THAT WAS A DISTRACTION IN EVERY SENSE OF THE WORD.
JESUS! YOU ARE FUCKING PARANOID! SERIOUSLY, DAD--
YOU SAID IT YOURSELF--THE FBI SHOWING UP WAS JUST A COINCIDENCE!
SORRY, SON...
BUT THERE'S NO SUCH THING.

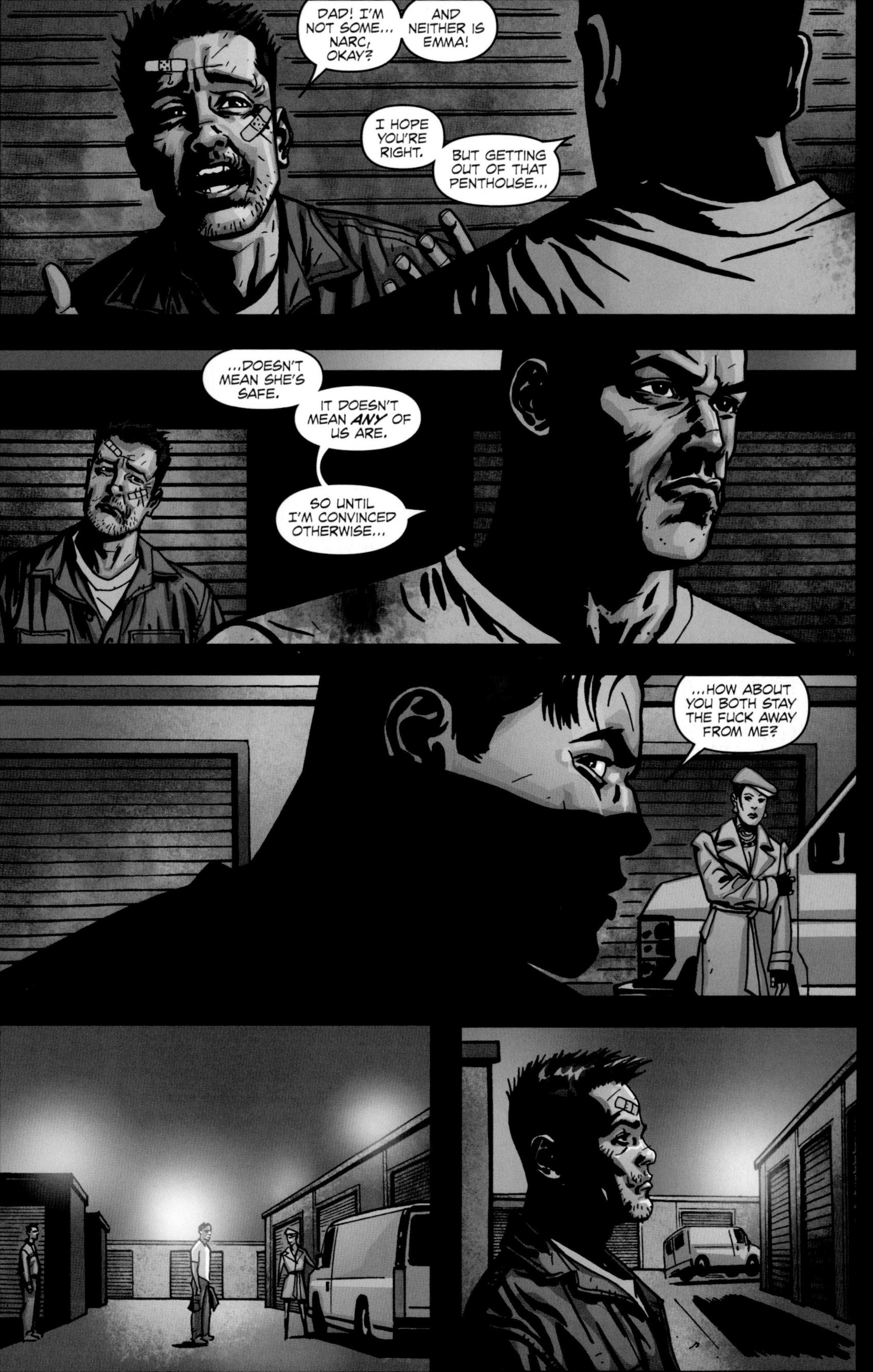
DAD! I'M NOT SOME... NARC, OKAY?
AND NEITHER IS EMMA!
I HOPE YOU'RE RIGHT.
BUT GETTING OUT OF THAT PENTHOUSE...
...DOESN'T MEAN SHE'S SAFE.
IT DOESN'T MEAN *ANY* OF US ARE.
SO UNTIL I'M CONVINCED OTHERWISE...
...HOW ABOUT YOU BOTH STAY THE FUCK AWAY FROM ME?

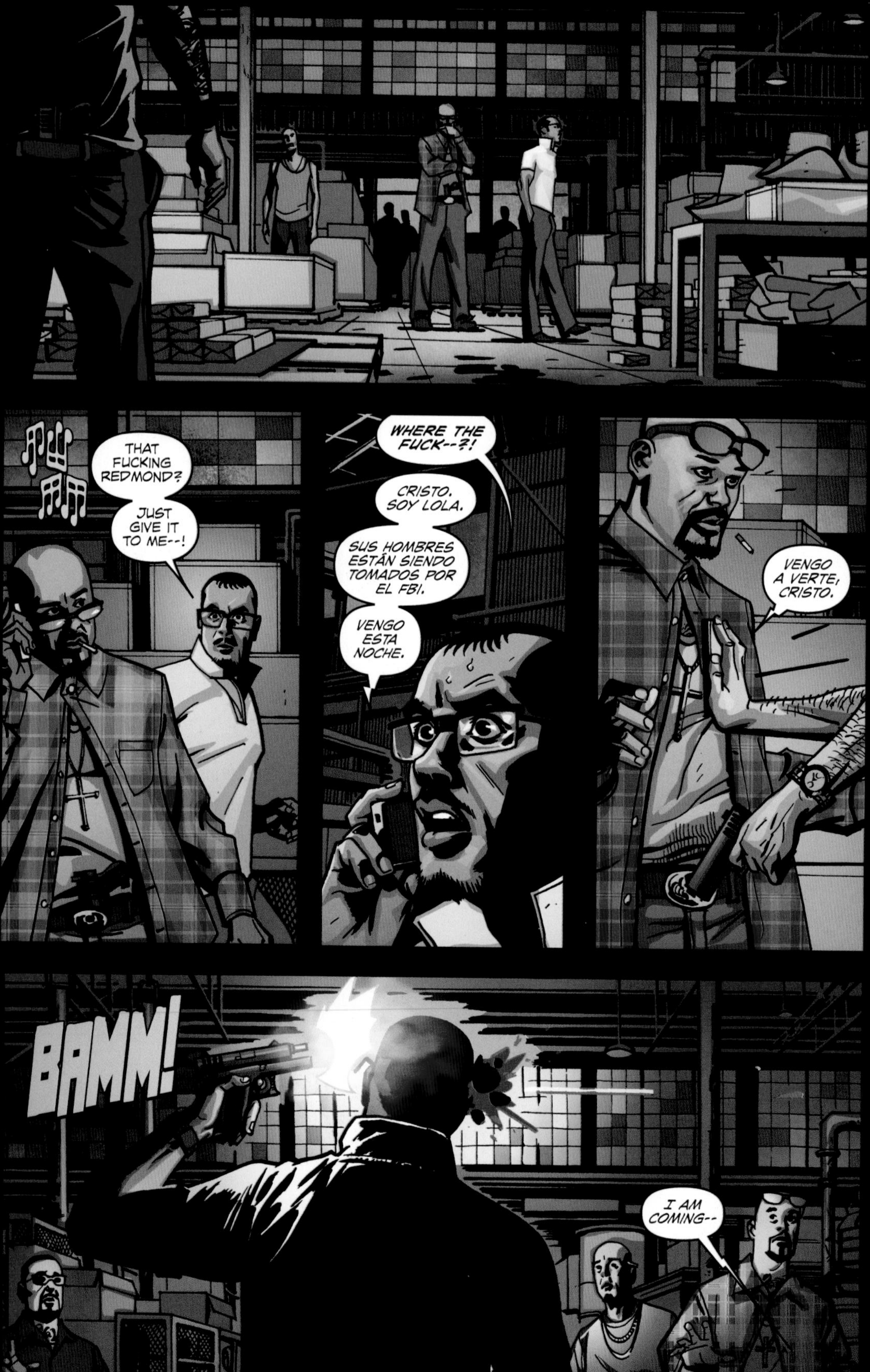
THAT FUCKING REDMOND?
JUST GIVE IT TO ME--!
WHERE THE FUCK--?!
CRISTO. SOY LOLA.
SUS HOMBRES ESTÁN SIENDO TOMADOS POR EL FBI.
VENGO ESTA NOCHE.
VENGO A VERTE, CRISTO.
BAMM!
I AM COMING--

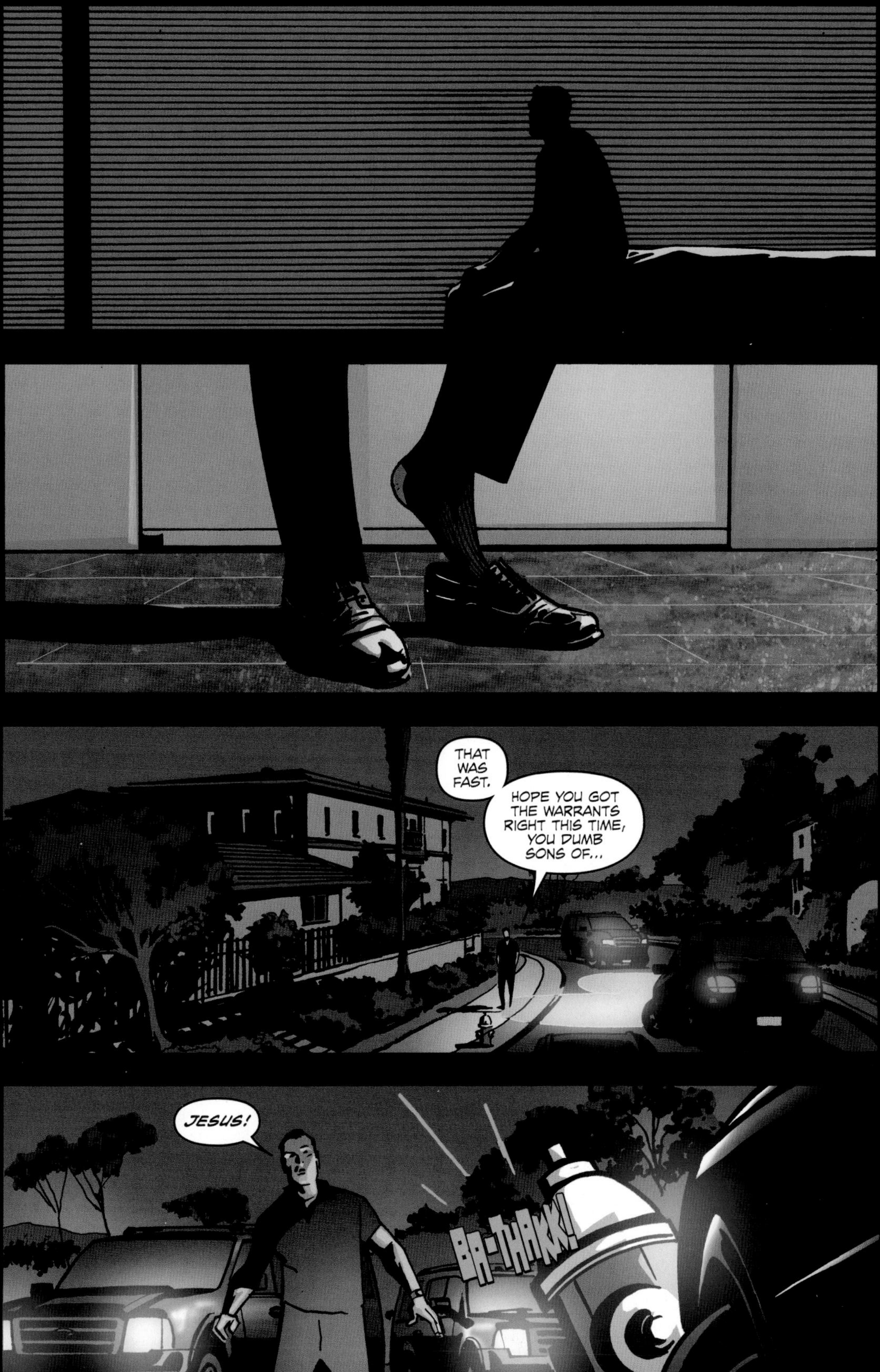
THAT WAS FAST.
HOPE YOU GOT THE WARRANTS RIGHT THIS TIME, YOU DUMB SONS OF...
JESUS!
BA-THAKK!

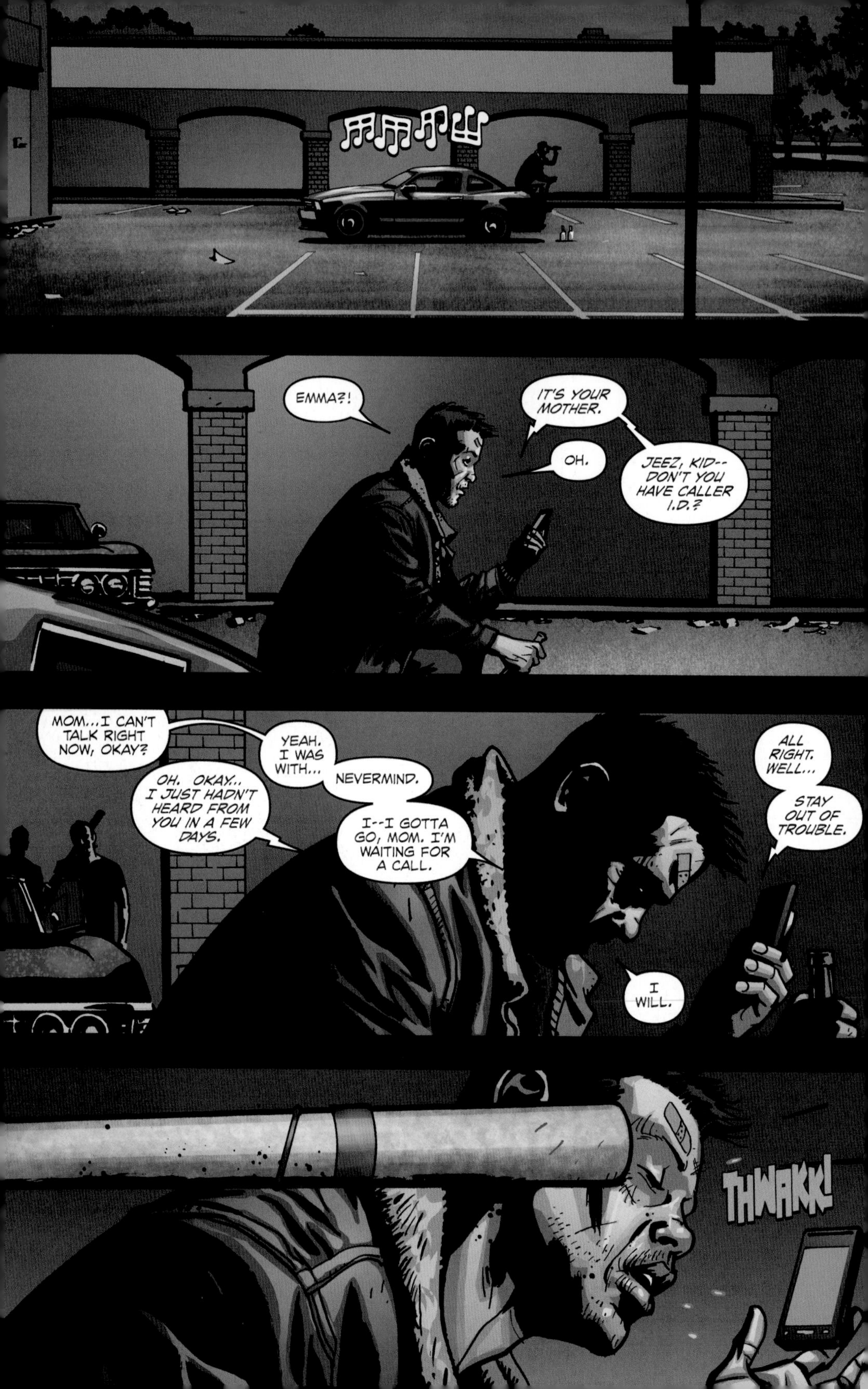
EMMA?!
IT'S YOUR MOTHER.
OH.
JEEZ, KID-- DON'T YOU HAVE CALLER I.D.?
MOM...I CAN'T TALK RIGHT NOW, OKAY?
OH. OKAY... I JUST HADN'T HEARD FROM YOU IN A FEW DAYS.
YEAH. I WAS WITH...
NEVERMIND.
I--I GOTTA GO, MOM. I'M WAITING FOR A CALL.
ALL RIGHT. WELL...
STAY OUT OF TROUBLE.
I WILL.
THWAKK!

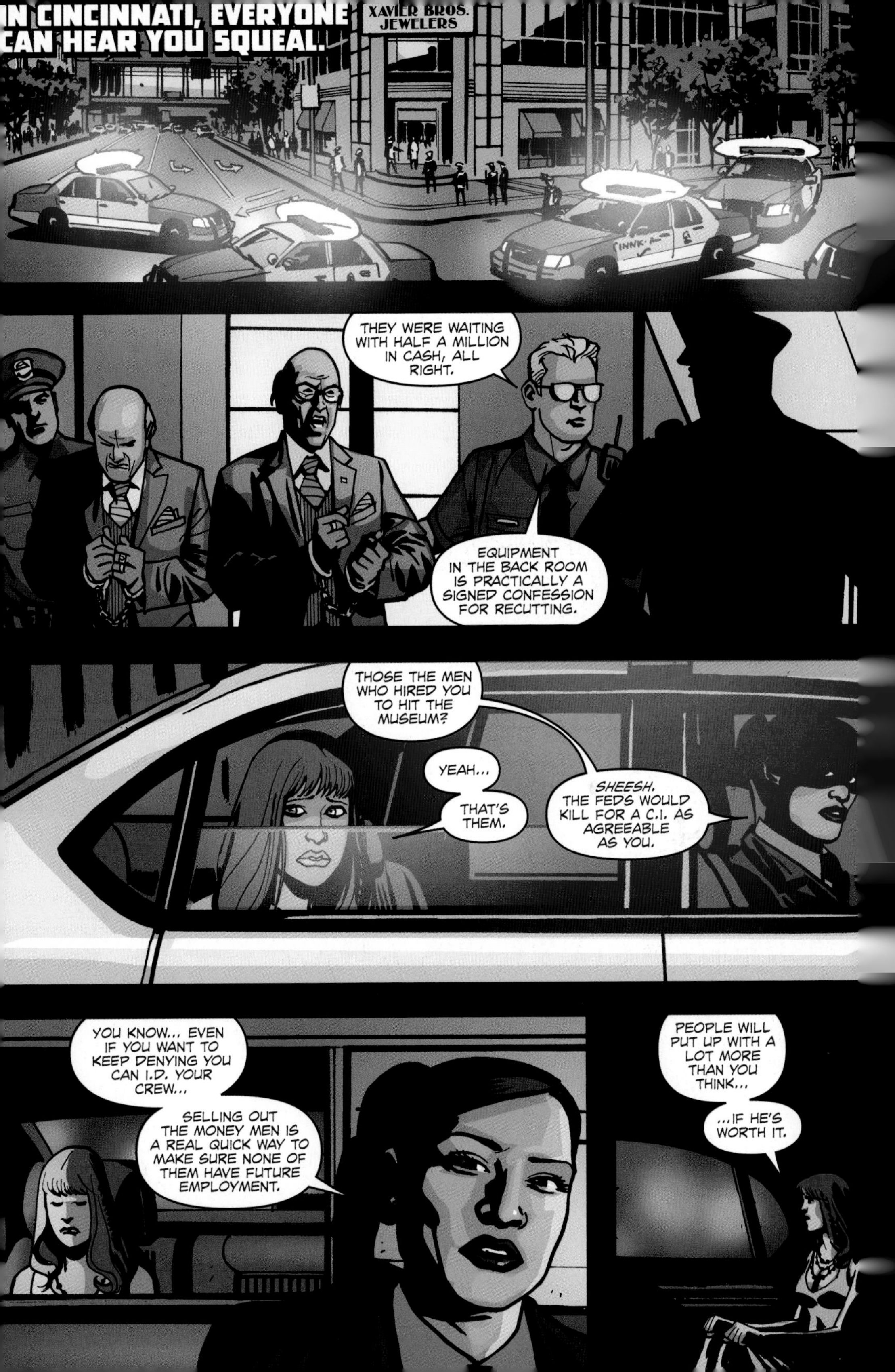

IN CINCINNATI, EVERYONE CAN HEAR YOU SQUEAL.
XAVIER BROS. JEWELERS
THEY WERE WAITING WITH HALF A MILLION IN CASH, ALL RIGHT.
EQUIPMENT IN THE BACK ROOM IS PRACTICALLY A SIGNED CONFESSION FOR RECUTTING.
THOSE THE MEN WHO HIRED YOU TO HIT THE MUSEUM?
YEAH...
THAT'S THEM.
SHEESH. THE FEDS WOULD KILL FOR A C.I. AS AGREEABLE AS YOU.
YOU KNOW... EVEN IF YOU WANT TO KEEP DENYING YOU CAN I.D. YOUR CREW...
SELLING OUT THE MONEY MEN IS A REAL QUICK WAY TO MAKE SURE NONE OF THEM HAVE FUTURE EMPLOYMENT.
PEOPLE WILL PUT UP WITH A LOT MORE THAN YOU THINK...
...IF HE'S WORTH IT.

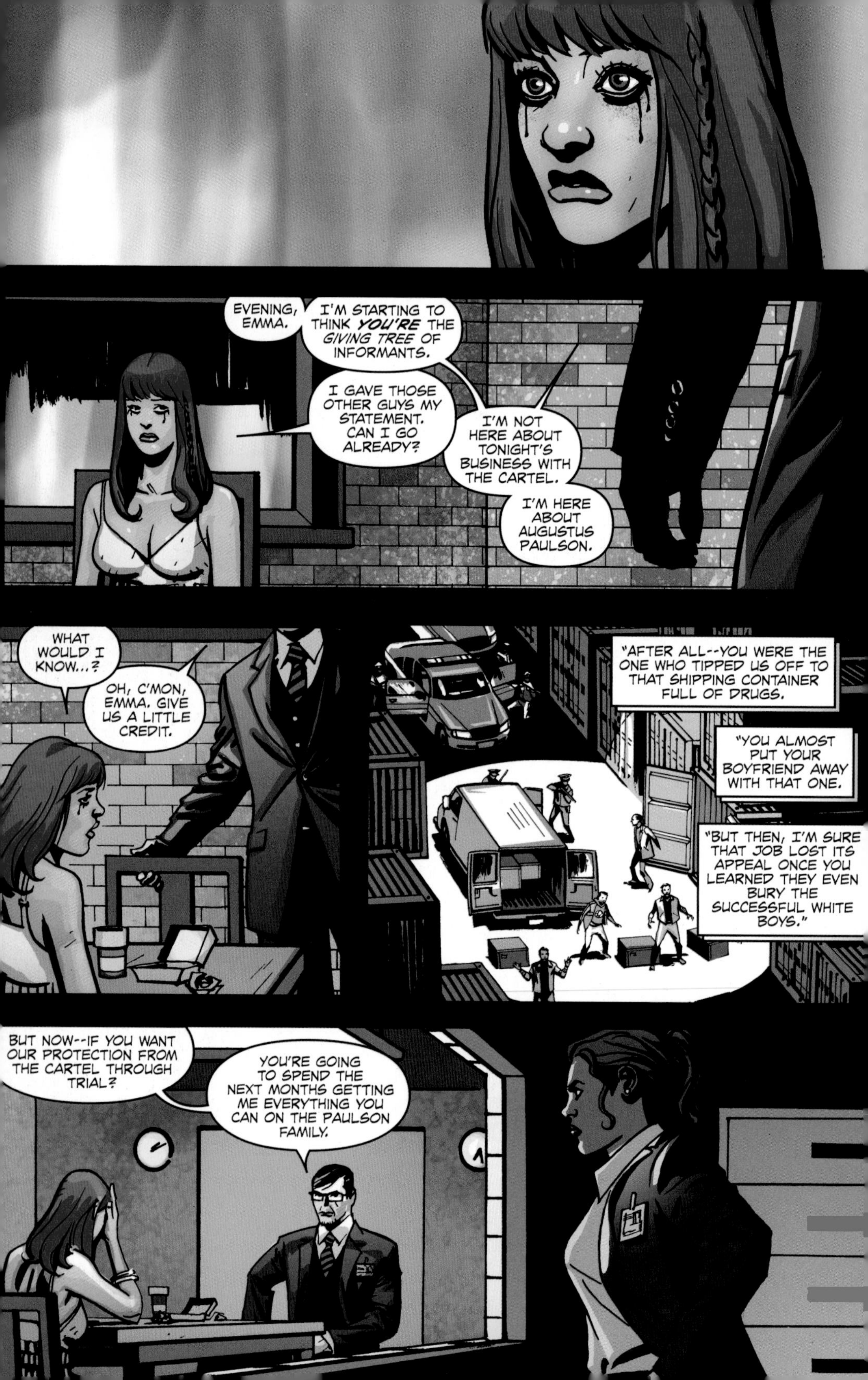

EVENING, EMMA.
I'M STARTING TO THINK *YOU'RE* THE *GIVING TREE* OF INFORMANTS.
I GAVE THOSE OTHER GUYS MY STATEMENT. CAN I GO ALREADY?
I'M NOT HERE ABOUT TONIGHT'S BUSINESS WITH THE CARTEL.
I'M HERE ABOUT AUGUSTUS PAULSON.
WHAT WOULD I KNOW...?
OH, C'MON, EMMA. GIVE US A LITTLE CREDIT.
"AFTER ALL--YOU WERE THE ONE WHO TIPPED US OFF TO THAT SHIPPING CONTAINER FULL OF DRUGS.
"YOU ALMOST PUT YOUR BOYFRIEND AWAY WITH THAT ONE.
"BUT THEN, I'M SURE THAT JOB LOST ITS APPEAL ONCE YOU LEARNED THEY EVEN BURY THE SUCCESSFUL WHITE BOYS."
BUT NOW--IF YOU WANT OUR PROTECTION FROM THE CARTEL THROUGH TRIAL?
YOU'RE GOING TO SPEND THE NEXT MONTHS GETTING ME EVERYTHING YOU CAN ON THE PAULSON FAMILY.

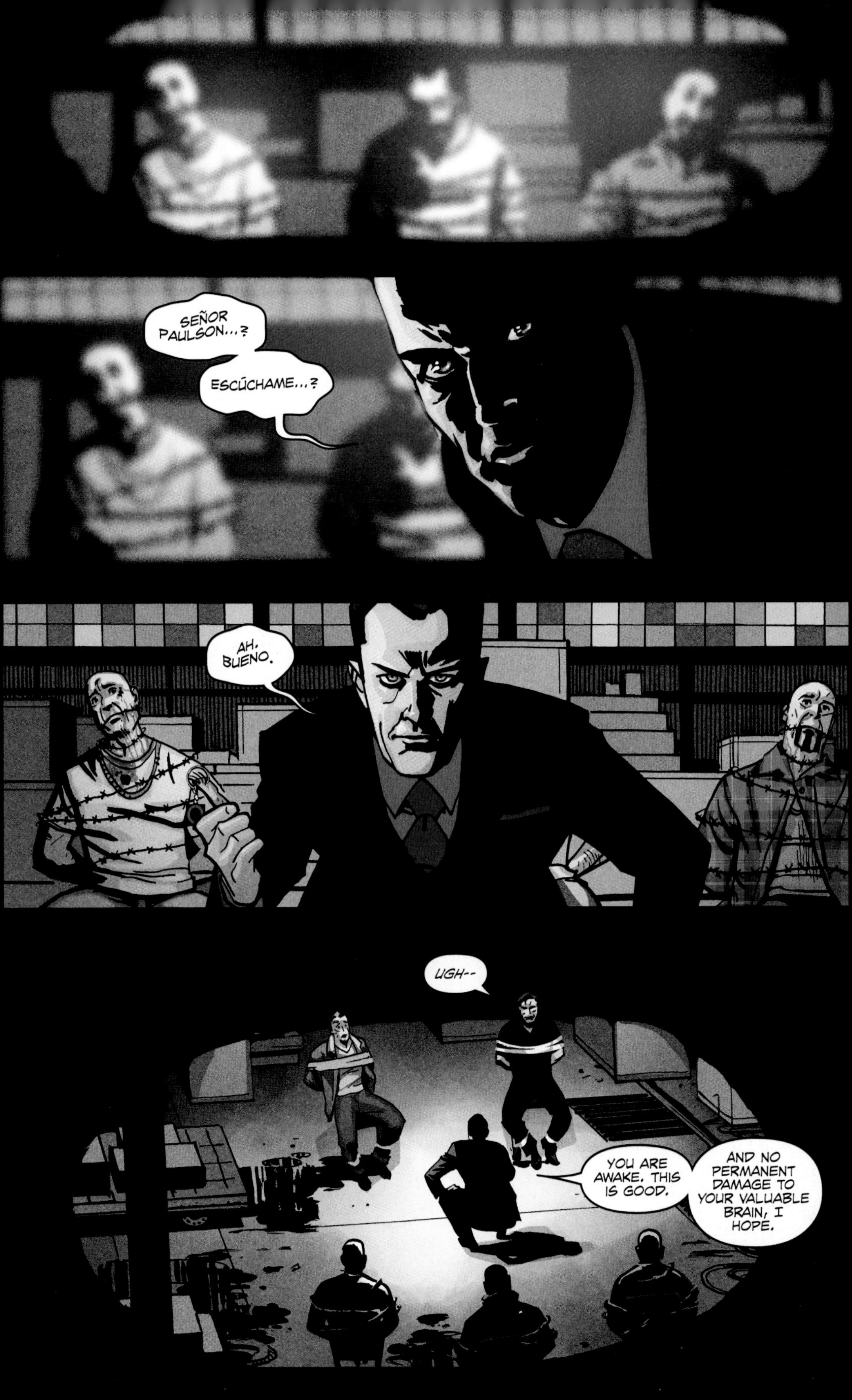
SEÑOR PAULSON...?
ESCÚCHAME...?
AH. BUENO.
UGH--
YOU ARE AWAKE. THIS IS GOOD.
AND NO PERMANENT DAMAGE TO YOUR VALUABLE BRAIN, I HOPE.

AFTER ALL, THE ONLY THING THAT KEEPS MEN LIKE YOU ALIVE...

...IS TO BE OF MORE *VALUE* THAN YOU ARE *TROUBLE.*

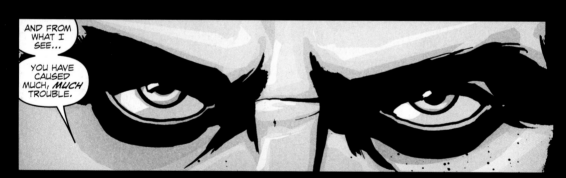

AND FROM WHAT I SEE...

YOU HAVE CAUSED MUCH, *MUCH* TROUBLE.

THESE MEN, HOWEVER, HAVE BEEN MY DEDICATED SOLDIERS.

SELFLESS.

CLEAN.

LOYAL.

...BUT THEY MAY BE COMPROMISED TO YOUR FBI.

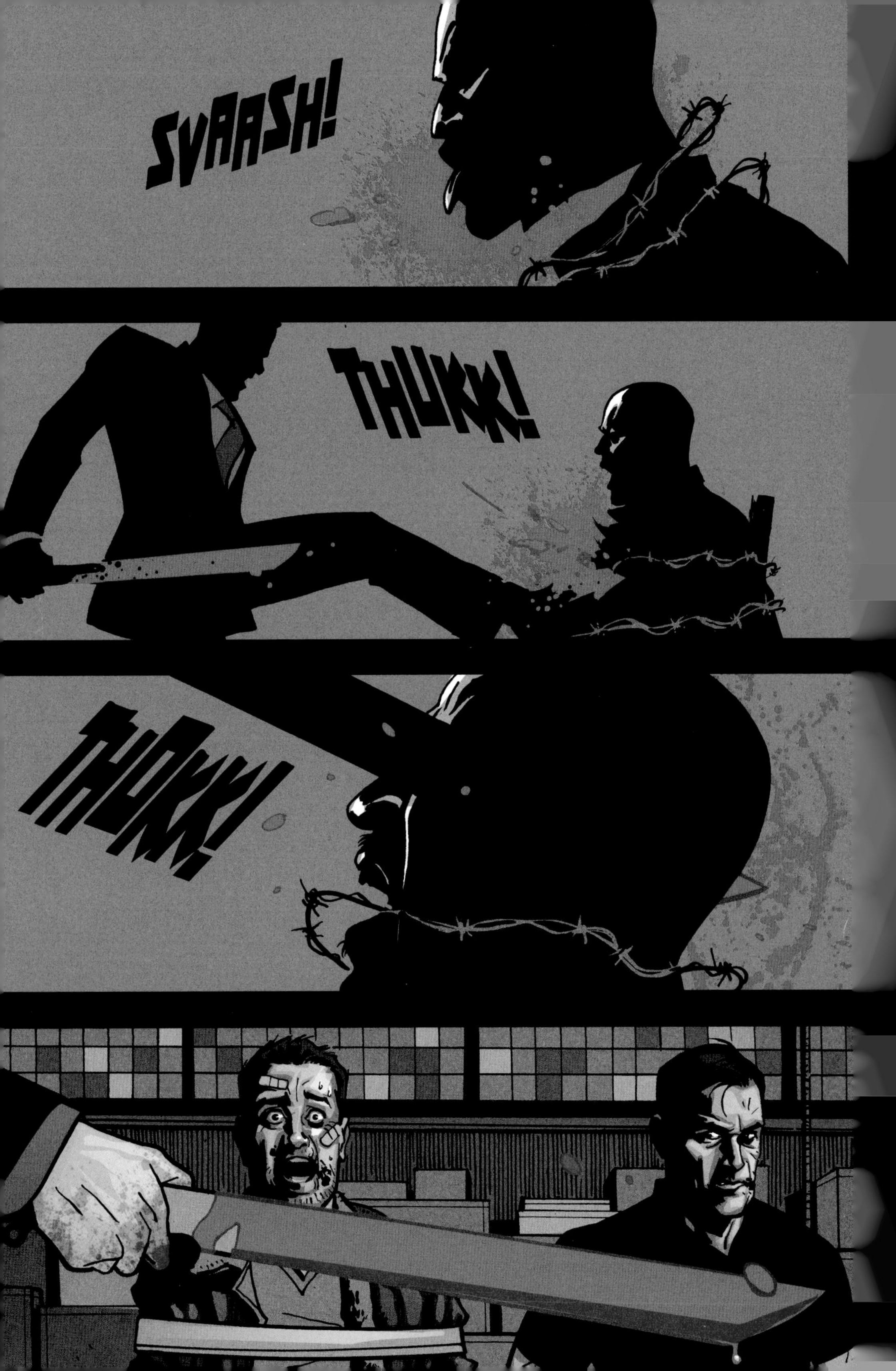
SVAASH!
THUKK!
THUKK!

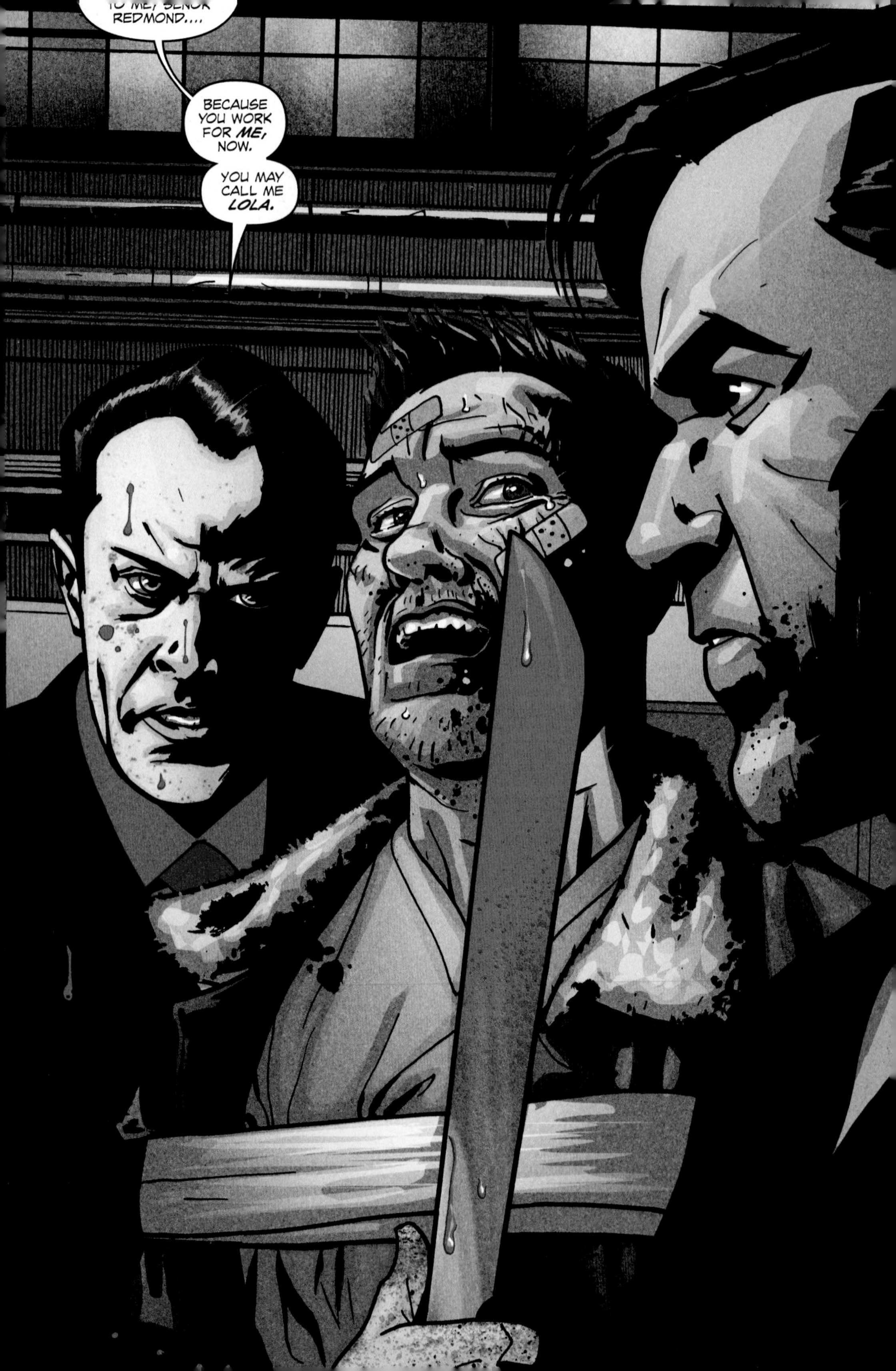
REDMOND....
BECAUSE YOU WORK FOR *ME*, NOW.
YOU MAY CALL ME *LOLA*.

TO BE CONTINUED...

MORE BOOKS FROM
ROBERT KIRKMAN
AND SKYBOUND!

TO FIND YOUR NEAREST COMIC BOOK STORE, CALL:
1-888-COMIC-BOOK

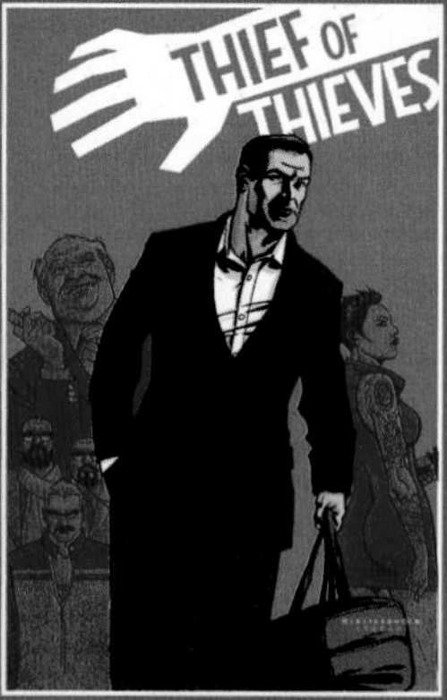
THIEF OF THIEVES

THIEF OF THIEVES
VOL. 1: "I QUIT."
ISBN: 978-1-60706-592-0
$14.99
VOL. 2: "HELP ME."
ISBN: 978-1-60706-676-7
$14.99

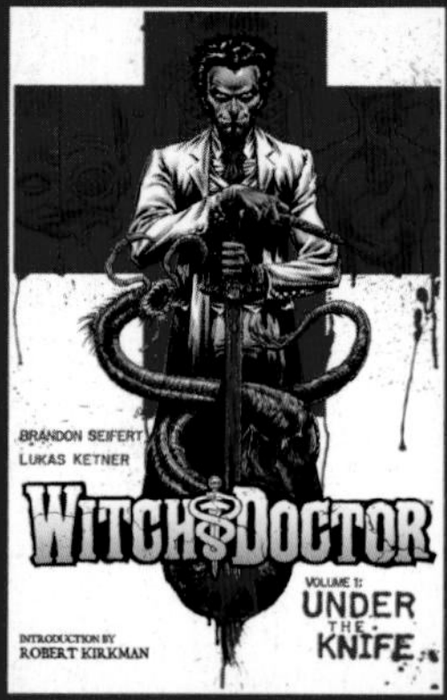
BRANDON SEIFERT
LUKAS KETNER
WITCH DOCTOR
VOLUME 1: UNDER THE KNIFE
INTRODUCTION BY ROBERT KIRKMAN

WITCH DOCTOR
VOL. 1: UNDER THE KNIFE TP
ISBN: 978-1-60706-441-1
$12.99

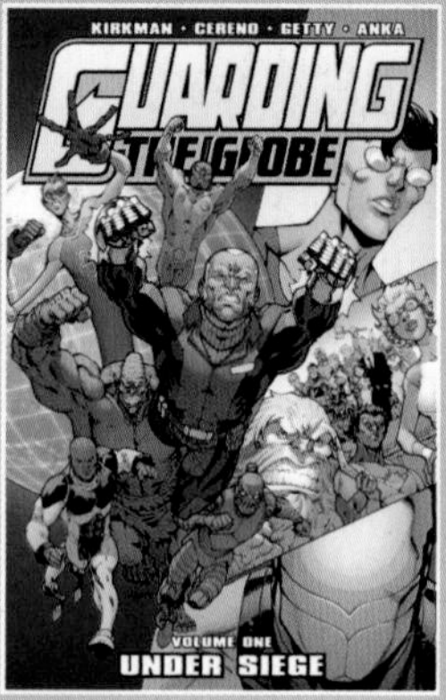
KIRKMAN · CERENO · GETTY · ANKA
GUARDING THE GLOBE
VOLUME ONE
UNDER SIEGE

GUARDING THE GLOBE
VOL. 1: UNDER SIEGE TP
ISBN: 978-1-60706-356-8
$16.99
VOL. 2: HARD TO KILL TP
ISBN: 978-1-60706-673-6
$16.99

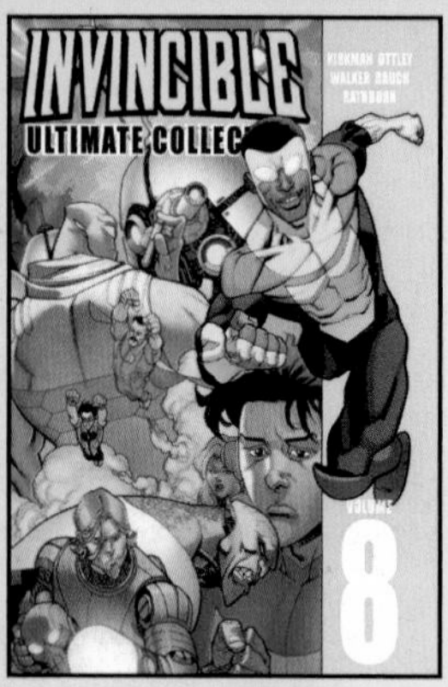
INVINCIBLE
ULTIMATE COLLEC
VOLUME
8

INVINCIBLE
VOL. 1: FAMILY MATTERS TP
ISBN: 978-1-58240-711-1
$12.99
VOL. 2: EIGHT IS ENOUGH TP
ISBN: 978-1-58240-347-2
$12.99
VOL. 3: PERFECT STRANGERS TP
ISBN: 978-1-58240-793-7
$12.99
VOL. 4: HEAD OF THE CLASS TP
ISBN: 978-1-58240-440-2
$14.95
VOL. 5: THE FACTS OF LIFE TP
ISBN: 978-1-58240-554-4
$14.99
VOL. 6: A DIFFERENT WORLD TP
ISBN: 978-1-58240-579-7
$14.99
VOL. 7: THREE'S COMPANY TP
ISBN: 978-1-58240-656-5
$14.99
VOL. 8: MY FAVORITE MARTIAN TP
ISBN: 978-1-58240-683-1
$14.99
VOL. 9: OUT OF THIS WORLD TP
ISBN: 978-1-58240-827-9
$14.99
VOL. 10: WHO'S THE BOSS TP
ISBN: 978-1-60706-013-0
$16.99
VOL. 11: HAPPY DAYS TP
ISBN: 978-1-60706-062-8
$16.99
VOL. 12: STILL STANDING TP
ISBN: 978-1-60706-166-3
$16.99
VOL. 13: GROWING PAINS TP
ISBN: 978-1-60706-251-6
$16.99
VOL. 14: THE VILTRUMITE WAR TP
ISBN: 978-1-60706-367-4
$19.99
VOL. 15: GET SMART TP
ISBN: 978-1-60706-498-5
$16.99
VOL. 16: FAMILY TIES TP
ISBN: 978-1-60706-579-1
$16.99
VOL. 17: WHAT'S HAPPENING TP
ISBN: 978-1-60706-662-0
$16.99
ULTIMATE COLLECTION, VOL. 1 HC
ISBN 978-1-58240-500-1
$34.95
ULTIMATE COLLECTION, VOL. 2 HC
ISBN: 978-1-58240-594-0
$34.99
ULTIMATE COLLECTION, VOL. 3 HC
ISBN: 978-1-58240-763-0
$34.99
ULTIMATE COLLECTION, VOL. 4 HC
ISBN: 978-1-58240-989-4
$34.99
ULTIMATE COLLECTION, VOL. 5 HC
ISBN: 978-1-60706-116-8
$34.99
ULTIMATE COLLECTION, VOL. 6 HC
ISBN: 978-1-60706-360-5
$34.99
ULTIMATE COLLECTION, VOL. 7 HC
ISBN: 978-1-60706-509-8
$39.99
ULTIMATE COLLECTION, VOL. 8 HC
ISBN: 978-1-60706-680-4
$39.99
COMPENDIUM VOL. 1
ISBN: 978-1-60706-411-4
$64.99
THE COMPLETE INVINCIBLE LIBRARY, VOL. 2 HC
ISBN: 978-1-60706-112-0
$125.00
THE COMPLETE INVINCIBLE LIBRARY, VOL. 3 HC
ISBN: 978-1-60706-421-3
$125.00
THE OFFICIAL HANDBOOK OF THE INVINCIBLE UNIVERSE TP
ISBN: 978-1-58240-831-6
$12.99
INVINCIBLE PRESENTS, VOL. 1: ATOM EVE & REX SPLODE TP
ISBN: 978-1-60706-255-4
$14.99

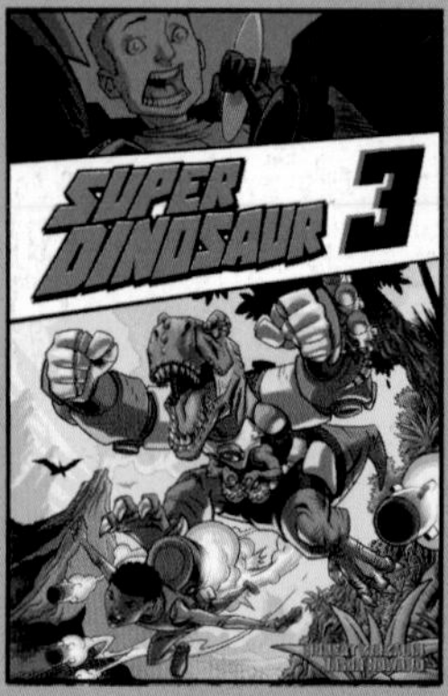
SUPER DINOSAUR 3

SUPER DINOSAUR
VOL. 1
ISBN: 978-1-60706-420-6
$9.99
VOL. 2
ISBN: 978-1-60706-568-5
$12.99
VOL. 3
ISBN: 978-1-60706-667-5
$12.99
DELUXE COLORING BOOK
ISBN: 978-1-60706-481-7
$4.99

THE ASTOUNDING WOLF-MAN
VOL. 1 TP
ISBN: 978-1-58240-862-0
$14.99
VOL. 2 TP
ISBN: 978-1-60706-007-9
$14.99
VOL. 3 TP
ISBN: 978-1-60706-111-3
$16.99
VOL. 4 TP
ISBN: 978-1-60706-249-3
$16.99

BATTLE POPE
VOL. 1: GENESIS TP
ISBN: 978-1-58240-572-8
$14.99
VOL. 2: MAYHEM TP
ISBN: 978-1-58240-529-2
$12.99
VOL. 3: PILLOW TALK TP
ISBN: 978-1-58240-677-0
$12.99
VOL. 4: WRATH OF GOD TP
ISBN: 978-1-58240-751-7
$9.99

BRIT
VOL. 1: OLD SOLDIER TP
ISBN: 978-1-58240-678-7
$14.99
VOL. 2: AWOL
ISBN: 978-1-58240-864-4
$14.99
VOL. 3: FUBAR
ISBN: 978-1-60706-061-1
$16.99

CAPES
VOL. 1: PUNCHING THE CLOCK TP
ISBN: 978-1-58240-756-2
$17.99

HAUNT
VOL. 1 TP
ISBN: 978-1-60706-154-0
$9.99
VOL. 2 TP
ISBN: 978-1-60706-229-5
$16.99
VOL. 3 TP
ISBN: 978-1-60706-552-4
$14.99
THE IMMORTAL EDITION, VOL. 1 HC
ISBN: 978-1-60706-241-7
$34.99

THE INFINITE
VOL. 1 TP
ISBN: 978-1-60706-475-6
$9.99

SUPERPATRIOT
AMERICA'S FIGHTING FORCE
ISBN: 978-1-58240-355-1
$14.99

TALES OF THE REALM
HARDCOVER
ISBN: 978-1-58240-426-0
$34.95
TRADE PAPERBACK
ISBN: 978-1-58240-394-6
$14.95

TECH JACKET
VOL. 1: THE BOY FROM EARTH TP
ISBN: 978-1-58240-771-5
$14.99

FOR MORE OF THE WALKING DEAD

TRADE PAPERBACKS

VOL. 1: DAYS GONE BYE TP
ISBN: 978-1-58240-672-5
$14.99
VOL. 2: MILES BEHIND US TP
ISBN: 978-1-58240-775-3
$14.99
VOL. 3: SAFETY BEHIND BARS TP
ISBN: 978-1-58240-805-7
$14.99
VOL. 4: THE HEART'S DESIRE TP
ISBN: 978-1-58240-530-8
$14.99
VOL. 5: THE BEST DEFENSE TP
ISBN: 978-1-58240-612-1
$14.99
VOL. 6: THIS SORROWFUL LIFE TP
ISBN: 978-1-58240-684-8
$14.99

VOL. 7: THE CALM BEFORE TP
ISBN: 978-1-58240-828-6
$14.99
VOL. 8: MADE TO SUFFER TP
ISBN: 978-1-58240-883-5
$14.99
VOL. 9: HERE WE REMAIN TP
ISBN: 978-1-60706-022-2
$14.99
VOL. 10: WHAT WE BECOME TP
ISBN: 978-1-60706-075-8
$14.99
VOL. 11: FEAR THE HUNTERS TP
ISBN: 978-1-60706-181-6
$14.99
VOL. 12: LIFE AMONG THEM TP
ISBN: 978-1-60706-254-7
$14.99

VOL. 13: TOO FAR GONE TP
ISBN: 978-1-60706-329-2
$14.99
VOL. 14: NO WAY OUT TP
ISBN: 978-1-60706-392-6
$14.99
VOL. 15: WE FIND OURSELVES TP
ISBN: 978-1-60706-440-4
$14.99
VOL. 16: A LARGER WORLD TP
ISBN: 978-1-60706-559-3
$14.99
VOL. 17: SOMETHING TO FEAR TP
ISBN: 978-1-60706-615-6
$14.99

HARDCOVERS

BOOK ONE HC
ISBN: 978-1-58240-619-0
$34.99
BOOK TWO HC
ISBN: 978-1-58240-698-5
$34.99
BOOK THREE HC
ISBN: 978-1-58240-825-5
$34.99
BOOK FOUR HC
ISBN: 978-1-60706-000-0
$34.99
BOOK FIVE HC
ISBN: 978-1-60706-171-7
$34.99
BOOK SIX HC
ISBN: 978-1-60706-327-8
$34.99
BOOK SEVEN HC
ISBN: 978-1-60706-439-8
$34.99
BOOK EIGHT HC
ISBN: 978-1-60706-593-7
$34.99

COMPENDIUMS

COMPENDIUM TP, VOL. 1
ISBN: 978-1-60706-076-5
$59.99
COMPENDIUM TP, VOL. 2
ISBN: 978-1-60706-596-8
$59.99

SPECIALTY BOOKS

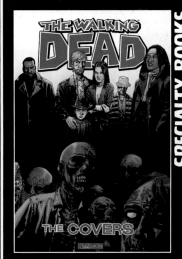

THE WALKING DEAD: THE COVERS, VOL. 1 HC
ISBN: 978-1-60706-002-4
$24.99
THE WALKING DEAD SURVIVORS' GUIDE
ISBN: 978-1-60706-458-9
$12.99

OMNIBUS

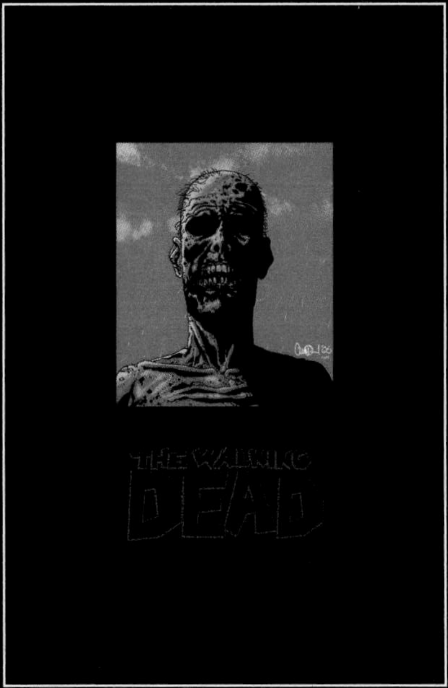

OMNIBUS, VOL. 1
ISBN: 978-1-60706-503-6
$100.00
OMNIBUS, VOL. 2
ISBN: 978-1-60706-515-9
$100.00
OMNIBUS, VOL. 3
ISBN: 978-1-60706-330-8
$100.00
OMNIBUS, VOL. 4
ISBN: 978-1-60706-616-3
$100.00

THE WALKING DEAD™ © 2013 Robert Kirkman, LLC

THE WALKING DEAD.com

NEWS

INTERVIEWS

SNEAK PEEKS

CONTESTS

BEHIND THE SCENES INFO

CHARACTER BIOS

STORY COVERAGE

MERCHANDISE

SKYBOUND